Understanding Life After Death

An Exploration of What Awaits You, Me and Everyone We've Ever Known

AFTERLIFETOPICS.COM

AFTERLIFE

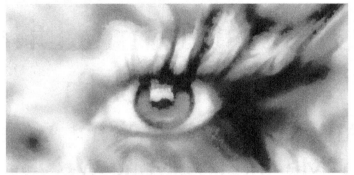

TOPICS

Developed Life Books
4884 W. Hardy Rd
Tucson, AZ 85704
US

First Printing – 2015

ISBN-13: 978-0692529171 (Developed Life Books)

CONTENTS

Introduction

The essence of what you are about to read is an argument in support of the existence of life after death, and an examination of its ramifications. As an open-minded skeptic, I understand the importance of both sides to an argument being presented accurately and fairly, and only then can a determination be created. As part of your education on something that will ultimately affect all of us, I present to you the proponent's side of the story.

Firstly, if you have already made up your mind that this subject does not, or cannot exist—I am unsure what you will benefit from reading these pages. My desire is to explore what I consider a most important topic for all of us, including new research, as well as a better understanding of the philosophical and conceptual ideas that surround our existences post physical death. For some, however, no amount of data will convince them. I am not here to spin my wheels to try and win over the people who already made up their minds. Some won't be convinced, especially if there is preconceived bias present. If you're such a person, maybe this is not the topic for you.

Secondly, I hope that this book presents a reasonable, albeit secular, case for life beyond the physical body. Some may read this text and feel aghast that there is no mention of redemption or Jesus or scripture. To these people I say this: life after death seems a reality that transcends a religious interpretation. You may still be able to fit this information through a Biblical prism, and it is your right to do so.

Such an opinion would argue that religion is the tool to guide a person through this confusing subject in-order to find the truth. I personally don't believe this, but it's a viable interpretation for the theologically minded, and it's certainly one method to process this subject (although not one I would use).

Regardless, understanding the afterlife is an important and forgotten part of our education. It is the subject of "What happens next?" and "Where do my family members and loved ones go after I bury them?" To say this is an important topic is an understatement. It is arguably more important than making money, politics, careers and vacations. Our lives are stunningly short, and very soon—you are going to die—whether from a disease like cancer, an auto accident, or hopefully a natural passing in your sleep. Given this reality is fast approaching, it makes sense to begin committing time to understanding it, so that the moments you have left can be enjoyed without having to worry so much about mortality—because what we understand, we do not fear.

A myth currently pervades society that we do not—and cannot—know what happens beyond the great, dark doorway. To those of us who have delved down this rabbit-hole and made it through to the other end of it, we can testify that this is not the case. The information is there, the experiences can be accessed, and the only thing stopping this information from being more widely accepted is our own limitations of comprehension.

At the heart of this topic is consciousness. Awareness of the self is the thing that defines us, and it's what must persist to make an afterlife possible. You may hear terms in this book like veridical perception or "consciousness outside of the body", because these are the key phenomena that indicates life beyond the body, and it's the starting point to try and understand it. If there has even been one case in history of a person's mind drifting away from the confines of the brain, then some type of argument can be made that the afterlife exists. As you'll find out, there have been far more than one or two cases of this happening—rather, it seems an overlooked fact of nature that consciousness is only merely tethered to the brain and the body, but hardly dependent on it. What if we (mankind) have been simply living with blinders over our eyes all this time? What if death was never supposed to be what we have culturally defined it as?

In this book I hope to take the exploration of this subject to the next level. There are many books about the afterlife on the market, but there is a lack of information about the exact, literal conditions of the afterlife. Ghosts, ethereal people, "the Light", and other vaporous ideas do not clearly define exactly the types of things you and I will be doing in a hundred years from now, how the astral universe works, and what we can really expect. This is where I hope this book will satisfy those of us who long for details and an understanding that goes beyond the murky theoretical. Later in the book I will begin trying to finally piece together the great afterlife riddle, using numerous sources (as well as personal experiences) to create a picture of astral existence that anyone can use for a coherent understanding of the next, perfectly natural phases of our existence.

Finally: I dedicate this book to open-minded skeptics. As a millennial writing this, I understand very well how it's fashionable for my generation to doubt all types of subjects that are heaped on the "supernatural" dog pile. There's a great fear to be considered irrational, or unable to cope with reality the way it "really is". On the other hand, it takes a degree of bravery to approach the unknown and try to come to terms with it.

Some of my generation's disdain for the supernatural is born from rightful distrust of religion and its vague links to even the secular cases for the "soul". As a non-religious, secular person myself—I can perfectly understand this distrust. But we must be careful not to allow our disillusionment with religion to poison all spiritual concepts, and we must also be cautious in adopting drastic, antithetical philosophies with no benefit to us. It was Stephen Hawking who recently was quoted as saying that in the light of science, "philosophy is dead", because his definition of "reason" is such that subjective interpretations of life, meaning and purpose are irrelevant in a cold, mechanical universe. The irony of Hawking's statement is that what he is saying is, in itself, a philosophy—and not a particularly meaningful one. This attitude precludes concepts like the afterlife and spirituality even in lieu of evidence and reasonable arguments to support such topics. It creates a cynical, depressing, and wholly unnecessary point of view.

As I went down the rabbit-hole of exploring literal and rational spirituality, I found cynicism to gradually disappear from my mind. Tiring, negative philosophies naturally went away and were replaced by more meaningful views of life, the universe, and our purpose. And that, to me, is the greatest benefit of exploring this topic. Despite popular belief, to experience the supernatural is not inaccessible. It is something that is real, and can be experienced even by you. In fact, the overall picture of life after death, once fully examined, is as crystal clear as any other established area of the physical sciences. And most importantly, this information has a direct, unavoidable relationship with your own life.

I hope that you'll enjoy this book, and that ultimately it will provide to you some peace of mind as you better grasp this most complex of all topics.

Acknowledgements

- Special thanks to my parents, brothers, and the rest of my family and friends who, for the most part, have no idea I wrote this book (perhaps I should pick more conventional and less controversial topics next time).

- The entire crew who runs the *Spiritual, Skeptic? Evidence for the Existence of the Afterlife* Facebook group, including Marcus, Caroline, Rae and Victor (and any other mods I am forgetting to name), as well as Amy Kristine, Brian Shennan and others for their contributions.

- Especially a "thank you" to Victor and Wendy Zammit, who helped to spur my interest in the afterlife over 15 years ago, and who continue to make dedicated weekly reports about this most important subject.

- Jan and Marta, Dexter, Harsh, Josh "Maverick" and all of the others in my publishing circle who helped me understand the art of writing a book. As Marta says, writing the book is only 5% of the work.

- Open-minded researchers everywhere who are leading us on this mind-bending new frontier; including consciousness pioneers at my school, the University of Arizona.

I – The Death Debate

Death is often unspoken of among regular conversation, but it's vitally important. Before this topic even appeared on my mental radar, I was driven by a desire to understand the primal fear and shadow that lingers over all of our lives. I could feel death, a penultimate boogeyman, as soon as I learned to walk, talk, and form coherent ideas.

From when I was as young as five or six years-old, I had a vague sense that religion—as taught by my eclectic and pseudo-religious parents—was a bit more like "playing pretend". It was easy to get caught up in its throes, but I knew that beneath religious philosophy was a very grim prospect—no one really knew what the hell was going on (least of all, my parents).

When I was an adolescent, my thoughts turned to the existential. How could non-existence be rationalized? Yearning to make sense of the impossible, I started putting it into numbers.

"Well, I'd only 'not exist' for so long as I didn't exist before I was born. Whatever mathematical anomaly made me exist in the first place is bound to repeat itself, even if it takes a trillion years and the universe dies and begins again," I thought to myself. *"As I would have no awareness of the time in-between my existences, I will literally just die and exist again as something else!"*

My "revelation" provided some comfort and my mind could focus on other, teenage related things. At 13 and 14, I was a fairly hard-nosed skeptic of paranormal alternatives. I'd read the Wikipediaderived skeptic's opinions long before I'd ever touch the resources of what I felt were self-deluded believers.

It was my brother, his wife, and their foray into the supernatural that made me start to wonder if my skeptical shell was not just blocking out important information. In particular, it was his claims of going "out of his body" that I found most interesting.

He would describe a shadowy "astral" realm that he could enter after tedious practice. I eavesdropped on him discussing this realm to his friends:

"Slowly, I floated from my body. The world around me was dark, but almost iridescent, like exploring the negative on film. I could look down, and see my hand, and it was translucent. I made it down the hallway until I was pulled back to my body."

From these tales I was drawn to Usenet newsgroups about out-of-body experiences, as I attempted to glean more understanding from his reports. It was there I also learned, for the first time, about out-of-body states that occur among the terminally injured.

I would delve much deeper into the topic of the near-death experience (NDE) in coming months; but my initial reaction to the exploration of such esoteric ideas was the sensation of being simultaneously fascinated and mortified.

The ideas were mortifying because, unlike my theory of "mathematical immortality", the business of going out of one's body raised a thousand more questions than it did answers, including some particularly unpleasant ones, such as:

Does this information mean ghosts are real, and we become them after we die?

How can we live and enjoy ourselves in the shadowy, out of body dimension that my brother described?

Do we maintain our individualities, or do we become something else?

How can we leave our bodies if our minds are controlled by our brains? What is the mechanism?

The existential thoughts once again bubbled up into my mind and I couldn't shake them away—except now, bizarre accounts of the occult were scrambling my ideas of reality. Often, I would switch between hats of "believer" and "skeptic" on the internet; trying to figure out which hat fit me the best—and which version of reality bore merit.

At this point, I had started what would become a long-term "career" in the matters of life beyond death, spending a portion of my time every-day exploring the topic; sometimes as a skeptic, sometimes as a proponent.

The first place I turned to, in an attempt to understand the "believers", was the still brilliant resource by Kevin Williams, www.near-death.com, which was quite active back around the year 2000. The near-death experience, and the research into the many fascinating areas of this—like veridical perception, perception among the blind, etc—presented a solid case for the reality of these topics.

As I would learn, countless thousands of people from around the world report "going toward the light" and the phenomenon is the source behind many little cultural sayings, from "is there light at the end of the tunnel?" to "my life flashed before my eyes". The NDE is interwoven within the human cultural narrative. And as such, life after death is also interwoven in a way that is more powerful than any religious interpretation. Indeed, religions, as it would turn out, are merely interpretations of something that is consistently encountered in all cultures.

In the 21st century, the shadows are being pulled away, and after so many millennia—these spiritual topics can now be studied with scientific scrutiny. Various extraordinary subjects are now providing a great deal of information about the phenomenal powers of human consciousness, transcending far beyond the mortal confines of the brain.

You may wonder how different so-called paranormal topics, from telepathy to mediumship, can relate to a concept as grandiose as survival of human consciousness. It's my view, as an amateur researcher, that the majority of credible "paranormal" topics are like spokes on a wheel, and the wheel is the persistence of consciousness. A topic like telepathy or remote viewing indicates that, at least in some cases, the mind operates outside of the brain. If this occurs even once, it calls into question if the mind really needs a brain, at all. Then, when we go into the world of near-death experiences and after death communication, a body of evidence begins to accumulate that not only can our consciousness go outside of the brain; it appears that it can thrive in such conditions. Later in this book, we'll explore in more detail just what these conditions are like.

Life after death is the direction that most research leads, and it's an exciting but also intimidating subject to try to understand. It's also no surprise that the gatekeepers of science and academia guard the mainstream institutions, and may use labels like superstition to denigrate the information. The reason is that a paradigm shift this drastic will not be embraced so easily. There are many moral considerations for a world that is effectively "post death". For instance, if humankind knew beyond reasonable doubt that death simply means a transition to a potentially better state of consciousness, in a new Earth-like environment that is altogether quite pleasant—then what's to stop mass suicide and a wavering of morality? It's the finality of death that serves as Western culture's moral reminder and authority. And, it makes sense. What is finite is what we seek to preserve and protect—what would we do if even mankind itself is no longer finite? When the existence of the astral is proven, suddenly the universe and its astral counterpart would appear limitless—and perhaps the material would become disposable.

On the flipside, a world that is post-death would also mean a generally happier civilization. The intense suffering caused by the uncertainty of the "great mystery" would be lessened. It would mean that mainstream institutions would take the topic seriously enough to put funding behind it. If certain scientists today are to be believed, there could then be technological innovations that allow two-way communication to the deceased. Imagine the strange world where the dead are a phone-call away at your local post-mortem communication center.

And then there would be the entire matter of religious upheaval. Religion has, since tribal times, maintained a monopoly on matters of cosmic destiny. Judging by the state of devout religiosity in the early 21st century, it is not likely that a widespread acceptance of the afterlife would occur easily. No, I would suspect it would be met with shouts of heathen and more than one or two suicide bombs detonating.

Regardless of these hard to swallow, moral and societal implications, life after death is the direction that so many of these topics point toward. Whether it's a reality that's convenient or not, there is still a large amount of evidence to suggest that it is nonetheless true, and for those of us willing to try to understand this information— we must begin to conceptualize the consequences of these facts.

It is also an intimate, personal reality for every single one of us. No single subject in the world is more immediately important. You are going to die, so am I. Your family is going to die, and so is mine. In general, death is regarded as a dark, horrible aspect of reality. It is therefore of some significance (to put it mildly) to point out that the only evidence that exists about what death really entails leads us toward conclusions that are the exact opposite of dark or horrible. I admit that this point of view is grounded in the philosophical, and even—dare I say—the realm of belief and anecdote. However, I see no moral objection to belief if it's grounded in data, science and investigation versus blind faith.

To Keep a Critical Mind

As a proponent of life after death, I think it's extremely important to approach this topic with a critical mind, while abstaining from cynicism or personal bias. One important point is that many of the skeptics, who fight against charlatan psychics, are quite justified, because many psychics and mediums are exactly that—charlatans.

This is a phenomenon that has been occurring, I presume, since civilization began. The reason is that as shadows and hints of the so-called spirit world pervade society, and as people feel desperate to understand details so they may understand the fate of loved ones, so do the manipulators of the world descend upon the prey. The scam is as old as people. Step forward, claim to have the answers, and ask for money in exchange.

Self-deception also pervades the borderlands between the spiritual and the literal. There are many examples of this, especially in the New Age genre. Self-deception typically preempts falling into the arms of one of the aforementioned con-artists. An example could be reading the writings of a charlatan channeling-medium who claims to have the answers for mankind. A credit card payment later, and the self-deceived victim is flying to Sedona for a $5,000 personal reading and a $12,000 retreat with others who also believe they are going to be swept away by celestial beings.

16

Sometimes self-deception is more subtle. Don't even get me started on some of the electronic voice-phenomenon ghost apps floating around the iTunes stores. One such app, EchoVox, claims to be able to detect spirits as they try to talk, by giving the spirits randomly generated sounds that they can manipulate somehow into full sentences. So, what the app essentially does is that it blurts out sporadic noises that sound like variations of broken speech.

I won't hate on the ghost researchers who designed the app. The theory seems to have some merit in parapsychological circles who have tried to perfect EVP techniques. The problem is that people download the app and start to presume that the software's randomly generated noise interface is, in fact, the voices of departed souls. If the smartphone running EchoVox is set anywhere, it will begin spitting out noises that could be interpreted as words or even sentences. It does this randomly, and at no point should any of these voices be considered departed souls. However, fans of the app get excited, making themselves believe that "Mffmmsru" was General Custer repenting for his mistreatment of Native Americans.

To literally experience the astral world is powerful when it happens, and it's also unmistakable. Whether it's the apparition of a loved one, a near-death experience, or even an EVP recording where, in an isolated environment without background interference, a mysterious voice calls your name. However, these profound experiences are rare. In fact, some believe they're rare intentionally, as how could we learn the lessons of our human lives if we are constantly bombarded by the astral dimension? As a result of the general obscurity of such phenomena, those desperate for evidence use their imaginations to fill in the blanks. The truth is stretched and flights of fantasy are manifested to accommodate the sudden existence of all manner of supernatural experiences.

The reason progress in the understanding of the astral is so limited is directly because of these ancient tendencies. Some try to blame organized skepticism and the critics of the immaterial theories, but this gives the generally boredom-inducing atheist / skeptic community way more credit than they're worth. The real culprit behind why advancement is slow is the paranormal community itself. It's the New Age genre in the bookstore where potentially credible information is heaped in with books that self-promote psychics who, in fact, probably have no legitimate psychic talent. It's the fake mediums who give real mediums bad names. It's the general culture of shadowy manipulation and trickery that surrounds these topics.

Venturing down this rabbit-hole means you must guard yourself with open-minded skepticism and critical thought. While you should not believe every morsel of information that comes your way, at the same time, there is no shame in taking some of the information and deciding that it is of benefit to you. Understanding, and dare I say believing in, life after death can have an enormously positive effect on a person's life.

Some people I've known, even after directly experiencing these other worlds will spend years wrestling with the experience, shifting between acceptance and denial. Their refusal to accept is often spurred by peers who tell them they were hallucinating, and their attempt to "be rational" keeps them from admitting what they know inside. Yet, the more they try to dismiss what they experienced, the deeper they are hiding from it. When I see this, I wonder why there has to be so much struggle. Just embrace what it is. Embrace the evidence, and the reality of this topic. More and more people are coming forward with stories that range from direct communication with the deceased, to amazing episodes of clairvoyance or astral travel.

For those of us willing to accept this evidence, it opens up a world of possibilities. Of course, if it's not something that you want to necessarily accept—that is your right. All things in life are inherently subjective until personally experienced. If you are a fence-sitter, then enjoy the view from that fence. I hope this book gives you a comfortable place to sit on it.

The Culture War

Any attempt to study realms of spirituality or the supernatural will put you into the battle-ground of skeptics versus believers, and the explosive division created between scientific philosophies of materialism versus non-materialism. And so, this is a topic we have to tackle before we begin the exploration of the objective evidence for the afterlife. I think it is important to have an understanding of this debate, because many times people with a growing interest in the subject change their minds very early after a few encounters with skeptical friends, books, or TV shows. However, it's critical to not take anyone's word for what the facts are, and to do your own research. In this subject, you will encounter many people who refuse to follow the direction of empirical evidence, and instead cling tight to prejudices, philosophizing endlessly about how something cannot exist without possibly considering the other side of the story.

I learned early that my adolescent hobby of studying the esoteric meant that I had unwittingly stepped foot into a full-fledged war between mainstream institutions versus so-called "proponents", with an endless amount of vitriolic arguments across the wires.

The narrative pushed by the opposing-side of the cultural debate is that all things dubbed "paranormal" should be shoved aside in a select box, such that people are allowed to discuss their woo-woo topics at California crystal conventions or on the phone to Ms. Cleo, but keep topics like out-of-body experiences or psychic powers *the hell away from science, academia and mainstream institutions*!

I learned how there are entire organizations, namely the Committee for the Scientific Exploration of Claims of the Paranormal (CSICOP, "psi-cop", get it? They're now called "CSI") whose sole purpose is to aggressively censor any topic that is on a list of subjects they deem as taboo. Or, even more maddening, they will try to take a the "neutral" approach of looking at the "belief" in paranormal topics as some type of psychological condition (a tactic seen in books like *Why People Believe Weird Things* by Michael Shermer). Condescending to the extreme, this attitude by default rejects people's personal experiences as well as the highly evidential research (which will be outlined in this book) and goes straight toward the assumption that a belief that goes outside their consensus should be treated as a psychiatric problem or mass delusion. It sure is fun when you are trying to debate with these people, and as you are citing scientific evidence to support a "paranormal" topic—they are nodding sympathetically before trying to convince you to see a doctor to treat your condition.

Over the decades, organized skepticism has done a phenomenal job of separating people with even nominal interest in "paranormal" matters into black and white camps—heretics versus rationalists, heathens versus good scientists. Somehow, this opinion has become the mainstream consensus. Should someone who is highly versed in a particular subject (be it NDEs or reincarnation) assert in public that there is validity to these notions—they will be ostracized (even by those who have no understanding of the subjects in question). This has created a black hole where objective research should belong. The culture is so politicized and hostile that people with interest in such phenomena, or who have had their own spiritual experiences, feel paranoid to reveal such things to the public, as they risk having their careers ruined.

This type of behavior would be scorned if it concerned the physical sciences—imagine, for instance, an organization whose purpose is to squelch taboo geological concepts. This would be considered unscientific at best, and censorship at worst. However, these exact types of organizations, as well as the blogs and followings of known career skeptics, are given the good graces of very powerful names who feel that it is a charitable cause to suppress information that promotes (what they believe are) pseudo-scientific theories or superstition.

The Two Sides

After you are finished with this book, there are many resources by people with esteemed surnames, like Shermer and Myers, on up to figures as great as Dawkins and Hawking, who will present very articulate counter-arguments against non-materiality or the special properties of consciousness. These arguments are typically centered on the strictly biological idea that the human entity is a pile of meat and sinew; and consciousness is a fleeting byproduct. Probably the best modern resources to support this notion are the arguments made by career skeptic up-and-comer Keith Augustine, who co-wrote *The Myth of the Afterlife* with Michael Martin and various contributors (2015, available on Amazon). In it, a lot of philosophical positions are argued that the mind is created by the brain, therefore the mind is a physical object, and an afterlife is impossible. From mentally degenerative diseases like Alzheimer's, to the personality changes incurred by brain injury, the skeptical position uses what they believe is the heavy hand of science to debunk superstition.

The supposition of materialism, or more specifically eliminative materialism (the belief that all behavior is pre-determined based on biological processes) is firmly rooted in post-enlightenment era academia; which has become a powerful institution, and materialism itself is arguably the force that greases the gears of modern civilization. The skeptical acolyte of this institution may wonder how something as fundamental to the laws of nature as the non-locality of consciousness could somehow be missed by the collectivity of all the great minds across the world. By contrast, something proven and embraced, like materialism, has led to modern medical science that allows us to lead much longer, richer lives right here on Earth.

For the longest time, I personally wrestled with these notions. Between proponents and skeptics, I finally found the proponent side to be the most sensible. The reason is clear: the problem with the materialist position is that despite how the materialist side presents rock-solid, seemingly scientific arguments, there is a deep flaw I could not ignore. It's the same flaw that has not been addressed in the last 15-20 years that these debates have raged across the web. Nor has it been addressed in the last century and a half since Darwin and the rise of materialism.

The flaw is that the materialist side attempts to argue that because X exists, Y cannot exist, however, Y continues to exist despite the existence of argument X. The materialists believe that by simple virtue of explaining how something cannot happen (and then philosophizing about it endlessly), then that subject therefore no longer happens / cannot occur. A logical fallacy that pervades most of their arguments. When the phenomena continues to happen despite their very cognizant arguments that it's impossible, the researcher encounters a type of information gap that cannot be accounted for, and the materialist argument starts to look very shaky.

As an example, a professional skeptic, somebody like Keith Augustine, may cite temporal lobe epilepsy as an argument against the existence of what he views as a soul. This condition, when it gives rise to Geschwind syndrome, involves a chronic, accelerating change in the seizure victim's personality[1]. This provides a scientific basis that personality appears to be a neurological factor, and therefore completely physical. If personality is physical by nature, then the soul does not exist. A materialist proponent would consider this to be damning evidence against all esoteric subjects from the near-death experience to the powers of the mind as they extend beyond the brain.

21

The argument contends that Y cannot exist because X exists. Because Geschwind syndrome and similar conditions compromise the fabric of who we are, then it appears what we are is both flimsy and entirely dependent on the blind mechanics of the body. This argument can be dug down even deeper, as materialists love to eventually delve into true eliminative materialism which contends that consciousness itself is an illusion, and that we do not even really exist, at all!

The previously mentioned flaw is that when an argument like this is presented by the materialists, it discounts that *consistent phenomena contradict their assumption.* Veridical perception during a near death or out-of-body-experience, or veridical information obtained through a spirit communication, are just a couple of examples. Just because the skeptic states that these types of things cannot exist because of the nature of the brain and consciousness, does not make these occurrences just magically disappear. In the materialist's perfect world, once their explanation has been put forth, all of these experiences and reports would simply fold like a bunch of paper tigers, built on superstition and wishful thinking, but without real substance or merit.

However, the burgeoning dilemma of the skeptic is that despite their crystal clear arguments that phenomena cannot exist, those same annoying contradictions continue to occur, and they do not have the consistency of paper tigers, at all. Near-death experiencers continue to have cosmic otherworldly experiences despite flat-lined EEGs, parapsychologists continue to conduct impressive experiments, and true mediums continue to provide veridical information that cannot be attributed to chance. This does not mean the materialists are wrong. In fact, they're correct. These things should not occur. Based on neurological data, it's absurd that extra-physical properties of consciousness are real. But absurd or not, if the phenomena continues, the only logical explanation is that there's some unidentified "X" factor that explains the contradiction and links materialism to the so-called supernatural. The materialists make the great mistake of attempting to pretend something either does not exist or is not valid simply because they can't figure out this X-factor. This is very unscientific, especially considering the reason they cannot find the X-factor is because they refuse to acknowledge such a thing could even exist in the first place.

In case you are confused, think about it this way: an Alzheimer's patient who develops aggressive tendencies may be considered as an argument against the existence of a soul. However, the veridical near-death experience, as well as the anecdotal strength of all such reports, provides strong evidence that consciousness, in spite of Alzheimer's disease, still manages to travel outside of the body. Just because these two subjects contradict each other does not invalidate either one. It simply means our current breadth of knowledge is limited. In some way we don't understand, the brain and brain-induced consciousness states exist separately from post-brain experiences where the mind can function outside of the physical organ. In the far future, scientists may unlock what this link is. This would be a major development for medical science. Imagine the ability to trigger an out-of-body experience so that a patient can simply leave their body during a period of intense trauma. Or, imagine being able to induce such a state in a patient with severe amnesia, so they can interact with family members while their consciousness is separated from the brain and not reliant on the memory function of synapses.

Until that day comes, is it really wise to resist the existence of the contradictory information? The reason I became permanently turned off to the subculture of the skeptic materialist movement is because of their reliance on philosophy disguised as credibility. If you present these people with evidence of non-materialism, they reject it because they know that even if they cannot explain the occurrence, it must be attributed to some level of fraud, incompetence, brain-washing or sloppy reporting that simply hasn't been uncovered yet. So, if they fail to provide an adequate explanation, they can just say, "Someday we'll figure out why this isn't real. It's probably wishful thinking, fraud, or a misinterpretation of data." Which is their reliable ticket to escape being cornered.

Unfortunately, in this book we cannot attempt to address every single professional skeptic or blogger's opinion. There is a rebuttal attempt for every paranormal topic in the world, and it would take a very large book to examine each one and pull out the truth from the fiction. These rebuttals are regularly found on Wikipedia. A group of moderators called the Guerilla Skeptics go to great pains to ensure all topics they deem as superstition are edited to ensure either the phenomena or the researchers are cast in a negative light. As a result, it's extremely hard to find balanced reports on things like psi or mediumship. The majority of all pages about supernatural topics, including almost all biographies by researchers who even dabble in such fields, are laced with debunking agendas by these pseudo-editors.

As any law student knows, a counter prosecutorial argument can be presented for literally anything. If an incident of psi arouses legitimacy and it's reported on the Wikipedia pages, it will immediately be edited to cast doubt on the claims, even if those claims are not particularly well thought out. For instance, a medium with a long history of positive hits or working successfully with a police department will have a single negative incidence blown out of proportion. While other topics on Wikipedia are debated with alternate theories shown, this is impossible for paranormal subjects, as the moderators practice censorship and do not allow dissenting opinions.

I think this is a problem that does, eventually, need to be addressed, given that Wikipedia is the first source for information that most people on Google come across. But, this is too much for this book to handle. For now, we can only hope that people who are truly seeking information will find it outside of Wikipedia. If you want a book that completely tackles this topic, then I suggest to read *Psi Wars: TED, Wikipedia, and the Battle for the Internet* by Craig Weiler.

Wow, These Skeptics Really Want to Suppress Information. It Sounds Like a Conspiracy!

Before we start making tinfoil hats, I think it's important to address that I don't feel there's a conspiracy in the truest sense. The behavior by skeptics may seem like an organized effort to suppress information, but all that's really occurring is a phenomena known to psychologists as "group think".

Groups of people, united around common ideas and beliefs, will tend to merge together, reinforce those ideas, while beginning to distrust the perceived "other". As the ideology deepens and perceived enemies multiply, the behavior becomes the unfortunate basis behind everything from religion to armed militants. This tendency seems to be built into our genes, and it may stem from our instinct to form tribes, as if we were still living in a barbaric society. Tribal lines based on spiritual experiences are to be expected as anthropologically, the mystical has always existed. Any topic that concerns a spiritual nature automatically draws these tribal elements out from their primordial origin. Skepticism is also historically common as communities decide to either embrace (sainthood) or reject ("burn the witch!") those with outlandish spiritual tales.

So, what causes these types of divisions? As for skepticism, for the longest time, I've tried to understand the motivations behind rejecting all spiritual experiences and their implications. Although I used to be a skeptic, my reasoning process is very different today than how it was when I was 14. Fueled by cynicism, I can understand why I sneered at many accounts of a spiritual nature. But this didn't last. Eventually I objectively assessed what was in-front of me, and learned to be less distrustful of the experiences of others. Why is it then that some people never shed this phase?

This mystery was perhaps partially solved when I moved to the Czech Republic followed by the Balkans (Croatia, Bosnia and Macedonia) in 2015, and came to discover just how much a culture can sway your personal beliefs. I came to find that built into the roots of many places in Central and East Europe is an aversion to spiritual topics. This is a subjective observation that did not apply to everyone I met, but it did for a substantial portion. I recall a young woman I briefly dated who immediately began screening me: "I don't like any guy who believes in supernatural nonsense or is into things like science fiction or fantasy, I am a very down to earth woman" (to her dismay I not only write about the paranormal, but I am also an avid science fiction and fantasy writer). She was not the only person I met who had this point of view, and I realized there was a pattern.

The attitude could be understood because countries recovering from Soviet rule experienced a type of institutional atheism that literally forbade spiritual beliefs. However, I think the motivation runs deeper. The further East one goes in Europe, on through Russia, there is a prevailing attitude of being "tough". Part of this toughness includes rejecting hopeful or "nice" things if they could be viewed as naive, as this would indicate an inability to cope with the harshness of life. The more one can tolerate our cold, grim reality (sometimes with the help of vodka), the more respectable you are considered. There is usually no room for spirituality in this atmosphere.

Ironically, many of the people I met in this part of the world were actually by definition, more spiritual than my fellow Americans, if you would define spirituality by principles like not being materialistic, caring about your neighbors and family, being free of egotistical attachments, enjoying the small things, and overall kindness. It was the literal spirituality that they rejected, while they maintained a strong sense of the philosophical golden-rule kind.

Now, it is no longer much of a mystery to me why segments of the population are automatically avoidant of such topics. The topic of life after death, in particular, has such a deep impact on our view of how reality works that it is entangled with personal philosophy, religion, and culture—and it's very hard to separate the two. Even a scientist, academic, or an otherwise trained smart person may be completely swayed by prejudices, and sometimes without fully realizing it.

Therefore, the information that you will be learning about in this book simply isn't for everyone, and it might not be something you'll enjoy learning about. For cultural, philosophical, and personality related reasons, the concept that not only are we more than our bodies—but life is perhaps far more mysterious and *positive* than we imagine it to be, is not a pill everyone wants to swallow.

So there's no reason to hold a grudge against skeptics, either. Cultural prejudices can be infectious, and they can completely hijack our sensibilities. Of course, it is a shame that some people unite under their disbelief to cause damage to the honest work and research of people not affected by such prejudice, which is the challenge that the afterlife researcher faces in an attempt to bring this information into the broad daylight. However, in all this time, not a single skeptic has been able to successfully refute the more convincing areas of afterlife evidence. They operate through broad assumptions, sweeping generalizations and dismissals; but when one examines the evidence under a magnifying glass, it becomes clear that the reason skeptics fear delving too deep is because beneath their broad dismissals are those annoying specific incidences and facts that would be impossible in a court of law to refute. And when concrete anecdotal and scientific evidence is combined with the macro-perspective of an entire phenomenon, then its existence becomes as self-evident as any other established area of nature.

Finally, I've discovered that all prejudices—whether personal or cultural—are weakened in light of the revelatory nature of personal experience, which is what makes endless debate and discussion about the afterlife blur into the background among those who already know because they've literally been there (as in the case of profound near-death experiencers). As I've embarked on this journey myself, I, too, have had enough convincing experiences to help me see that all this "culture war" business and endless debate are just the angry throes of a threatened, outdated paradigm that is now being challenged.

II – The Evidence of the Astral

Throughout history, there have been shadows and glimpses of something unseen and marvelous. It has been interpreted as religion, as the paranormal, and as many other things. Very slowly, and with the help of science, mass communication, and post-enlightenment cultural shifts, the real story is beginning to emerge.

Before we go any further, we must first analyze how the presumption of an astral realm, one that we will presumably reside in after our Earthly deaths, even exists. Admittedly, somebody sheltered from the evidence of this realm could find the concept absurd. The idea of another world that we cannot immediately see or feel but that we can somehow merge into while preserving our own unique identities does, at first glance, seem outstanding.

However, there is far too much evidence to discount the possibility, and the conclusion of life outside the bounds of death—no matter how absurd—must be looked at seriously. Most of the areas of evidence I am about to present—when a bit of critical thought is applied—seems to point in one direction: *the existence of the astral universe*. It's the most logical explanation, as it's the single theory that unites all of the so-called unexplained topics together, adding explanations to where there would otherwise be a lot of confusion, murky theories about mass hallucination, and just general impossibilities to comprehend.

28

The following is a list of subjects with very basic summaries about each one. Understand that every topic here could involve an entire volume of content and research. My aim is simply to show what subjects are most often cited as evidence of the astral world.

As Victor Zammit, author of the very popular book and website *A Lawyer Presents the Case for the Afterlife* says, this type of evidence is meant to be taken *as a whole*, which when put together offers a strong case in support of life after death. The wrong way to approach this topic is to focus on one subject and then use that single area of evidence as the deciding factor of whether or not an afterlife is possible. The problem with looking at the material narrowly is that any particular subject can be picked apart indefinitely. No conclusions can be made from just one area of evidence. If, for instance, the only afterlife evidence a researcher is familiar with is the near-death experience, this poses a problem because NDEs, while convincing on their own, would pose the question of why something so important and fundamental to the universe would be confined to one single phenomenon. This by itself would raise some alarm bells about the possibility of hallucination / self-deception. Further, it's not enough data by itself to be able to hang your hat on it.

The big picture is that there are many different linked phenomena that can be connected to each other based on similarities that relate to some type of astral world. If you feel that an area of evidence in one subject is lacking, there are countless more subjects that can be researched. In fact, there are so many topics that relate to life after death it would take an entire education to familiarize oneself with all of them on a sophisticated level. The amount of research needed to comprehend this topic is one reason I discount armchair skeptics, as I have no doubt they're not properly educated in these matters to even begin to scratch the surface with their criticisms. (This is not to say there are not educated critics, there are—but there are also many who refuse to do their homework.)

AFTER DEATH COMMUNICATION (ADC)

The ADC is a wide and varied subject, which includes some of the more interesting cases of spirit contact from the astral. Many of these reports are anecdotal in nature, although no less profound. An ADC is usually characterized as a specific, personal experience by someone who recently lost a loved one to death. It could be feeling or hearing the departed, an intense dream that provides some level of verifiable information, synchronicities, or even witnessing the sudden physical materialization of the deceased.

An ADC could be as subtle as a whiff of perfume, a strange sign such as a significant number repeatedly appearing, a dream, or other small clues. As it's believed to be hard for an astral person to make contact across the barrier of another universe, perhaps this is all that they can do. However, this style of evidence is limited and not that evidential of an afterlife. More substantial accounts include witnessing a materialized form of the deceased or being provided veridical information through spiritual contact.

. The very term after death communication was coined by Bill and Judy Guggenheim. Throughout the USA and Canada, they interviewed over 2,000 people, chronicling experiences with the deceased ranging from the subtle to the in-your-face literal. Guggenheim estimates that 60 million Americans have had encounters with the deceased.

Most staggering are perhaps when ADCs directly affect the world around us by assisting with an emergency situation. Bill himself, a former Wall Street broker and overall skeptic, was set into motion for this type of work due to his own profound experience. One afternoon in his home, a voice materialized and said "Go outside and check the swimming pool". He stepped outside, found the gate open, and his two year-old son unconscious, floating in the deep end. He saved his son through resuscitation. Despite child-proof doors and locks in the home, his son somehow escaped and would have drowned if not for the mysterious voice, which Bill believed was a spirit's intervention. Bill went on to claim that the same voice would reappear, and it urged him to take up work chronicling other people's encounters with communication from beyond.

For a very interesting time, browse through the archives at http://adcrf.org/. There are many more important cases of veridical ADCs similar to Bill's, where an apparition, dream or vision informs the recipient of previous unknown information; such as the death of the loved one who has appeared, or the news of a different loved one's passing. Such information makes it hard to dismiss these accounts as hallucinations.

APPARITIONS

Apparitions take various forms, including crisis apparitions and after-death communication attempts. By its very nature, this phenomenon is highly veridical and evidential. A crisis encounter in particular is when a person encounters the materialization of a deceased person shortly after that person's death. Typically, the experiencer is unaware that the individual has passed away, and after the strange occurrence they may receive a phone call informing that the same person had just died.

Apparitions, of course, may appear at any time, for any reason—usually in the context of the deceased trying to make contact with a living friend or family member. One of the most well-known incidences was recounted by death and dying pioneer Elizabeth Kubler-Ross. Kubler-Ross will always be well-regarded in the field of terminally ill patient care, as she coined the stages of grief that most of us are familiar with. Kubler-Ross also had a strong interest in near-death experiences and after death contacts.

In her 1997 autobiography *The Wheel of Life*, Kubler-Ross describes waiting outside of an elevator with a colleague, when she noticed a woman in the room with her, a patient who had died some ten months before. She could see this apparition, but her colleague could not. After her coworker left, the apparition approached her and engaged her in a dialogue. The apparition encouraged Kubler-Ross to continue her work on the study of death. Kubler-Ross, fearing that she was experiencing some type of psychotic episode or hallucination, asked the apparition to leave behind some type of proof. She claims the figure then procured a pen and wrote a thank you note for another colleague, asked "Are you happy now?" and then vanished.

These types of apparitional encounters are more commonly reported among bereaved spouses and parents. Apparitions may even appear to rectify a wrong, such as providing authorities the name of the person who killed them. One of numerous examples of this can be found in the Society for Psychical Research records. Since the 19th century, the SPR's American and English branches have investigated and documented the most authoritative incidences of otherworldly contact. In 1911, the American team sent a researcher, James Hyslop, to investigate the incidence of a woman in Portland, Oregon who reported being continuously contacted by sudden apparitions of her deceased son. Her son, an army officer, had reportedly committed suicide. The apparition, however, told a different story, and reported that in reality he had been beaten to death by his fellow officers, and described in detail the locations on the body where he was beaten. The body was exhumed, and the damage matched where the apparition said he suffered the injuries. The death was then considered a homicide, however evidence from a ghost was not credible enough to lead to any convictions[2].

DEATHBED VISIONS & SHARED DEATH EXPERIENCES

"Oh wow, oh wow, oh wow" were the now famous last-words of Steve Jobs, and this experience is hardly isolated. According to researchers like pediatrician Melvin Morse, deathbed visions are a common occurrence, when a dying patient begins to see extraordinary things moments before passing away, but maintains enough lucidity to report them. Their experiences may tie closely to the near-death experience, where the dying patient reports being drawn to a light, or acknowledges deceased family members circling the bedside.

One of the most interesting facets of this phenomena is the shared death experience. Dr. Raymond Moody's 1977 book *Life After Life* brought the near-death experience into common vernacular, and he once again broke new ground over 30 years later with the publication of *Glimpses Of Eternity*. In this book, Moody explores the phenomenon of healthy loved ones or medical staff sharing in the supernatural experiences of a sick and dying patient.

According to Moody's research, the SDE may involve seeing the soul of the dying patient leave the body; perhaps in the form of a smoke or mist that rises upward. The SDE may also include sensing a presence, feelings of peace, witnessing a golden light, or even communication with an astral entity who has come to the bedside of the dying.

Research conducted has shown that these experiences can be very comforting for both the dying and the loved ones who are surrounding the dying patient.

This phenomenon may occur hand-in-hand with terminal lucidity, which I will talk about momentarily.

GHOST CONTACT

Ghost research is an interesting field that is still steeped in paranormalism and entertainment. However, there appears to be a real phenomenon underneath.

Logically, if the material presented is true, and if astral worlds exist outside of our perception, it would make sense that sometimes the astral will "bleed through" into this universe. This may explain a large amount of anomalous incidences throughout the ages. Everything from Bigfoot to sightings of women in white dresses in old houses could be attributed to dimensional glitches and astral bleed-through.

Where things become murkier is defining a ghost versus a spirit—that is to say, an astral intelligence. It would be of disservice to this entire area of study to lump "ghosts"—things that go bump in the night—with communication with astral humans, who are very much not phantoms or wraiths or any of those types of things. That being said, according to ghost experts, there does appear to be "non-human" hauntings; which are more like recordings that playback indefinitely; another kind of "glitch" in our reality interface. An example could be a civil war battle that seems to reoccur in the old cornfields on a dark night.

Perhaps this is why the afterlife has incurred something of a bad reputation through the ages. Misidentifying a ghostly after-image as a regular human who's passed on could create the impression that the astral is a shadowy realm, full of phantoms and unrealities. It would be a grim prospect indeed to imagine that what awaits us after death is a step below what we experience here; and that we fall into some type of illusionary dream world, repeating our actions forever in some cornfield.

Fortunately, there is no reason to assume such things, whatsoever. The ideas of phantasms, specters, ghosts and goblins can all be put aside as irrelevant to the topic of what happens when you— a healthy, conscious human being—passes away. Ghost experts have distinguished between "residual" hauntings where an anomalous event seems to have etched itself into the fabric of reality, and legitimate communications by astral entities.

"Ghost tech" (EVP devices, light diode communication tools, thermal readers, etc) has allowed for some improved communication with such astral entities. However, much of the field is hard to test scientifically, which is why the very mention of ghosts arouses skepticism in many people. As it's hard to put a ghost in a box and examine it, for now this field consists mainly of compelling anecdotal accounts.

And, these anecdotal accounts should not be dismissed just because of their fleeting, personal nature. Sometimes an encounter with an invisible presence can be so compelling that it can completely change a person's worldview.

Further, these encounters fit perfectly with every other area of research, including mediumship. Often, different aspects blend together, and mediums can assist with communication with astral entities in the environment for the purposes of assisting them move on, or for relaying information to the living.

INSTRUMENTAL CONTACT

If you've ever watched a ghost hunting reality show, you've probably heard the acronym "EVP" (electronic voice phenomenon) or seen it in action as ghost hunters wave audio recorders and other devices. My initial impressions about EVP years ago was skepticism and eye-rolling. People obtain garbled sounds and interpret them as spirit communication. My feeling was that EVP was going to hurt the credibility of real afterlife contact.

Herein lies the problem with jumping to conclusions without first gathering all of the evidence. In reality, EVP can be used half-heartedly, or it can be a tool of mediumship; allowing a channel for astral entities to possibly communicate. Delving deeper, I discovered how EVP has been studied for decades, with the concept first introduced by a name you may have heard before: Thomas Edison

"I have been at work for some time building an apparatus to see if it is possible for personalities which have left this earth to communicate with us," Edison is quoted as saying in an October, 1920 issue of *The American Magazine*[3]. Other scientists, like television pioneer John Logie Baird, were actively involved in early EVP signal technology, as well[4]. Later scientists picked up where these great minds left off, bringing the subject of EVP into the light of day. Researchers like Konstanine Raudive, who published the book *Breakthrough* in 1971, recalled detecting voices even after isolating sounds and preventing the possibility of stray radio signals. At its height, over 400 people were involved in Raudive's research.

The issue with EVP is the paraeidolia effect, where random sounds can be interpreted as intelligent speech. As mentioned before, I used to rule out EVP as afterlife evidence because of this possibility, but certain cases of EVP experimentation have caused me to rethink. One of the best examples are Class-A recordings, which are voices dubbed by researchers as crystal clear. To further rule out some type of stray radio signal, the voice would also need to be dynamic and interacting with the experimenter. These criteria have occurred among investigators, notably within the Big Circle group.

In this instance, EVP was used almost as a tool of mediumship for Martha Copeland and the rest of the experimental group. Copeland suffered the loss of her teenage daughter Cathy in a tragic 2001 car accident. Motivated to find answers among other bereaved, a group was formed from the AAEVP.com forums (now the Association for Transcommunication, an EVP / ITC research group) that began seeking ways to make contact with the other side, including through EVP sessions. As they diligently performed experiments, it wasn't long before they were obtaining Class A recordings. Some of these recordings were (reportedly) picked up while the recording apparatus was idle in a room with the experimenter gone. In one instance, a pet dog is barking and the anomalous voice (that reportedly sounds just like Cathy when she was alive) can be heard scolding it ("Doja! No!").

As for the stray radio signal theory, this is not an unreasonable theory. However, in the case of Copeland's group, the voices were clearly that of deceased loved ones, something that is self-evident even when heard by outsiders. Further, something researchers do not detect in their experiments are bits of music, sports announcements, or other types of sounds heard on the radio. Rather, EVPs tend to be very short, concise messages as if the one relaying the message understands they only have a moment to be able to get a communication across.

Whatever the case is with EVP, it's just another interesting piece of the puzzle. It might not provide proof of the afterlife on a standalone basis, but when combined with other areas of evidence, incidences such as the Big Circle recordings create the possibility that something extraordinary could be possible, especially if there is a bond between the communicator and the experimenter.

I highly suggest searching for the documentary *Calling Earth* to explore more areas of research into ITC / EVP.

MEDIUMSHIP (Veridical)

Mediums are not just TV entertainers of dubious credibility. Mediumship includes the ability to sense information from an anomalous source (reputedly, the deceased in the astral). For this reason, police departments around the world continue to use talented mediums to obtain veridical information to help crack hard to solve cases. These practices are met with a lot of criticism, but because the results speak for themselves—mediums are still employed. The topic of psychic police work will be explored in much greater detail in the next chapter.

MEDIUMSHIP (Physical)

One of the most interesting (and hotly contested) areas of research is physical mediumship. This is the ability of a medium to enter a trance state and produce psychic phenomena inside of a séance setting. Traditionally physical mediumship was widely reported in the 1900s, producing many questionable black and white photos of ectoplasm and floating trumpets. However, it's wrong to make the assumption that psychic séance phenomena was just relegated to 1900s sensationalism. In the 1990s, the Scole experiments in England were a heavily documented account of physical séance phenomena, which were attended by scores of highly qualified scientists who used rigorous protocols to confirm true paranormal phenomena. Today, physical mediums like Kai Muegge continue to demonstrate very unusual, photo and video documented phenomena, including the levitation of objects, the materialization of phantom body parts, and even direct communication with materialized entities, who appear in the dark or dim light while the medium is closely monitored or tied as a protocol against fraud.

Perhaps most impressively, however, has been my personal investigation of private physical mediums, where supernatural occurrences become casual weekend events for the sitters. However, due to the nature of the work, such mediums operate outside of the public spotlight to avoid the unending ridicule and scrutiny; instead opting to host phenomena for closed groups to help regulars reconnect with deceased loved ones (and they don't make a dime from this work). For privacy issues of the mediums, this is not information I can go into detail about at the moment, however I hope to be able to expand on this with a greater investigation in the future.

Some who have experienced certain physical mediums claim it is the ultimate proof of life after death; that they are able to talk to, sit with, and even hold their deceased loved ones who fully materialize in the room with them. I'll be the first to admit that this is a very hard subject to accept at face-value because it's so extraordinary in nature. In the next chapter, we'll talk a lot more about physical mediums.

MEDIUMSHIP (Direct Voice)

Yet another form of mediumship, similar to physical mediumship. The most well-known of direct voice mediums would be Leslie Flint, whose career spanned from the 1940s to the beginning of the 1990s when he passed away. Leslie would produce disembodied voices in a dark room that were often recorded on tape. Personalities came through, with claims of being famous old artists like Oscar Wilde and Chopin, as well as a wide variety of regular people or deceased friends and family of the sitters.

Armchair critics and Wiki pages immediately dismiss Leslie as a fraud, but deeper investigations affirm the existence of some type of paranormal or mediumistic ability that goes ignored by the critics. Notably, the case of a man's deceased wife who returned, in her normal voice, and which allowed him to continue his relationship with her for well over a decade. Many of these interactions were recorded, where they discuss intimate details. More information about this incidence and Leslie Flint séances will be discussed later, as well as some of the incredible information about what the afterlife is like— described over decades of séances and hundreds of hours of recordings.

THE NEAR-DEATH EXPERIENCE

No area of afterlife evidence has been more influential to popular culture than the NDE. This is probably because of both the mainstream attention the phenomenon has received, as well as the frequent nature of the experience. Presently, thousands of user submitted NDEs can be browsed at http://www.nderf.org. A great misnomer about the NDE is that it's relegated to a few authors trying to make some bucks. While I find the NDEs of some popular authors, like Eben Alexander, to be highly evidential—we cannot forget the millions of stories that have not been published as mainstream books, but are relegated to private sharing on forums and in the notebooks of researchers like Parnia, Kenneth Ring, Michael Sabom, Penny Sartori, Jeffrey Long, and many more.

The NDE is, in a nutshell, an individual's experience journeying into the planes outside of Earth as a result of cardiac arrest or trauma. They occur about ten percent of the time among cardiac arrest patients[1]. According to researchers like world leading cardiologist Sam Parnia, the phenomena is probably even more common than we realize, but heavy amounts of post operation drugs and sedation may inhibit patient memories.

Exploring the NDE world is truly eye-opening. Surrounding the NDE are so many amazing stories of veridical information, consciousness arising even during complete brain non-functionality, encountering deceased loved ones whom a patient was unaware had even died, and much more. I dedicate a later chapter to this phenomenon where you can learn much more about it.

OUT-OF-BODY EXPERIENCES

What if it were possible to explore another plane without being close to death? Out-of-body experience practitioners claim they can do exactly that. It also opens a window into having your own experiences within the astral dimensions, which may be hard to believe but is certainly another one of the most important areas of afterlife research.

The "university" for out of body exploration is the Monroe Institute, based in Faber, Virginia. The institute describes itself as a center for the exploration of human consciousness, but make no mistake: the faculty firmly believe that their consciousness exploration involves separating from the physical body and experiencing the rest of the inhabited universe in an objective way.

---

[1] According to the Lancet and AWARE studies.

During an OBE, a person may find they experience an electrical sensation over their body, followed by sudden visual awareness of their surroundings despite the fact their eyes are closed. They may then be able to move from their body and into the bedroom, while the physical body remains asleep (and visible) on the bed. A more advanced OBE may lead to an awakening in another type of plane, where it's not uncommon for practitioners at places like the Monroe institute to report encountering astral guides, deceased loved ones, or just random astral residents, in varied locales that range from temples, cities, to non-physical dimensions.

A critic may rightfully wonder if the OBE is a real experience, or some type of dream, especially given that induction of the OBE state often involves the manipulation of sleep states, or even entering the state via lucid dreaming, whereby the dream environment will fade into the astral environment.

My personal experiences, which I will explore in more depth later, suggest that the OBE is a mixture. We are both disconnecting from our physical body, while at the same time being bombarded by dream imagery hallucinations. The skilled OBEr develops the ability to resist the brain's influence, bypass the sleep states completely, and experience out of body perception in a similar way as during the NDE.

Of course, the only way to test that this is really happening is if veridical (verifiable) information can be obtained during the OBE state to prove that consciousness is really disconnected and separated. This can be challenging, because of the aforementioned ways that the OBE realm is mixed with dream imagery; and this can taint perceptions of normal reality. However, veridical information has indeed been recorded.

The best known case would be the experiments conducted by Charles Tart in the late 1960s with an anonymous OBE practitioner identified only as "Miss Z". Z, an unmarried college student in her early 20s, was picked for the experiments due to her ability to frequently enter OOB states.

In the report, Tart says:

"Miss Z's OOB experiences were almost all of one kind. She would wake once or twice during a night's sleep. Each time she would find herself floating near the ceiling, but otherwise seemingly wide awake. This

39

condition would last for a few seconds to half a minute. She frequently observed her physical body lying on the bed. Then she would fall asleep again and that was all there was to the experience. As far as she could recall, these experiences had been occurring several times weekly all of her life. As a child, she had not realized that there was anything unusual about them. She assumed that everyone had such experiences during sleep, and never thought to mention them to anyone. After speaking about them to friends several times as a teenager, however, she realized that they were looked upon as 'queer' experiences, and she stopped discussing them."[5]

Using a sophisticated sleep laboratory, Tart began monitoring Miss Z over the course of several months. During this time, Tart concluded that some type of parapsychological events were occurring, which included both apparent episodes of clairvoyance (Miss Z's psychic connection to a nearby murder) as well as veridical OBE perception. This was obtained through Tart's careful placement of a series of numbers that could not be seen unless observed through an out of body perspective.

"...At 5:57 A.M. the slow wave artifact was lessened and the record looked somewhat like Stage 1 with REMs, but I could not be sure whether this was a waking or a Stage I record. This lasted until 6:04 A.M., at which time Miss Z awoke and called out that the target number was 25132. This was correct (with the digits in correct order), but I did not say anything to her at this point; I merely indicated that I had written the number down on the record. I then told her she could go back to sleep."

At the end of the study, Tart concluded that there was a remote chance of Miss Z cheating if she were to somehow use an apparatus of hidden mirrors that she snuck into the laboratory, but Tart believed it was very unlikely given his protocols; and he concluded a parapsychological explanation was the best fit.

I should note that recently there has been an article trending which claims to have debunked the OBE phenomenon (Neuroscientistnews.com: "Brain scan reveals out-of-body illusion", reporting from the *Current Biology* journal). Or at least, skeptics are using this article to make such a claim. Unlike the experiments with Miss Z, this experiment did not actually involve OBE practitioners inducing their own experiences. The study was simply a recreation of the sensations that could be reported during an OBE state. This was done using head-mounted displays, and then the scientists observed how participants experienced a sensation of bodily disconnection, with brain scans verifying that the mind became confused about its location in relation to the body.

In no way did this study involve participants actually inducing OBE states. In an attempt to disprove a phenomenon, these scientists created an entirely separate phenomenon and then incorrectly tried to link the two together.

PSYCHIC ARTISTRY

Sometimes I am asked "What can you show me in video or photo form that could sway my rigid skepticism?" This is, of course, a tall order to fulfill. All manner of media related to the "supernatural" is typically dubbed unconvincing, especially in the age of consumer level special-effects software.

However, something that can't be faked so easily are the incredible talents performed by people who claim to be psychic channelers, either drawing inspiration from planes beyond—or having their hands literally guided by unseen intelligences while the medium slips away into a trance.

Luis Gasparetto, from Sao Paulo, Brazil is one such artist. His extraordinary claim is that after he began visiting Spiritualist churches in Brazil with his family, he found that an allegiance of astral intelligences were trying to make contact with him. Soon, he felt these same entities were attempting to control his limbs using their own thoughts; essentially possessing his body. As he developed his relationship with them, it became known that the spirits were a host of world-renowned artists who had banded together in an attempt to bring their talents back to Earth. This included entities claiming to be Van Gogh, Picasso, Monet and even Leonardo DaVinci.

Of course, as they say extraordinary claims require extraordinary evidence. The absolutely brilliant paintings produced by Gasparetto, all in exact likeness of the original artists in question, are created while Gasparetto is in a state of trance. During a documentary investigation, Gasparetto was seen creating four beautiful paintings at once, using a separate limb for each apparent spirit (one painting performed by his right foot, left foot, right hand, and left hand). In addition, Gasparetto is seen to work while his eyes are closed and he is in a trance, while he is looking away, or in complete darkness. Finally, he works so quickly that he confounds modern artists who cannot understand how he can create an original masterpiece in just minutes, with no mistakes.

To watch an early 1990s documentary investigation about him, please follow this YouTube URL: http://tinyurl.com/pynhwfx.

Gasparetto is not the only type of psychic artist. Another example is U.S. artist Akiane Kramarik. This young woman born July 9th, 1994 is considered a former child prodigy and is currently one of the world's most recognized artists due to her mind-blowing achievements in realism and poetry. Not long after Akiane first learned to walk, she began playing with the pencil and creating sketches that her parents quickly realized were not ordinary. By age 8, she created "Prince of Peace", a stunningly accurate depiction of a man interpreted to be Jesus. A realistic portrayal that defies many of the church-influenced depictions:

Finished at 8 years of age.

Unlike Gasparetto, Akiane does not claim that her limbs are being operated by any unseen entity. In fact, it would appear her talent is entirely her own (she produces helpful video tutorials for artists available to watch on her Facebook page, as well). Despite starting her career as a little girl, Akiane says that her skill required a great amount of training and practice to master. However, she frequently cites visions, dreams, and a connection to a divine realm as her guiding power. And like spirit-influenced Gasparetto, Akiane can complete a masterpiece extremely quickly, with some of her most well-known paintings finished in as little as two hours.

While there is no outright supernatural claim, browsing Akiane's site (www.akiane.com) and observing how her art has evolved from as young as age 3, it really causes one to pause and consider the other areas of spiritual evidence, like reincarnation. Akiane, on a totally subjective level, seems completely beyond the maturity and skill of anyone else her age. Her art continues to evolve, and represents a wide spectrum of both the human experience, and spirituality. In addition, Akiane herself seems committed to philosophical messages for the benefit of mankind, which can be studied within her words and poetry. After researching her, I believe her body's age does not match what may be a very ancient soul.

The great thing about these psychic artists is that talent cannot be refuted. Even people who are allergic to spiritual ideas can still look at a painting and be moved in the same way.

PSYCHIC ENERGY

Another area of evidence that strongly indicates both the existence of a non-material physics, and the immediate benefits of research into that area, is that of psychic energy and its implications for healing.

For thousands of years, eastern practitioners have referred to the energy systems of the body as "qi"; a force that can be channeled for peaceful or aggressive purposes. Qi is used among martial artists to amplify the power of their attacks, and it is also used by healers to sooth and restore our cells.

There is a long and ancient history of documenting qi energies. However, one of the more interesting investigations aired in a 2007 BBC documentary. A journalist discovered a man in Java, Indonesia who claimed some extraordinary abilities and worked as a healer, channeling qi energy into his patients to fix a myriad of conditions. Many years later, the filmmaker brought a documentary crew to research him. He wished to remain anonymous, so they dubbed him "DJ" (or "Dynamo Jack").

Intrigued by footage and personal accounts of DJ touching patients and causing their bodies to instantly react to the energy, the crew decided to bring along a team of highly trained scientists to investigate him, including Dr. Grey Simpson, a physicist from Albert Einstein University.

The team, skeptical, were quite shocked (pun intended) to discover that DJ was so proficient at the use of qi-energy that he could immediately provide powerful currents into their bodies just by touching them. Determined to sniff out any fraud, the team used an airport-grade metal detector to check for any devices DJ may be using, and he came up clean.

They then isolated DJ in a random location of their own choosing to further rule out any variables related to the environment. Even in these isolated environments, DJ continued to generate powerful electrical currents that, despite their strength, could not be detected through any regular voltage detection meters. He then proceeded to power a light-bulb with his hands. Other feats included generating fire and allegedly pushing a chopstick through a table. To watch the entire documentary, please follow this YouTube link: http://tinyurl.com/o4rbva6.

It's important to be wary of the skeptical claim that these types of incidences have never been properly scientifically studied, replicated, analyzed, and explored in controlled conditions. It simply isn't true. Although unrelated to qi-energy, a comprehensive study was carried out in 1998 and published in the Western Journal of Medicine to study whether distance-based or psychic healing had any real effect or not. Experiments were carried out on groups of advanced AIDs patients with 6 month follow-ups. The experiment was randomized and used double-blind protocols. 40 healers were used, who were picked for having extensive training in holistic healing techniques. When final results were compared with control groups, the experimenters determined the following: "Over the 6-month study period, the [distance healing] group experienced significantly fewer outpatient doctor visits, fewer hospitalizations, fewer days of hospitalization, fewer ADDs, and a significantly lower illness severity level"[6]. In other words, "prayer" seems to work.

Among all the topics covered, the subject of distance or energetic healing is most likely to rouse the ire of the skeptic community. And they are somewhat justified in this anger. The reason is that fraudulent healers have been known to dupe people out of seeking conventional treatments when they are necessary, seeking large payments for fake healing that kills the patients. However, scientific investigations have proven human energy systems are real, and thought-based actions can indeed cause improvements. It's useless and damaging to let the anger caused by some of the charlatans to bleed into the reality of the topic, and worse yet to accuse those with legitimate abilities of fraud.

For more about the powers of the mind over physical reality, please see chapter 13 of this book.

REMOTE VIEWING

Remote viewing is the ability to obtain knowledge and / or create an influence on the environment through a distance. Unlike out-of-body experiences (astral projection), remote viewing is performed during a regular albeit focused state of consciousness. The effects can be produced at any distance, including the other side of the globe.

There is a long history of remote viewing practice that spans through the cold war, and into the present day. The primary book that explores in detail the history of remote viewing by major world governments is "Remote Viewers—The Secret History of America's Psychic Spies" (1997) by Jim Schnabel. Other highly informative books include "Mind Trek (1997) by Joseph McMoneagle, and for an in-depth analysis of modern remote viewing research, please see "Mind at Large" (2002) by famed psychic scientist Russell Targ and edited by Charles Tart and Harold Puthoff.

Remote viewing and other types of psychic behavior is effective enough that world governments have taken the subject very seriously. As is documented in Jim Schnabel's book, in 1978 a U.S. remote viewing operation successfully located a downed spy plane, with President Jimmy Carter confirming the obtainment of the coordinates.

The following is an excerpt from a 2006 *GQ Magazine* interview with Carter by Wil S. Hylton. Hylton asks Carter about his promises to investigate the Roswell incident during his time in office, and if he ever did. Carter decides to go off point and talk, instead, about another area of "paranormal" interest.

"...There was only one instance that I'll talk about now. We had a plane go down in the Central African Republic, a twin-engine plane, small plane. And we couldn't find it. And so we oriented satellites that were going around the earth every ninety minutes to fly over that spot where we thought it might be and take photographs. We couldn't find it. So the director of the CIA came and told me that he had contacted a woman in California that claimed to have supernatural capabilities. And she went in a trance, and she wrote down latitudes and longitudes, and we sent our satellite over that latitude and longitude, and there was the plane."

An interesting thing to note about this interview is Carter's choice of the words *"There's only one instance that I'll talk about now"* which could be translated as there being other instances which Carter *cannot* talk about. What other forays into psychic technology are our governments hiding for national security reasons?

Critics may wonder why this information is not used to catch terrorist leaders and things of that nature. I ask: how do we know it isn't being used for those purposes as we speak? It would seem that governments take this topic very seriously, as it's the ultimate method of spying. If an opposing government suspects that their rivals have given up their psychic spying program, this would give that nation an advantage of secrecy. Under this rationale, it is no surprise that despite the types of hits they were receiving, the U.S. military "officially" ended their use of these techniques, shutting down the Stargate program in 1995. In addition to the location of the spy plane as recounted by Carter, other Stargate "hits" on record include:

- The 1987 attack on the U.S.S Stark by an Iraqi warplane which killed 37 personnel was predicted 48 hours before the attack.

- A downed Soviet TU-22 bomber was located in the jungles of Zaire.

- A kidnapped marine was located and rescued in Europe.

- A Soviet "Typhoon class" submarine was identified and located.

- A successful operation was carried out by Stargate to locate nuclear weapons material stolen in South Africa by paramilitary forces.

- An operation to locate nuclear and biological weapons material in North Korea was deemed a success.

Contrary to popular belief and reports by professional skeptics, the scientists who were tasked with reviewing the Stargate program did not consider remote viewing to be "bogus" or "debunked". Professors

Jessica Utts and Ray Hyman were tasked with evaluating the project. Hyman, although a noted career skeptic, did acknowledge statistical anomalies, as did Jessica Utts, who wrote in a report published in the Journal of Parapsychology that "the statistical results of the studies examined are far beyond what is expected by chance".

This leaves the question of why such a successful program would be shut down. Aside from the possibility that Stargate remains operational on a higher, more covert level—there is also the possibility of conflict the program caused based on moral and religious grounds in the Defense Intelligence Agency. However, this is entirely speculative.

In a 2000 interview with Anthony LoBaido of *World Net Daily*, Anthony asked Utts, a professional statistician, about possible religious bias in the U.S. intelligence community. Utts, avoiding a clear answer, responded:

> "...I have also become much more convinced by the data that there is something unusual going on, that doesn't fit our current understanding of science. But I reserve judgment on what that is. I think those who put this into either a religious or New Age framework are making a leap into what they think the mechanism is. For instance, fundamentalists might think it's the 'work of the devil' and New-Agers might think it's that we are all somehow interconnected. Either theory could be right but that's a matter of faith, not science."[7]

In the end, Utts and Hyman recommended for Stargate to end, which influenced the removal of the program. In the *World Net Daily* interview, Utts explained that the rationale for ending Stargate was that remote viewing is not understood enough yet as a phenomenon for it to be operational for military purposes. However, even the woman who was considered the nail-in-the-coffin for Stargate determined, as a statistician, that remote viewing is a real occurrence. These facts are conveniently omitted by the skeptical portrayals of the program.

Remote viewing is therefore one more proven phenomenon of the mind possessing powers that extend outside of the brain. It can be safely added to the body of evidence toward this book's thesis of the survival of human consciousness, as a mind that can exist outside of the spatial boundaries of the brain also suggests a mind that does not require a brain to be able to thrive.

REINCARNATION

Some of the strongest evidence for life after death exists within the modern body of research into past lives. Dr. Ian Stevenson, the former head of the Department of Psychiatry at the University of Virginia, spent 40 years researching reincarnation. Stevenson took a different approach from his peers who used hypnosis to unearth past-life memories. The issue with hypnosis-based past life recollection is how there is a possibility that memories could be implanted by the hypnotist. Instead, Stevenson opted to investigate the past lives of children; narrowing his focus to incidences such as children who are born with anomalous memories or born with a mysterious comprehension of foreign languages.

Stevenson was known for impeccable research that attracted serious attention by those who would otherwise call themselves skeptics. The late Herbert S. Ripley, former chairman of the psychiatry department at the University of Washington in Seattle, was quoted in the Journal of Nervous and Mental Diseases as saying, "We are lucky to have someone of his ability and high integrity investigating this controversial area. Either he is making a colossal mistake, or he will be known as the Galileo of the twentieth century." [8]

Among Stevenson's work, there is extensive physical evidence documentation in the form of birthmarks. The following is an excerpt from a journal published by Stevenson in the Department of Psychiatric Medicine at the University of Virginia:

"Among 895 cases of children who claimed to remember a previous life (or were thought by adults to have had a previous life), birthmarks and/or birth defects attributed to the previous life were reported in 309 (35%) of the subjects. The birthmark or birth defect of the child was said to correspond to a wound (usually fatal) or other mark on the deceased person whose life the child said it remembered. This paper reports an inquiry into the validity of such claims."

The journal continues with the results of Stevenson's in-depth investigation:

"[A] Burmese child said that she remembered the life of her deceased aunt, who had died during surgery for congenital heart disease. This child had a long, vertical linear hypopigmented birthmark close to the midline of her lower chest and upper abdomen; this birthmark corresponded to the surgical incision for the repair of the aunt's heart. (I obtained a medical record in this case.) In contrast, a child of Turkey had a horizontal linear birthmark across the right upper quadrant of his abdomen. It resembled the scar of a surgeon's transverse abdominal incision. The child said that he remembered the life of his paternal grandfather, who had become jaundiced and was operated on before he died. He may have had a cancer of the head of the pancreas, but I could not learn a precise medical diagnosis."

Many of these eye-opening cases can be found in Stevenson's book *20 Cases Suggestive of Reincarnation*, which is available on Amazon or your local bookstore.

My personal thoughts: A big point about reincarnation research is that these people can remember their past lives. Reincarnation could exist from a materialist point of view, but it would be impossible to remember previous lives because your old neurons that hold memories are destroyed. This phenomenon shows that memories, therefore your mind, must be able to exist outside of the space of your brain.

TELEPATHY

Telepathy does not, by itself, lend evidence directly to support life after death. However, it's another "spoke on the wheel". If it's possible, in even just one instance, for a person's mind to operate outside of the brain and have some type of reaction on the objective world, then it calls into question the mechanical nature of the mind that modern materialists believe. Telepathy, today, is harder to discount. It's becoming more and more apparent that the mind can influence the world at a distance, or allow certain gifted people to perform surprising abilities.

One brand-new study into telepathy relates to the surprising powers of autistic savants. This research is being explored by Dr. Diane Powell and will, in the near future, be published into a full report. However, in the meantime, her early findings suggest autistic children can perform feats that would be impossible without some type of telepathic skill[9]. Examples include having the power to immediately understand the cube root of a six-figure number, randomly generated, without hesitation and without prior knowledge of mathematics.

Taking this well-known phenomenon of the powerful processing power of autistic savants, she setup experimental designs to discover if telepathy is the function of their abilities. A highly autistic, nonverbal nine year-old girl was selected for the potential telepathy demonstration, as therapists had reported telepathic experiences with her in the past. In the experiment, therapists worked outside of the child's view, and were presented with a series of randomly generated images, followed by the therapists writing their descriptions of the images. The child was asked to "read the therapist's mind" and dictate answers via her stencil communication. Further, the child was asked to report the answers to mathematical equations that were being performed by the experimenter, again out of view. The experiment resulted in many conclusive hits, with 100% accuracy being reported multiple times on both the mathematical equation and visual description exercises—a feat that is far beyond any possibility of chance.

This experiment has shown what could be a significant leap forward in the study of telepathic power. Beyond this experiment, however, telepathy has remained a subject of debate and research.

From the theories of biologist Rupert Sheldrake that telepathy is the function of migratory flocks of birds, to the experiments of Russell Targ through the 1970s, 1980s and into the present day which are strongly indicative of an innate ability for human consciousness to detect, influence and create change at a distance. Telepathy becomes a powerful argument in support of non-material properties of physics, which can be connected directly to the support of how consciousness can manifest outside of the body.

TERMINAL LUCIDITY

A phenomenon that may go hand-in-hand with deathbed visions and near-death experiences is terminal lucidity. Explored by psychiatrist Bruce Greyson and biologist Michael Nahm, and currently undergoing extensive research at the University of Vienna, terminal lucidity is reported as the anomalous ability for an Alzheimer's patient, or a patient with a similar damaging condition, who regains full cognitive ability shortly before death[10]. This phenomenon has been reported for a long time anecdotally by critical care nurses and loved ones at the bedsides of the dying. It's currently very hard for mainstream science to reconcile how this could occur, but it fits perfectly with a non-material model of consciousness where awareness levels returns to normal, functional levels as the connection with the physical brain ceases.

According to research by Greyson, there exists in medical literature people who not only lost the ability to think or communicate, but who were discovered after their autopsies as having had degenerated or even completely non-functional brains for a long period of time before their eventual death. And yet, these same patients were able to regain lucid awareness.

Terminal lucidity has occurred among sufferers of:

- Brain abscesses
- Tumors
- Strokes
- Meningitis
- Alzheimer's
- Dementia
- Schizophrenia

- Mood disorders

And yet, despite even physically deteriorated and completely inoperable brains, such sufferers regain full lucid awareness within minutes, hours, or even days leading up to their physical deaths.

Greyson collected cases of 83 confirmed terminal lucidity accounts as documented in mainstream journals, although the incidences are considered quite rare. However, he believes the actual number could be much higher than initial estimates, as in a UK based study, 70% of caregivers to the dying reported stories of patients returning to full lucidity in the hours before death[11].

According to Greyson, there is no known physiological mechanism for terminal lucidity, and so it is placed into the realm of consciousness acting separate from the brain. Greyson hypothesizes that as the brain begins to fully die, consciousness is able to release itself from the brain's confines, and in these uncommon cases the "released" consciousness is still able to interact with the rest of the physical body; while no longer requiring the body to manage the function of processes like memory.

MANY MORE

This short list was designed as a primer for understanding the mere fundamentals of afterlife and psychic phenomena. This is not the complete list. There are many more types of phenomena that can be explored. The breadth of this knowledge is not resting only on the credibility of one or two odd phenomena; but a great assortment of evidence which often consistently points in a particular direction—the existence of some type of astral universe that is wrapped around our own.

III – A Closer Look at Mediumship

In the previous chapter, I introduced many different topics. One of the most varied, as you may have realized, is mediumship. It is also among the most important of the afterlife topics. In this chapter, we'll dig deeper to try and understand mediumship in its various forms.

The skeptical consensus is that all mediums are either deliberate or unconscious frauds. This presumption unfortunately scares people away from a highly evidential field without fully understanding the facts.

Very strong cases of mental mediumship represent an area of parapsychology that is hard for even the most ardent skeptic to fully disprove without resorting to the claim that some form of psi usage occurred.

Even casual observers of the world of mediumship may be familiar with terms like "cold reading", which is the ability for a hoaxer to glean information through subtle hints, cues, body language and assertions to create the illusion of having psychic powers. No one can deny that cold reading is one method to dupe people; historically performed by gypsies in caravans and people trying to make a buck at the local psychic reading boutique. By contrast, there is also "hot reading" when a fake medium finds some way to research the client ahead of time and provide facts to that person.

The best illusion of all, however, is the idea that all mediumship falls into these categories (which is pure intellectual sleight of hand). Practices of blind protocols and scientific scrutiny eliminate these possibilities. And, legitimate psychic mediums are able to overcome the factors that would make a hoaxer crumble apart. When a skeptic says that all mediumship are tricks—don't be duped.

The Medium 7 Research…and the Case of the Donkey Dick

As I searched for the perfect example of mediumship in action, with testable results that are available for digital viewing, I came across the Medium 7 project, a series of research experiments that are profiled in the book *Medium 7: Evidence for the Afterlife and Predictions* by Donna Smith-Moncrieffe (iUniverse, 2013) and with accompanying YouTube videos. For this project, Moncrieffe investigated ten psychic mediums and their clients in an attempt to understand the truth of the situation, while applying scientific protocols to ensure results without threat of trickery or bias. In the process, Moncrieffe carries out in-depth interviews with clients (some rather skeptical initially) and pieces together the accuracy of the readings.

One of the experiments was specifically tailored for non-believers. In this experiment, a client named "Chad" was interviewed who had never met Moncrieffe nor the medium before in his life and had no contact with either of them beforehand (it was a completely blind study to rule out hot-reading). Chad participated in a series of readings by the medium Chris Stillar, and it was moderated separately by Moncrieffe.

In the interview, which takes place about an hour after the psychic reading finished, Moncrieffe asks Chad for his opinion on the topic of mediumship itself prior to the reading. "I thought it was bullshit," Chad responds. "I didn't believe in it at all, I just thought it was lies and a mind-scam," he continues. But after the reading, Chad describes the accuracy of Chris Stillar as "amazing" and that it left him in "shock".

During the reading, Chad describes being given specific information about a recently deceased friend that was totally outside of the realm of chance or cold reading; with firstly his friend's love of pickles being relayed. However, what blew the lid off the case for Chad was when Chris Stillar mentioned the phrase "donkey dick".

According to Chad, "donkey dick" was part of a crude joke that was only known between Chad and his deceased friend, and that it was impossible for the medium to have picked up this information without having known them both personally.

Another piece of accurate information provided by the medium was that Chad had recently been involved in a near accident on the highway when a tire on his work truck blew out. However, there were fewer details about this incident (comparatively speaking).

Aside from being shocked and stunned, Chad reported that the highly verifiable information brought a great sense of closure that his friend was fine[12]. (You can find the entire interview by searching for the Medium 7 project or Donna Moncrieffe on YouTube.)

The Medium 7 project is host to a wealth of additional information and veridical information, as well as this case. It's worth researching for anybody looking for the strongest evidence available of legitimate mental mediumship.

Mediumship is Consistently Reliable in Laboratory Conditions

Aside from donkey-size...*ahem*, mediumship has a long history of verifiable information. The skeptical approach is to find the failures of mediums and cling on to them while ignoring substantial hits like the above case. However, in reality, if even one highly accurate (beyond chance) reading is performed, with blind protocols established, it immediately calls into question the narrative that all mediums are hoaxers, and it requires reassessment of the information.

One place to begin delving into this information would be the Scottish Society for Psychical Research. Tricia Robertson and the late Archie E. Roy worked extensively to determine whether the typical criticism against mental mediumship, that all information provided by psychics are broad generalizations, was worthy of any merit. They carried out one of the largest studies of mediumship ever conducted.

At the end of their projects, the final reports from papers 1 and 2 were published in the April 2001 and July 2001 editions of the Journal of the Society for Psychical Research, with a later third paper published, as well.

In the first paper, experiments were carried out between 440 participants and 10 mediums, and the reduced chance of the skeptical hypothesis being correct were "millions to one" (sspr.co.uk)[13]. In the second and third papers, the investigators began applying varied strict experimental designs to prevent body language inference by the medium, and various other factors, including the seating placement of the participants, all of which could be construed into skeptical arguments that some type of elaborate cheating took place. The final results, with new protocols established, were still favorable to the mediums and the chances of their hits remained at millions to one against the skeptical hypotheses. The papers can be accessed online at the SPR website (www.spr.ac.uk).

Other studies continue to verify the authenticity of certain mediums, utilizing strict protocols including triple and quintuple blind studies. My hometown of Tucson, Arizona has become a hotbed of such mediumship research in recent decades. The Windbridge Institute, founded by Julie Beischel and her husband Mark Boccuzzi, continued the field of afterlife research after the University of Arizona VERITAS lab closed in 2007 (VERITAS, directed by Prof. Gary Schwartz, was where many positive mediumship experiments were carried out, as documented in the book *The Afterlife Experiments*).

In a 2010 report, Beischel, the Windbridge director, describes the protocols involved for their mediumship experiments in order to eliminate all of the variables that could create incidences of fraud or bias, as proposed by skeptics[14]. Beischel uses quintuple blind studies. This means the names of the deceased are provided to Beischel through e-mail from a colleague, with the sitter (the participant of the reading) blinded to any direct contact with Beischel and the medium. Beischel then asks the medium a series of specific questions related to the deceased person. Later, a different sitter and a different deceased subject are used for a second experiment. The names are hidden, and the two sitters are then asked to score each reading without knowledge about which hits by the medium belonged to which sitter. The experimenters working with the mediums and sitters are also blinded about which experiment was which. Using this protocol, the accuracy of the readings can be determined by interviewing both sitters. In the event of broad information (cold reading), then there would not be a difference in the accuracies of each reading as they apply to the specific sitters.

Since the founding of Windbridge, the institute has been slow, methodical and highly scientific in its approach to studying mediumship in this way. Using increasingly rigorous and blinded studies, Beischel and associates have spent considerable time organizing experiments and analyzing data. The institute refers to the acronym AIR to describe their main working hypothesis (anomalous information reception), and an early experiment at the institute with mediums provided data that supported AIR and mediumship as a legitimate phenomenon; however, according to Beischel "In science, it doesn't happen until it happens twice," as one "positive" experiment can always be discounted as some type of fluke. Therefore, to follow up their initial experiments, in March 2015 Beischel published the results of a second large mediumship experiment. In this experiment, a total of 20 specially certified Windbridge mediums participated with a total of 87 sitters, including the blinded conditions mentioned previously. According to the subsequent paper published in the journal *Explore*, the hits provided by the mediums was beyond the realm of chance and that a non-local source of information transfer was the most likely explanation[15].

According to the Windbridge website, the institute is continuing expanded research into both psi phenomena as well as specific afterlife related areas. Currently in progress there is research being carried out to explore the claims of instrumental contact with the deceased, and several studies have already been performed investigating different aspects of ITC / EVP work. In addition, Windbridge also researches areas of grief support / psychological counseling related to mediumship. To stay up to date with Windbridge, please see www.windbridge.org.

Mediumship as a Law Enforcement Tool

A question arises that if psychics and mediums can obtain information from unseen sources or telepathic means; then why don't they use their powers to help solve criminal cases? The answer is that police agencies have had a long history of utilizing psychic case work. It is, however, a complex and sometimes frustrating subject.

According to the investigations into psychic police work, as chronicled in the book *Psychic Criminology: A Guide For Using*

Psychics in Investigations by Whitney Hibbard and Raymond Vorring, the use of a psychic typically begins with the psychic making a phone-call to the precinct after he or she received some type of information purportedly from the deceased, which often occurs when the police are making no headway in solving a recent death. This, however, is an awkward venture because the psychic must deal with an unsympathetic deputy who is not ready to waste the time of him(her)self or other officers listening to somebody who they might regard as some crackpot or circus gypsy. Officially speaking, precincts do not admit that they use the aid of psychics. Off the record, however, it's well established that sometimes even an unsympathetic police station will, as a last resort, turn to the aid of a medium—and find surprising results. According to Hibbard and Vorring, numerous police chiefs have been known to secretly employ psychic help for hard to solve cold-case files, and that the positive results have led to other police stations seeking out the same psychic assistance; all while trying to keep it formally off the record so as to avoid scrutiny. The authors argue that given the enormous benefit that mediums and psychics have provided to law enforcement, and the increasing pressure on police departments to implement them, then it's time for their usage to become established and in the open.

There are many cases of psychic detectives cracking mysteries and providing veridical information. Special thanks to contributor Eteponge for highlighting some of these cases on his paranormal research related blog. One psychic that Eteponge brought to my attention is Dorothy Allison who deserves special mention here[16].

The Work of Psychic Detective Dorothy Allison

Allison (1924-1999), was a New Jersey housewife, talented from an early age with the ability to see, hear, and communicate "beyond the veil". According to her Los Angeles Times obituary from 1999, when Allison was a child, neighbors thought she was a witch because she had a vision of her father's death shortly before it occurred[17]. Not allowing the negative connotation to deter her, Allison continued to hone her psychic abilities. Her mother, who shared some of her talents, warned that her gift should not be used for profit. As a result, Allison claimed she would never accept any money in return for her assistance with numerous cases of missing children and other cold case homicides.

Her first major experience occurred in 1967[18]. Living as a housewife and a mother of four, she had a dream where a blonde, blue-eyed boy in a green snowsuit, with his shoes on the wrong feet, had drowned in a pond, with his body getting stuck in the drainpipe. A month later, a boy's remains whose description had never been publicized was found in a drainpipe, green jumpsuit and shoes on the wrong feet.

In 1974 Randolph Hearst asked for her help to find kidnapped daughter Patricia Hearst. She made several accurate predictions in this case, including that she was hiding in Pennsylvania and then New York, and then she would go on to join her captors as a bank robber herself (an example of a premonition).

Later in December 1974, Allison was asked by the police to assist with a missing person. A businessman boarded a train, but he never got off at its stop—simply disappearing. Some suspected that he fled after an embezzlement operation, or that he eloped with a mistress. Allison, however, was convinced he was dead. The body would later be discovered, as it would seem the man fell (or jumped) from the train into a riverbank as the train passed over a bridge. Allison provided spot-on accurate details about the location of the death, as well as the future discovery of the body. The information was noted by the precinct 3 months before the discovery.

-   Allison first suggested that he drowned after falling off the train, and that he was in a body of water. This was true.

-   That a bow and arrow was of note. As it turned out, a boy shooting a bow and arrow with his father near the scene accidentally shot an arrow across the riverbank, and the arrow landed next to the corpse, whereupon they called the authorities.

-   That the number 222 was significant. This was the date the body would later be discovered (February 22nd).

60

- She described a row of tires up on a hill, near an area where children played, and this was where the body was. These were all accurate descriptions of the area by the riverbank.

- That the numbers 166 were significant. There was an old tugboat stationed (permanently) directly below the bridge. The numbers 166 were written in large print on it.

- That "two guys" would discover the body. It was discovered by the father and son team.

Although she didn't solve the case herself, this could be attributed to a lack of diligence on the part of the police, as all of her information turned out to be correct in relation to the location of the body. Although perhaps the body was not meant to be discovered prior to February 22nd—the date that she predicted it would be found.

As for the next case, in 1976, 14 year-old Susan Jacobson disappeared from her home. After the police told her parents that she was a runaway, the parents came to Allison for help. First, Susan correctly identified the girl's birthdate and time of birth, and then proceeded to state that she had been strangled by her boyfriend—complete with providing the boyfriend's name.

- She described that the body was in a marsh area, with the word MAR written in big red letters.

- That there was a smell of oil.

- That the numbers 222 were present.

- There was an abandoned car nearby.

As it turns out, the body was discovered in a marsh, stuffed into an oil drum, with the numbers 222 on the drum. The words "MAR" were written on a rock about 100 yards from the body. There was an abandoned car in the marsh, as well.

Other visual clues were provided—including two sets of church steeples (a church was in view) and a nearby factory with

61

smokestacks (accurate). The boyfriend who murdered her was later caught and convicted of the killing.

Another noteworthy case in her long career of psychic police work occurred in 1991. Police called her about a missing girl. She returned impressions of a girl dismembered and encased in cement. She said there may be a body near a lake, and she drove by a lake in question. This grisly vision however did not yield any helpful clues as it seemed unrelated to the case the police were asking about.

It would seem it was a "miss", until several months later a different missing person case occurred in June, 1991. Two weeks later a girl's body was discovered in the lake, dismembered, and encased in cement. Much like the previous case, it would seem Dorothy was able to detect a murder before it had occurred, and was aware of the exact location and method of death months before it actually happened (this has some startling implications for the concept of pre-crime, like in the movie *Minority Report*).

Following this case, Dorothy told police a second body would be found, strangled underneath some brush. Another body was indeed found, just as she described.

This is only the tip of the proverbial iceberg. I would suggest to see Eteponge's blog (eteponge.blogspot.com) for a more thorough listing of many other incidences. According to her obituary, she died at age 75 after having predicted her own death exactly, and that her walls were lined with awards and certificates from the police stations that she assisted throughout her career.

If one were to consult with the Skeptic witch-hunting teams on Wikipedia and elsewhere, none of the information I've presented would be of any validity. As with any good psychic, there are misses as well as hits, and cases that she could not solve. Instead of looking at the information objectively, and understanding that some of the information is highly veridical and could easily pass in a court of law, the Skeptics in this situation have chosen to *ignore* her veridical information and instead attack her based on what appears to be a cherry-picked assortment of misses and skeptical opinions about her, spanning over the course of her very long career.

In 1981, James Randi (the historic and infamous Skeptic) "awarded" her a condescending "pig" trophy for charlatan psychics. A mean-spirited gesture that served no purpose other than to try and shame and bully those who attempt to go public with psychic talents.

Meanwhile, you can find Dorothy's Wikipedia page at the following address (https://en.wikipedia.org/wiki/Dorothy_Allison_(psychic). Take a look at it, and then ask the Guerilla Skeptic editors who control the biographies of all psychics on Wikipedia why none of the objective information listed in this book are provided for readers, and why the tone of the entry is that of defamation instead of an unbiased assessment. You can reach the Guerilla "Skeptics" at their blog (http://guerrillaskepticismonwikipedia.blogspot.com/).

Delving Deeper into Psychic Police Work

The next obvious resource that you should use as you explore more into the field of psychic police work is Victor Zammit's collected testimonies of police officers, as well profiles of many more psychic detectives who have been used to crack cases while confounding the skeptics. You can find this information at: www.victorzammit.com/articles/psychicdetectives.html

There is the possibility of this type of work becoming more mainstream. However, obvious challenges exist, especially as it relates to cultural taboos. Seasoned officers are reluctant to admit that they use psychics, and further the police must undertake the task of discerning credible psychics from less than talented ones who may phone in tips with no use to them. Finally, the mainstream climate in any professional discipline is very negative about psi, for reasons that have already been outlined.

However, there has been one interesting recent step forward in psychic work, when a renowned and seasoned criminal profiler—Deborah Schurman Kauflin (PhD)—came forward in November 2012 to announce that during her long career, she had often relied on her secret abilities as a psychic medium which gave her a special edge—allowing her to identify specific names, incidences and even future events (including the 2008 Mumbai terrorist attacks) through her link with the other-side.

In the 2012 *Psychology Today* article, Kauflin writes, "Many times shrewd detectives told me I was so accurate, it was eerie"[19]. Kauflin writes that she had kept her abilities as a psychic medium secret, as it's not yet a widely accepted branch of law enforcement. However, she claims that over the course of her long career, she could list many times that she'd witness cops and homicide specialists secretly working with psychics or even harnessing their own psychic / intuitive abilities to assist with hard cases. In fact, Kauflin claims that the "majority" of detectives that she'd work with over the years used some sort of psychic assistance.

Kauflin's revelation suggests that in the hardened field of law enforcement, there exists a taboo and unspoken field of psychic usage that is perhaps already more mainstream than we realize—however, it seems to exist in a shadowy, secretive way. The police know it works, but they also know they cannot speak about it openly or they would not be taken seriously by the people they are tasked to defend. And so, psychic police work remains a best kept secret of criminal profilers, detectives, and other branches of law enforcement.

The Television Interpretation

Popular TV shows have explored the psychic law enforcement world, such as "Psychic Detectives" and "Sensing Murder". Many episodes of these shows demonstrate cold case files cracked by psychic mediums, with interviews of both police involved, as well as the medium him / herself; often combined with dramatic reenactments. On these programs we see hardened officers of various rank testify to successful psychic involvement with police work. Critics have suggested the huge amounts of jaw-dropping case studies presented on such shows are invalid by nature that they are presented on television. This, however, is an unfair assumption given the methodical research that has gone into the production of these two shows in particular.

Firstly, let's establish whether or not the mediums presented on these programs are legitimate; or if we are dealing with some type of manipulation of facts and the presence of cold-readers. For this book, I spoke to Brian Shennan, who worked as the sound recording specialist on the New Zealand production of *Sensing Murder* in the early 2000s. Shennan is also recognized for his work in the field of audio engineering on countless major New Zealand productions since the 1970s, including popular movies like *The Lord of the Rings*. According to Shennan, it was his job on *Sensing Murder* that would become the most memorable—and life changing—of his entire career.

One of the episodes of the show involved an Australian psychic medium named Deb Webber whom was participating on an episode. On the first day of shooting, Deb told Brian "There's something not right with your prostate, promise me you will get it checked". Shennan did not hesitate to get to a doctor not long after the medium's pronouncement, whereupon they conducted an MRI. As it turned out, Shennan had the beginnings of prostate cancer, and in addition his left kidney was also cancerous, twice the size it should have been, and very close to bursting. A few days later he underwent an operation to remove the cancer, which would have killed him had he waited any longer. Well over a decade later, Shennan is alive and healthy.

Clearly, the mediums participating in the police investigations, and who are subsequently highlighted on these TV shows, are not merely fraudsters, as even the people who work around them during the productions are able to report profound experiences like this.

Brian also reports another incident with Deb. "We had a Detective Senior Sergeant insist on sitting in on a reading [with Deb, who was attempting to use her abilities to crack a case]. He sat there and at one point he had his head in his hands, shaking his head. After I asked why, he said that as the person in charge of the case he was the only one in the whole world who knew all the details, and Deb had come out with them and more. He was shaken."

I asked Shennan about his favorite case that he learned about on *Sensing Murder*. Shennan explained to me that the show provided opportunities to work closely with mediums, the families of murdered victims, and the police investigators, which resulted in a lot of "behind the scenes" experiences and stories that had a lasting impact on him and the rest of the crew. The following are Shennan's notes about his favorite incidence (this does not add strength to the subject of psychic police work, but it was just a great story that I wanted to share):

"A long time ago I interviewed a man named Keith Stewart [on the *Sensing Murder* set]. Keith and his wife ran a convenience store across the road from their local school. On this particular day he had to go to the wholesalers to get supplies for his shop. They had 3 children, the youngest of whom was their 6 year-old daughter, Lynley. Keith could only take the 2 elder children to help him as there was little room in his vehicle. He told Lynley to go across the road and play with the other neighborhood children that were still in the playground. When Keith returned a little later and found that Lynley was not at home, he went to the school to look for her. Although he searched and asked a few children if they had seen her, she was gone.

The police were called by dusk, and a search ensued. Some time later that evening they found Lynley's body under a school building. She had been murdered. When the police caught the person who had done it, it turned out the killer was a 12 year-old boy with extreme mental problems.

Now Keith aimed to be a good man of Christian principles, and after talking to the boy at a later date, forgave him. He and his wife couldn't sleep properly during those next 2 years after her death, as they so often wished they had had the chance to say goodbye, and kept thinking of the 'what if ' situations. One night he was lying in that half-awake state and suddenly he was on the greenest hill he had ever seen. He climbed to the top and looked down on the bluest sea he had ever seen. He could hear the squeals of delight coming from children playing in the surf. He walked down and into the sea, even though he couldn't swim and was afraid of the water. As he waded towards the children he saw Lynley. She saw him and screamed 'DADDY'. He swept her into his arms and held her tight. She pulled back and she said 'Who loves you Daddy?'. He said 'You love me darling'. She said, 'Yes, but Jesus loves you more' and with that he was back in his bed beside his wife. Although, he realized that awake in his arms suddenly was Lynley, alive and well. Solid and real. His wife awoke and got a frightful shock. They spent the next 2 wonderful hours talking and holding her and saying what they had wanted and wished they could have said to her.

Then, she said 'It's time. I must go. I love you...' and she faded away. Keith said it was the greatest gift Jesus could have given them. I was sobbing. The [*Sensing Murder*] crew were in tears, too. It was a great privilege to be there. But the story doesn't end there. The boy who was 12 years-old was sent off to a mental health unit in Levin specially built for him. He was the only occupant for some time. After many years of specialist help he was rehabilitated and released back into another community in the North Island. Keith got in contact with him on his release and spent many hours working with him to find him a job and set up a place for him to live. That man today is married and has children of his own. He took on spiritual values and is now a solid member of that community. Keith and his wife passed away some time later, to be reunited with their precious Lynley."

Although only a tale from the set of a TV show, this story is similar to other after death communication materializations that I've researched. Such accounts, as this one told by Keith, begin to lend credibility to the notion that, perhaps under guidance in specific situations, the dead can actually return to our world in full flesh and blood. This is the perfect opportunity to transition into the last area of mediumship—which involves attempting to enable such materializations under the carefully tailored conditions of the séance.

The Contested World of Physical Mediumship

As discussed in the last chapter, physical mediumship is one of the most compelling—albeit elusive—areas of afterlife research. It is also one of the most wrought with potential fraud. Skepticism surrounds the powers of physical mediums due to the extraordinary nature of their claimed abilities; however, there is no denying the great impact that physical mediums have made on people's lives, and the incidences that many have claimed to be "irrefutable proof" of the existence of the greater planar world.

Before we go further, let's try to conceptualize the types of experiences sitters claim to have. Imagine for a moment that you enter a small séance room with a few friends or neighbors, a researcher or two, and the medium. The chairs are arranged informally into a circle, and the medium may sit in-front of the sitters. Protocols against fraud may be taken simply as a measure to help properly document the experiences, and so the medium may have his or her hands tied together, mouth gagged, or sitters may elect to tie a string from themselves to the medium to ensure that the medium is not tampering with anything or moving during the seance, and that instead he is accounted for the whole time.

The lights are shut off or dimmed, and then there may be some element of "merry making"—singing, relaxing, and talking amongst each other. The purpose of this, so claims the etheric entities, is to lighten the "vibration" which makes it easier for them to make contact with the Earth plane.

Eventually, after some time passes, the medium will have entered a trance. Then, the sitters may find the temperature and "energy" in the room begins to change. They may, as documented in instances of ghostly contact, find the temperature to suddenly drop by a few degrees. They may hear a few unusual noises—whooshing or gargling—which is purportedly the ectoplasm being manufactured by etheric entities—and being removed from the medium, where it will then "coat" the astral bodies of the visitors. As this biological substance has the peculiar property of somehow existing in solid form in both universes at once, it allows a visitor to use it to manipulate and interact from beyond the veil.

Some physical circles are considered "developing", where the ectoplasm may result in just the formation of an unusual structure, an arm, or another limb appearing in the room and interacting with the sitters. These cases can be evidential in their own right, as a half-materialized form is arguably harder to fake than a full materialization. The fully developed accounts of physical mediumship, however, involve reunions with an entire materialized form appearing. In these instances, sitters may recount being embraced by the physical representation of a deceased loved one—matching in voice, body shape, smell, and many other details, as well as providing unmistakable evidence in the form of personal information relayed from the materialization to the sitter.

I would like to point out I have no way to verify the accounts of the most hotly contested physical mediums of yesteryear. This includes names like Helen Duncan, Eusapia Paladino, Eva Carriere, and others. Some historical physical mediums, despite being figureheads of Spiritualism, have less than sound reputations. There have been reports by independent investigators of 1900s physical mediums manipulating séances by using puppets, wires, and other tactics to simulate paranormal occurrences. This is one of the reasons that the Spiritualist movement itself remains viewed today with a great deal of skepticism.

Because of the shoddy history, every physical medium has been "officially" considered "fraud". But when you dig into the research, what you find are wildly conflicting reports. Proponents cite incredible experiences of objective, verifiable information and solid materializations of departed loved ones. Skeptics cite unfavorable experiences by investigators, who typically accuse the medium of orchestrating the whole thing with dual personalities. Most historical physical circles have had one or two researchers return with allegations that the whole event was made up, and these are usually the reports that lead to the cases being closed and the general consensus developing that said medium was a charlatan.

You can yourself venture further into this territory and make up your own mind and about who's a fraud, who isn't, and who exists in some nebulous in-between zone; however, I have no desire to comb over this literature when there are more interesting areas to investigate. I find a handful of physical mediums to be thought-provoking; and the modern forays into this field to be more reliable than what was presented in the heyday of Spiritualism. This is what I will focus on.

Further, in regard to some of the more famous cases of late 19th century and early 20th century physical séance circles, it's impossible to write about a topic with accuracy if no one living was present to experience it. All that's left in the end is conjecture and second-hand information based on historical records. Because of the extraordinary nature of the claims of such mediums, the entire topic has existed as a type of "low hanging fruit" among the skeptic community, who often use claims of fraud against physical mediums to paint the entire afterlife topic with an air of mischief. Obviously, this is as extreme a point of view as declaring all of the physical mediums to be genuine.

It's a truly bizarre subject because both the accounts of fraud and the accounts of legitimate abilities seem equally convincing. It makes one wonder if some strange miasma of both fraud and paranormal activity exists together in a type of symbiosis (see the book *The Trickster and the Paranormal* by George Hansen for more about this). Today, modern physical mediums whom I have researched, however, are far less interested in the spotlight or any of the types of activities of the mediums of yesteryear. In addition, they only charge as much money as needed to cover the costs of airplane travel and other expenses. This calls into question the skeptical assertion of fraudulent behavior, as what motive would a person have to devote their entire life to a dumb hoax—when they could make so much more money as a real magician, or a stage medium? This argument does not, however, refute allegations by skeptics that such mediums are perpetuating some kind of personal psychological delusion or multiple personality disorder.

My feeling is that it's impossible to know with certainty unless you discover a physical séance and attend yourself. The skeptic position can be extremely rigid and unyielding in its anti-parapsychology stance. But yes, believers can be prone to wishful thinking and flights of fantasy. There exists bias and flaws in both sides. The only real way to understand these things is to seek out a private physical séance and evaluate your own experiences.

Short of finding your own séance, my suggestion is to look into the accounts with an open mind, consider possibilities of mischief, but also don't completely discount the reports by credible sitters. Not everyone is gulled by wishful thinking. Most educated, critical thinkers would rather sit on a hot pike than allow themselves to have the wool pulled over their eyes. And, these same types of people have walked away from physical circles convinced of their authenticity.

How Physical Mediumship Influenced an Afterlife Activist

Michael Findlay Roll (b. 1938) from Bristol, England is one such person who was heavily affected by a physical phenomenon séance circle. In Michael's words, he advocates now for the secular case for the survival of human consciousness and the existence of the afterlife realms. Roll and the rest of his organization, the Campaign for Philosophical Freedom (cfpf.org.uk), believes that the afterlife is not a subject related to religion or mystical thought, but a tangible realm that is ruled by laws of physics, mathematics, and chemistry—the same as our universe. Indeed, it's simply another branch of the same universe that we exist in right now. Roll, a self-described atheist, sees no contradiction between secular, rationalist thought and the acceptance of the data for life after death.

For Michael Roll, his experiences were with the physical medium Rita Goold, who was most active around the area of Leicester, UK in the 1980s[20]. As with other physical mediums, Goold's alleged ability was to bring the dead through in their normal bodies, as apparitions—living and breathing.

Rita Goold was allegedly debunked by an SPR investigator named Tony Cornell. According to the book *Investigating the Paranormal* (Helix Press, 2002) Tony discovered that the materializations matched the size, shape and physical consistency of the medium herself, who he accused of stealthily changing her clothes in-between impersonations. Roll's report, of course, is a contradiction to Cornell's as he verified that the materialization were extremely different and identifiable on a level of personal detail, including the accuracy of the appearances of close loved ones which could be confirmed on a highly personal level. Cornell is no more reliable a witness than Roll (and others) who attest these facts about Goold's work.

According to Roll, he received "crushing proof" of the afterlife after attending some séances with Goold in Leicester in 1983. Unlike Cornell's impression, Roll found that the materializations were staggeringly accurate and of no relation to the physical form of the medium herself. As an example, pioneering scientist and psychical researcher Oliver Lodge purportedly would appear in the séance room. According to Roll, unlike the medium Lodge was a tall male over six feet. Further, although the séance was performed in the dark, illuminated clothes were allowed to be worn during the session. In Roll's account, Lodge dressed himself in glow-in-the-dark boots and a jacket, and then proceeded to walk around the room with a pair of drumsticks, tapping himself to show to sitters that he was real. He then proceeded, according to Roll, to defy physics by pushing the drumsticks straight through the table as a demonstration of etheric physics altering our physics (Roll describes it as a less than effortless process, as Lodge had to push it through the table like "a sharp knife through polystyrene" before it fully absorbed through the wood). Later, according to this account, the materialization then stepped *through* the table, sinking his body into it. This is all possible as a result of etheric life-forms possessing mental powers that are extremely powerful by our standards.

Further, Roll describes the appearance of Goold's famed spirit controller "Russell" who appeared as a nine year-old child, markedly different from any of the sitters in attendance or the medium herself[21].

Of course, the materialization of strangers, in this case Mr. Lodge and Russell, is less convincing by comparison to the materialization of somebody with whom you were personally acquainted in life. For Roll, his communication with his deceased father during the séances confirmed for him the validity of Goold's mediumship. Since these séances, Roll now runs the Campaign for Philosophical Freedom, which advocates for a secular case of life after death in a world where taboo subjects such as this are treated with hostility.

Roll is an advocate for early researchers who he says supported the secular argument for the afterlife. This includes Sir Oliver Lodge, Oliver Crookes, Arthur Findlay and the philosophies of Thomas Paine. The following is one excerpt from an interesting 2012 interview with Roll from Spirit Today:[22]

"It was very important for me to physically meet my 'dead' father at the Rita Goold experiment in 1983. I had to have this experience for a job I had to do on Earth – bring to millions the censored scientific discoveries that prove we all survive the death of our physical bodies. My job is now very easy, all I have to do is just point to what has been discovered but deliberately blocked. No prizes will be given to any person who guesses correctly which route the great mass of people will take when they have bothered to read Paine, Findlay, Crookes and Lodge:"

The Scole Experiments

No discussion of physical mediumship can be complete without mentioning the experiments performed in the basement of a cottage in Scole, England through the 1990s.

Understand that physical mediumship can include any host of phenomena occurring *physically* and produced through the tandem work of a medium and a team of etheric visitors, working through the medium to manifest into our universe. This may include lights, voices, faces, levitations, apports (mysterious objects dropping from the air), temperature changes, smells, and any number of paranormal occurrences happening in the controlled condition of a séance. Most of these many varied phenomena occurred for years through the Scole group.

Scole was primarily a physical mediumship circle that worked out of a farmhouse in Norfolk, England. It was organized by Robin and Sandra Foy, and Alan and Diana Bennett working as the mediums. It was an experimental research group open to all manner of scientific investigation, which is the reason Scole became a famous name in the legacy of parapsychological research. In attendance included esteemed professors like David Fontana, Montague Keen and Rupert Sheldrake.

Much of the phenomena of the Scole group was documented by Montague Keen of the SPR. It should be noted that some detractors may claim that the Society for Psychical Research, by nature of being a paranormal investigatory organization, is not a legitimate research group. However, the SPR is an impartial organization that has been instrumental in the *disproving* of psychic phenomena, with SPR members like Donald West who have historically worked to discredit physical mediumship. It is an organization of trusted academics and researchers that is keen to prevent any type of self-interest or fervent belief in a subject from contaminating an investigation. The Scole group remained under this high level of scrutiny throughout the course of the circle, and time and time again researchers were baffled by the phenomena documented within the cottage's old cellar.

The claim by the mediums of Scole is that they had established contact with a group of scientists who were living in the astral dimension. These scientists had been creating experimental

73

techniques to make contact with the Earth, using the séance as the conduit for their contact.

Keen described the investigation as follows: "Our objective was to obtain evidence of a permanent nature which could be experienced or examined independently outside the séance room, and was not wholly reliant on subjective assessment, experience, memory or feeling: evidence which had been produced in circumstances which precluded human interference and would satisfy external critics." (Keen, 2001).

According to the reports summarized by Keen, the following are some the phenomena experienced by attendees of Scole[23]:

- The manifestation of spirit lights that moved independently around the darkened room and interacted with sitters.

- These same lights would follow directions and communicate with attendees. They would bounce around the room, dive into crystal objects, cause small objects like tennis balls to move around—being pushed by an invisible force, cause crystals to levitate in front of the attendees faces, and penetrate through other objects.

- There was one report of the lights causing a crystal to "dematerialize"—a sitter was asked to pick a crystal up that had been manipulated by the light, and found that his fingers were passing through the phantom of an object that had formerly been physical.

- Some of the lights responded to "silent requests" by the sitters, indicating a type of telepathy occurring between the lights and the attendees.

- The moving of furniture by an unseen force.

- The presence of "shadowy floating figures" that would appear in the room. According to Keen's report, most attendees experienced light touches by these entities, from locations that would have been impossible to reach

74

through trickery. This also included the feeling of these materialized forms brushing past them, whereupon their light gossamer clothing could be touched.

- Successful experiments with photographic film. To preclude all possibilities of tampering, scientists would bring *unopened* cases of film, and upon later opening and developing it, they would find anomalous images and messages imprinted by the spirits. This included imagery of half-formed human faces and lines of obscure poetry that related to the context of the session that day.

- It should be noted that to further rule out fraud, these unopened film canisters were also placed into plastic security bags. Later, the experimenters even used a locked box to house the film, and the spirits continued to successfully imprint the evidence.

- Apports, or mysterious objects materializing within the séance room, falling into the laps of sitters.

- Entities manifested who possessed knowledge that appeared of a unique nature and which could not be replicated by the mediums themselves. One spirit reportedly had a discussion about advanced engineering concepts with another attendee. According to Keen, a subsequent cross examination with the mediums ruled out any knowledge on their part of such topics.

- Before the dissolution of the Scole group, many other strange phenomena were recorded by various sitters over the years, such as purported visitation from alien (non-human) entities.

Skeptical assertions were that all the phenomena were elaborate hoaxes performed by magicians. One common argument is that the mediums were using long, fiber optic cords to mimic the lights. The investigators found these claims lacking. A magician named James Webster had also been in attendance of at least three Scole sessions, and he concluded in an article in *Psychic World*: "I discovered no signs of trickery, and in my opinion such conjuring tricks were not possible."

Further, it was the conclusion of the trained researchers present that unopened rolls of film, doubly secured in protective seals and in the possession of the attendees, producing complex messages, often pertaining to the context of the current sitting, is not possible to be faked by any known means of trickery. Explanations outside of the realm of psychic influence appear impossible in this instance, making the *Scole experiments* a likely true account of physical mediumship.

For more on the Scole experiments, see the documentary by Tim Coleman: "The Afterlife Investigations".

Leslie Flint

As a matter of simply comparing positive versus negative evidence, I believe Leslie Flint to be one of the genuine physical mediumship examples. Flint will be discussed at length in a later chapter.

Physical Mediumship Theories

Physical mediums claim that in many cases, the primary conduit of their phenomenon is ectoplasm. According to the mediums, on the spirit side there are teams of scientists who discovered that all humans possess the ability to use masses of biological matter to help manifest material between dimensions. Observed as colorless blood cells and biological matter, the ectoplasm is taken from both the medium and sometimes the sitters, appearing as a white sheet like filament. Somehow, ectoplasm possesses the ability to cross between worlds. On the astral side, a person can interact with the ectoplasm in the same way as on the Earth side, and by stepping into it suddenly they appear solid and tangible in our world.

Not every physical medium, however, subscribes to or promotes the usage of ectoplasm. For instance, the Scole group seemed to manifest physical phenomena without using any, but still managed to produce spirit lights, the moving of objects, and even apparent materialization of entities.

Therefore, ectoplasm is just one way that physical séances occur. It would seem the backbone of the séance is the raising of the "vibration" levels. In most circles, music is played, people may joke and laugh, positive feelings are spread, and overall the "energy" in the room is raised to a point that, spirits claim, affects the very atmosphere and physiology of the world around us to such a point that they can make contact and enter into our dimension. This is, of course, not possible without the medium him or herself, who enters a trance and then becomes the metaphysical doorway between both realms; allowing his or her very psychic presence to somehow penetrate the barrier between dimensions; causing another world to pour through an invisible portal.

The most contentious element of the physical séance is, of course, the darkness. All séances are performed in either pitch blackness or, at best, dim lighting. This lighting may change once spirit induced lighting occurs, but leading up to this—no outside sources are typically allowed, with exceptions that occur with red lighting that may be turned on at different points during the séance.

Partial ectoplasmic structures like discarnate limbs, plus lights, moving tables and other phenomena have all been caught with both photography and videography (the *Felix Experimental Group*, a current physical séance research group, is especially consistent at capturing these things). However spirits themselves—that is, full materialized forms—seem oddly *shy* of showing themselves. This, obviously, sends the skeptics into a spin. If a fully materialized spirit has the power to walk around the room, why is there no photograph yet of such a spirit taking a selfie with a respected researcher?

I can certainly sympathize with the skepticism that these points generate. I personally have tried to figure this one out for a while, and I do not blame detractors for even going so far as to say all physical mediumship is bogus, which is the opinion I once shared, as well. Today, however, after researching this topic and even getting to know modern physical mediums personally, I do not think fraud is prevalent like skeptics think. The Scole group, for instance, proved that some type of real spirit contact seems to be occurring. However, even Scole did not prove the existence of full materialized forms. The matter of photographic proof remains contentious in this way, and alludes to some level of deception. But how could a séance be partially fraudulent, and partially real? Rationally, if there's a manipulation happening in a small way, then the whole experience must be fake, right?

I believe the answer is that something is going on that is too complex to easily understand, and that manipulation may be present—but I think that the manipulation is occurring through the realms of the astral and not the medium him or herself; who is mostly just a stationary, sleeping vessel being used by the manifesting powers.

To understand what I am saying, first let's look at the official explanation why light is not used in a séance. The reason is that light either disrupts ectoplasm, or disrupts the sensitive changes of energy being conducted by astral scientists present in the room (but invisible to you and me). It doesn't take long delving into the annals of spiritualism to encounter the famous story of Helen Duncan, the 1940s physical medium who was being hounded by the British authorities. One day during trance, the police barged into the séance room while she was conducting a materialization session, and the ectoplasm responded to the sudden impact of photons by surging back into the medium's body at such a high velocity it instantly killed her. Since this purported incident, physical séances always perform frisks of attendees to ensure they are not hiding flashlights that could endanger the life of the medium.

In some ways, this explanation suffices. The astral has, throughout history, always had a relationship with the dark. The famous saying isn't *things that go bump in broad daylight*. As we attempt to understand life after death, there are elements of physics that relate to the relationship between both worlds; and I suspect these elements are not fully understood by us mortals. One possibility is that the energy patterns of our photons simply do not correspond with theirs. The fewer of ours that are present, the easier it is for them to manifest. Further, ghost researchers have often speculated that phenomena occur as a spirit drains the energy from surrounding conduits, such as electronics. Then, as the battery in your phone drains and the air becomes cold, using that energy they may be able to manipulate matter or fully appear. In the light, however, there may be an overload of energy that makes manifestation impossible. It's possible these same laws experienced by ghost researchers are taking effect in the séance room.

There is one variable, however, that complicates matters, and is where the arguments in support of physical mediumship become complex, and the possibilities arise that we are not being given the full story; and it's the subject of night-vision. Modern night-vision is not an intrusive, high energy electronic operation. Low-light night-vision simply amplifies available light in the room to achieve better vision. A small electric field is used to accelerate electrons released by photons entering the photocathode, leading to a "field" of electrons enhancing the photon display. Now, it's not impossible to assume that this process could disrupt energies in the room too greatly and affect the integrity of the seance. However, given the very small amount of energy that's released, I find it unlikely that night-vision would really harm the medium or prevent the phenomena from occurring. Therefore, it would make sense that in the event of a full materialized form, one could simply equip night-vision and watch, in an historic moment, the spectacular event of ectoplasm swirling around the medium into the form of a living, breathing human being.

So, why hasn't this happened? I'll present a few theories about why this, or any other kind of "hard proof", is just so elusive.

- **Full Materialized Forms Do Not Exist**

I find this to be a shaky theory, given that the Scole experimental group did experience materialized entities, and all of the evidence suggests the authenticity of that circle. If we know that the materialization can occur in some cases, then it's certainly possibly it's happened in many cases.

- **The Materialization is the Medium**

This is not to say the séance is a fraud. However, what if some—or many—cases of materialization is the medium being in a sense *possessed* by the spirit, perhaps even taking on some of the forms and features of the possessor, but ultimately remaining in her body? There have been photographs of materializations over the decades, such as the famed Katie King picture, or Minnie Harrison's materialization of a deceased aunt. However, in these instances, critics rightfully point out that the materializations match the physical characteristics of the mediums way too much to be considered credible photographs. This suggests the entities are manipulating our perception of what is going on, perhaps because they are afraid if it's revealed that materializations are conducted in the medium's own body like a type of spirit possession, that it would spread distrust and resentment against the medium and disrupt the continued advancement of the circle.

• The Materialization Looks Ghastly

This theory is bound to please fans of horror movies. What if the process of converting an astral body into an ectoplasmic body doesn't always go right, and what appears is deformed or even grotesque? In this case, it would again damage the reputation of the medium or even cause public backlash if an image is caught of a terrifying representation of some poor sitter's dead father. However, this poses the question of why the spirit controls would not be honest about this fact. Or, allow videographic evidence to be produced on a private basis until a not-so-ghastly occurrence is fit for public consumption.

• We Are Not Ready Yet

This is a theme I will touch on later in this book, the *Prime Directive*, to use Star Trek terms, in action. What if the video footage that could be obtained during a full materialization would be so staggering, it would effectively hit society over the head with something that it wasn't yet able to handle?

Religions would be dismantled and mediums would be the target of terrorist attacks. Logically, astral civilizations must have the power to make full contact *if they chose to*, but it seems likely they are passing this responsibility to us instead, for the time that we are collectively open enough to receive their existence without it causing confusion, violence, and war.

While this is a fun theory, a solid rebuttal is that in the age of *Adobe After Effects*, any kind of stunning media evidence would, without doubt, be immediately dismissed as special effects and get relegated to the "bizarre news" section of a newspaper—or if lucky, a few thousand hits on YouTube. In other words, a proper video recording of a materialization probably wouldn't sway society.

• It's Just Too Dangerous

Finally, short of concluding fraud, the other possibility is that the mediums are telling the truth, and night-vision is too dangerous. While night-vision technology seems non-invasive to us, it still involve the use of electron fields and manipulation of photons. This is potentially all it takes to sabotage a séance or even endanger the medium or the sitters if there is ectoplasm present.

• Addendum

One final note, in defense of the proponents of physical mediumship, is that materializations *have* been witnessed in light; in particular glow-in-the-dark chemical lighting which spirits have concluded is a safe form of light emission. Sitters of contemporary physical mediums like Kai Muegge and David Thompson have reported seeing materializations through this dim glow, and have reported materializations picking up glow-in-the-dark objects and boards, placing their faces to them and showing their hands and other limbs.

Further, the Leslie Flint séances, which involved the creation of an ectoplasmic "voice box", was observed through seasoned Society for Psychical Research investigators using an infrared tube. This helped those particular researchers conclude that Flint used legitimate physical séance powers. I believe Flint to also be an authentic medium, and we will explore his mediumship and the messages conveyed in much greater detail later.

Another interesting phenomenon that I've heard about from sitters, which lends some credence to physical phenomena, is the materialization of deceased pet animals, such as dogs, cats and even in one case—a pet rat. Although purely anecdotal evidence, if such stories are true it would lend further credence to physical mediumship itself, as we enter the realm of absurdity to think magicians are researching the dog breeds that sitters used to own and then smuggling them into the séance room.

One thing I am certain of is that the physical mediums I know personally are not fakers. And, physical mediumship is a talent that regular mental mediums can (and should) develop as a way of taking their abilities to the next level. The nature of the séance, however, remains mysterious even to the mediums themselves. Perhaps, however, in coming years the physical séance will be even more explored, and some elusive photographic examples of full materializations will finally be unveiled.

Mediumship Conclusions

It's almost unfair for me to conclude this lengthy chapter at its current point, because there is so much more to cover. From the famous cross correspondences in the early 20th century that showed the power of spirit communication across vast distances and closed channels, to the remarkable mediumship work of Leonora Piper.

The main conclusion is that it's very hard to dismiss mediumship. The disinformation that you may have been familiar with up until this point is that mediums are California scam artists and television hucksters. This opinion has no basis in truth. Mediumship goes far beyond mainstream skeptical opinions and into a deep, serious topic that has for years attracted the attention of the most hardened and critically minded people alive—police detectives.

At this point, the powers of trained mental mediums have been proven as factual. The Medium 7 project alone has demonstrated irrefutable evidence of this. Physical mediumship, on the other hand has a way to go, and is more commonly met by skepticism. However, given the remarkable experiences witnessed at the Scole experimental group of England, it's possible that this subject is a "wild card" that may explode with interest in coming years.

Mediumship in any form involves a line of communication opening up between our world, and the astral. The best way that we can come to understand the mysteries of the world beyond the veil is through establishing these lines of communication and achieving information directly from the minds of those who live there. Trying to understand the specific dynamics of life in other planes through any other method is difficult. Even NDEs, although staggering journeys into the beyond, are extremely limited because they present only the initial stages of death, with few (if any) reports of what one's actual lifestyle is like after transitioning into a different, higher spectrum universe.

However, the NDE does still provide the most conclusive and scientifically valid afterlife evidence available. We'll explore this topic next.

Please wait—before you turn that next page.

The information age means that a book is no longer simply a book. We now have the ability to connect with what we read on brand new levels.

For this book, there are three resources that will allow you to get the most out of what you are reading, and the mysterious subject of life beyond the veil.

The Facebook Group
(https://www.facebook.com/groups/afterlifetopics) – I created the Afterlife Topics group where you can share spiritual experiences, ask questions, and meet others.

The Mailing List
(https://www.afterlifetopics.com/newsletter) – Access to afterlife related news and announcements (recommended).

My Author Page
(https://www.facebook.com/cyruskirkpatrickauthor)
You can "like" my little neglected Facebook page which will support the work that I do. You can also connect with me personally this way.

IV – A Closer Look at Near-Death Experiences

The near-death experience is ingrained into popular culture. You've heard the saying "Is there a light at the end of the tunnel?" which directly relates to the statistically uncommon but consistently reoccurring state of post-death awareness experienced by countless thousands who have undergone cardiac arrest, episodes of trauma, or other NDE inducing experiences and lived to tell the tale.

NDEs are commonly cited by afterlife proponents as one of the most concrete areas of evidence for post-mortem survival (but far from the only area). In my experience researching the NDE, I've found that these experiences offer a stunning—albeit limited—archive of temporary expeditions into the astral. The NDE is where the highest levels of debate arise in academia. It's a subject that has resulted in even hardened, trained medical doctors swallowing the proverbial red pill after encountering countless patients with similar stories, forcing such skeptics to rethink the possibilities of the astral universe's existence.

By now, most people reading this are familiar with the signs of NDE phenomena. An experience of leaving the body, going toward a bright light that possesses Godly properties, perhaps encountering some type of mystical being within the light, encountering deceased

85

loved ones, glimpses of a brilliant alternative dimension, reaching a barrier, and being told to return.

NDEs, however, routinely delve off the beaten path. Some people encounter only parts of the above experiences, some experience none of those things but have a totally original experience, while others have very negative experiences involving hellish beings or environments. There are really no surefire rules in regard to the NDE, as every experience is as unique as the person's own life. This is of course good news, because who would desire an afterlife that is uniform?

NDEs can be extremely beneficial for not only learning about the afterlife, but also for the purposes of recovering from grief. That being said, we also need to stay a bit cautious and critically minded as we explore this topic—being mindful that because of the personal nature of each story, a specific NDE does not necessarily reveal all the mysteries of the afterlife. Further, it's possible for somebody to experience a very detailed NDE that has been in some way prejudiced by personal opinion or belief, and they may use their experience to push a specific ideology.

Case in point: the recent trend of Biblical NDE accounts, being turned into profitable books or even movies like "*Heaven is For Real*". These cases typically involve meeting Jesus and being given the religious treatment—perhaps with a central message that involves spreading the gospel and converting more followers, as opposed to the more standard NDE messages of universal love, acceptance, and tolerance.

Aside from the fact that it's very likely such stories are either made up or heavily contorted to fit preconceived ideas of the experiencer (or the experiencer's parents), another important point needs to be addressed: the NDE is merely a glimpse of the astral, and it's very common to experience one's belief system made manifest. There are many theories about this, including the possibility that as "like attracts like", a dead person—far from being granted unlimited knowledge and Godly ascension—will die and still remain very ignorant in nature, and will attract other souls who live by the same dogma. As such, they may even experience a kind of illusionary heaven, constructed through that individual's own orthodoxy.

Researching NDE accounts requires careful consideration of these facts. It is not wise to simply absorb all of the many varied accounts as fact. There is no reason to assume that somebody who "sees the Light" automatically knows the answers to the universe. It's only a glimpse. Nonetheless, even with glimpses, we can begin to piece together a bigger, hopefully more factual, picture of what is going on.

Understanding the NDE

In 1975 the near-death experience (or the NDE) was coined by author Raymond Moody in the book *Life After Life*. The NDE had obviously existed long before this book, but it was Moody who brought it into the light, so to speak (no pun intended). His research involved cardiac arrest survivors—flatlined patients—who would report unusual experiences at the time of their clinical deaths before their resuscitation.

The experiences were not common. In fact, most people who undergo cardiac arrest do not recount any such incident. A percentage, however, do. The experience ranges from basic anomalous awareness—to fantastic tales of journeying into other worlds. The nature of the NDE would change greatly per interviewee, however some intrinsic elements would remain. One or more of the following aspects are commonly reported:

- A sense of separation from the body.
- An observance of the hospital or physical location from a vantage point of outside of the body.
- A feeling of peace or overwhelming love.
- Seeing a bright light, or a tunnel emerge (with a light at the end of it).
- Being drawn into the tunnel.
- Encountering a being who the experiencer identifies as a religious figure (Jesus, for instance).
- Encountering deceased relatives.
- Entering another world / dimension with Earth-like conditions (trees, mountains, flowers, etc) or with cosmic or alien properties (non-physical, energy-based, etc).
- Reaching a threshold point and being told they must return to their body

-      Being "sent back" into the body, and awaking to great pain.

Life After Life was the first book to chronicle these types of experiences, and the book was a sensation. Upon the influence of Moody's work, the International Association for Near Death Studies was formed in 1981, a non-profit organization whose mission is to provide information about NDE-related subjects[24]. In time, many other authors would add to Moody's pool of research. Kenneth Ring, Bruce Greyson, Pim van Lommel, and a lot more—including scientists and medical doctors.

This would thenceforth remain a niche topic; oddly blended in-between both medical research and the realm of the supernatural. No other topic perhaps crosses as many boundaries between accepted conventions and the taboo paranormal. In the NDE world, conventional scientists, physicians, spiritualists, paranormal researchers, the devoutly religious, and skeptics seem to all coalesce with similar interests. The unifying factor being, of course, an interest in the greatest mystery of the human experience: consciousness, death, and what happens after.

Today, the near-death experience and the countless individual stories account for a thriving field of research and investigation. Websites like Kevin William's Near-Death.com are popular hubs for information, while recent books like Dr. Eben Alexander's *Proof of Heaven* remain remarkably long on best-seller lists. Whether you're aware of it or not, you're already familiar with the NDE in some aspect of popular culture.

How Legitimate is the NDE Phenomenon?

As one tries to understand this topic at a glance, many questions will begin to arise. Namely, "Are people just hyping up made-up experiences?" This is a natural question to ask, given society's tendency to jump on bandwagon-induced hysteria at any moment (Y2K, anyone?). In addition, humans are known for flights of fantasy; with stories that range from lizard-men inhabiting offices of power, to being under surveillance by the New World Order who are watching us through our microwaves.

This first doubt can be dismissed because of two reasons: the prolific nature of the NDE dating back through the ages, and the scientific studies that have determined the percentage of NDEs that occur in the general public.

Both the Egyptian Book of the Dead and the Tibetan Book of the Dead contain descriptions of dying that seem to match NDE accounts. The Egyptian book describes the existence of subtle ("astral") bodies that progress through stages during the journey of death. The body identified by the Egyptians as the one that seems to be immediately available upon disconnection from the Earth body is the Sahu, and it houses the soul (Bahu)[25].

Another more recent, but still very old, text is the Tibetan Book of the Dead, also known as the Book of the Intermediate State, and it describes the afterlife in similar terms. This book dates from the 14th to 15th centuries and concerns the "bardo" state, a period that lasts between physical death and physical rebirth[26]. Tibetans view death as occurring in three steps:

The Chikai Bardo: The moment of death includes the dissolution from the earth elements and an encounter with "Clear Light", revealing one's Buddhist nature.

The Chonyid Bardo: A period of having visions of entities, and vivid encounters with hellish or heavenly realms. Judgments may also occur during this period.

The Sidpa Bardo: The stage when the soul decides to enter a new Earth body, and begin the cycle all over again.

These stages interestingly correspond with modern accounted near-death experiences. A first stage often includes seeing a bright light that corresponds to a transcendental expanse of consciousness, a second stage may include encountering a being interpreted as a deity and / or deceased loved ones, and a third stage could involve a choice to return to the physical body.

Not only do the NDE accounts appear to be historical in the east, but they are seemingly recognized through western history and have been interpreted through a religious prism. The painting "Ascent of the Blessed" by Dutch artist Hieronymous Bosch (1450-1516)

89

addresses the commonly perceived tunnel and light phenomenon among those close to death. The tunnel reflects the passage to heaven, with mortals in the throes of both angels and demons:

Anthropologically, it would seem the near-death experience and its accompanying imagery has been around for a long time. However, for the skeptical minded, this fact does not resolve the question of whether or not the experience is real or if the imagery and elements are just commonly parroted by those people prone to illusions. One argument that is sometimes proposed is that rather than the NDE always occurring naturally, they are now more common as a direct result of NDE popular culture, as we have all heard before about tunnels, life reviews, light, and heavenly figures which predisposes people to certain ideas that they fulfill during their imaginary treks through heaven. In other words, the NDE is a type of hallucination based on mental expectations.

These, and many more arguments are used by skeptics to try and dismiss a topic that is very much immune to this type of dismissal. For every purported skeptical explanation, there are countless holes in those theories, which keeps the skeptical side constantly struggling to tread water, especially as continual data only reinforces the so-called supernatural elements of the experience.

Examples of NDE Accounts

Many NDEs can be browsed at resources like nderf.org and near-death.com. I've included some fictional sample NDE excerpts of the types of experiences that people report. These are only examples, although they are based off some of the real stories that can be browsed online.

"I was guided by this being...through time and space. I could see planets, galaxies, clusters of galaxies. At the end, I encountered a border. I was no longer in a body, in a physical sense, but I could feel other beings around me, who were also without form or shape. I recognized one such presence to be my mother. Without words, I was telepathically told that if I went further, I'd never return. Thoughts of my family came to me. I knew I had to return, and before I could even finish those thoughts, I was gasping for air."

"A brilliant, golden light filled the room. My perception was keener, it was like I was more conscious and everything around me was brighter, more vivid. Suddenly, I was looking at my grandfather, who had joined me as I stared at my own body. He was coming out of what looked like a tunnel, where the golden light was coming from. I wanted badly to go with him, but he shook his head and told me it was not my time yet."

"I was in a room. It was not the hospital. It was circular in shape. People were all around me. I knew they were human, but also a lot more than that. Among the faces I could identify family members. My brother who had passed away, and my uncle. There was a great amount of love and warmth from all of them, but also seriousness. It is like they were judging if it was my time to be there or not. They decided it wasn't, and so I shot back into the operating room."

"As I floated through the tunnel, I found myself surrounded by familiar faces in a huge garden that looked like it was outside of a temple of some sort. All of the people I knew from my life on Earth, but who were deceased. Surrounding me was also the being of Light who presented such unconditional love to me. I was told without words that I had to return, but I did not want to—I wanted to stay there."

"Suddenly, I sped through space, and stars, whole galaxies, shot by me like blurs. Soon, I was outside of time and space itself, in a massive timeless void. Surrounding me were infinite amounts of other souls, being born or returning, as well, and I was a part of them, but they did not exist physically in any way. They were just there. At some point, the oversoul communicated to me, but not with words, that I had to come back to Earth with a specific message..."

"I was yelling frantically for help, but nothing could hear me. I felt an intense weight crushing down around me. It felt like I was in a chamber with the walls closing around me. Then I saw faces, and they were ugly faces. Like humans, but distorted. I felt they wanted to harm me." (An example of an LTP, or less than positive experience).

Science Seeks Answers

It wasn't until 2001 and 2014 that the results of comprehensive medical studies about the NDE were released. These studies have been able to effectively prove that the near-death experience is not a tall-tale recounted by fringe publicity seekers, but a phenomenon that is statistically unavoidable among cardiac arrest patients.

The first such study was published by a highly respected medical journal, The Lancet. In the study, 344 cardiac arrest survivors were profiled in 10 Dutch hospitals, and factors were included such as psychological and pharmacological conditions[27]. Among the survivors, 62 patients (18%) reported unusual experiences (some form of awareness or supposed out of body perception), and twelve percent of this group (41 patients) experienced "full blown" NDEs with core elements, which includes reports of journeying out-of-the-body or appearing in other worlds. The study did not draw any correlation between drugs administered or psychological states. The patients were then followed up over the course of several years, and the study discovered positive psychological effects among the groups of experiencers compared with the non-experiencers.

Some of the study's researchers, including their chief Dr. Pim Van Lommel, are sympathetic to the idea that the NDE may be a genuine phenomenon of mind separation from brain. Van Lommel is quoted as saying:

> "How could a clear consciousness outside one's body be experienced at the moment that the brain no longer functions during a period of clinical death with flat EEG? . . . Furthermore, blind people have described veridical perception during out-of-body experiences at the time of this experience. NDE pushes at the limits of medical ideas about the range of human consciousness and the mind-brain relation." [28]

However, psychologist Chris French was also published in the Lancet report with a skeptical position, suggesting that the patients who reported NDEs may have created false memories based on expectations or pre-cardiac arrest perceptions. This murky explanation does not account for veridical evidence, where these alleged expectations arise from, or why so many people seem to create the exact same types of "false memories".

Some years following The Lancet report, another more publicized study began. AWARE (Awareness During Resuscitation) was launched by a group known as the Human Consciousness Project and spearheaded by a British doctor, Sam Parnia. Parnia is a former critical care specialist at the University of Southampton, current Director of Resuscitation Research at the State University in New York, and is the world leading researcher on consciousness at the time of death. According to Parnia, the goal was to better understand what the mind experiences during the point of death, and to more accurately distinguish between what really constitutes death versus so-called near death states.

In October 2014, the results were published in the journal *Resuscitation*. The study tracked 2060 cardiac arrest patients, of whom 16% (330) survived. Of this amount, only 160 consented to be interviewed, and of that group 39% experienced episodes of unexplainable awareness during cardiac arrest (a similar number to the Lancet's), but without the elements of an actual NDE. Of these 55 patients, 46 described anomalous memories (frightening or unusual experiences, but incompatible with NDE criteria), while the remaining nine had "full blown" NDEs that included reports of leaving the body or entering an unearthly other-world. Among these nine, two patients reported direct out-of-body experiences. Of the two, Parnia recounts one gold-mine.

According to Parnia, this one case resulted in full and accurate identification of hospital staff and many other details that would have been unknown to the experiencer, all of which was perceived during an out-of-body vantage from across the room in the midst of a flat-line (sans brain activity). The patient also used an "auditory correlation" by recounting two beeps from an EEG machine that only goes off every three minutes.

Dr Parnia concluded:

"This is significant, since it has often been assumed that experiences in relation to death are likely hallucinations or illusions, occurring either before the heart stops or after the heart has been successfully restarted, but not an experience corresponding with 'real' events when the heart isn't beating. In this case, consciousness and awareness appeared to occur during a three-minute period when there was no heartbeat. This is paradoxical, since the brain typically ceases functioning within 20-30 seconds of the heart stopping and doesn't resume again until the heart has been restarted. Furthermore, the detailed recollections of visual awareness in this case were consistent with verified events."[29]

In the end, Parnia also concludes that the study cannot definitely determine the reality of out-of-body perception due to the low incidence of OBE states (2%), but the study points out the need for further unprejudiced research.

The results of the study were certainly controversial. The Telegraph, a UK newspaper, broke the story as "the first hint of 'life after death' in biggest ever scientific study"[30], a headline that helped the article go viral with thousands of Facebook and social media shares. Some argued that this was an inaccurate assumption, as The Lancet study compiled similar results years before AWARE.

Reception was also expectedly mixed. Due to the veracity of such claims, many skeptics are quick to dismiss the report, and many other news pieces, blogs and opinion articles skewed the study as the wasting of time and resources, continuing with the same drumbeat that the NDE has already been explained away as either an hallucination brought upon by the dying brain's electrical discharges, oxygen depravation, or temporary bouts of awareness combined with false memories. However, for researchers and doctors like Parnia, Van Lommel, Bruce Greyson, and a growing number of other medical doctors and academics, the subject is, at the least evidence of anomalous brain activity with important relevance to resuscitation studies. And, at the most, evidence that consciousness may in fact exist independently of the brain, paving the way for the possible objective existence of a life after death, independent of any religious or spiritual persuasion.

The ramifications are large, and for proponents of a spiritual world, these diverse experiences are icing on a cake of other topics; all pointing in the same direction. We are not yet at a point where any type of consensus is drawn about the NDE. However, as we are exploring in this book, there are good reasons why the NDE has completely changed the dynamic between material science, materialist philosophy, and the spiritual. For the first time in history, traditional medical science and potential higher realities are face-to-face, with opinions ranging from neutrality to seething skepticism and outspoken support. If nothing else, one thing can be agreed upon—these are changing times.

Strongest Features of the NDE

There's a reason why, today, the NDE is widely considered the most compelling "supernatural" phenomena of all time. Let's explore a few of the reasons why.

Veridical Information

The inner skeptic yearns for something more concrete to answer the doubts of whether the NDE is a hallucination or a real experience in the objective world. It's an elusive phenomenon, and it was the primary focus of AWARE to catch in action (and which succeeded, at least on a minor level with a single account). Veridical information remains the element that separates the NDE from possibilities of mere hallucinations. Both the AWARE and Lancet studies cited earlier resulted in small amounts of veridical information being reported, proving that albeit rare, even under scientific scrutiny the NDE's OBE phenomenon remains a credible part of the experience.

Beyond just these controlled studies, there are plenty of veridical accounts that can be found across NDE literature. One of the first NDE researchers to take especial interest in veridical out-of-body perception was Kenneth Ring, a professor of psychology at Connecticut University. Following his reading of Moody's *Life After Life* in 1977, Ring began a process of collecting letters and interviewing ND experiencers (102 in all) and later published *Mindsight*, which included his research into another highly evidential topic—OBE perception that supposedly occurs among the blind.

Ring's research led him to another investigator named Kathy Milne. Kathy was not an experiencer herself, but a nurse working at Hartford Hospital. Milne had an interest in NDEs and began talking to the recently resuscitated at her hospital, in an effort to collect NDE accounts for research. One day she was interviewing a woman who had previously been brought back to life:

> "She told me how she floated up over her body, viewed the resuscitation effort for a short time and then felt herself being pulled up through several floors of the hospital. She then found herself above the roof and realized she was looking at the skyline of Hartford. She marveled at how interesting this view was and out of the corner of her eye she saw a red object. It turned out to be a shoe ... [S]he thought about the shoe... and suddenly, she felt "sucked up" a blackened hole. The rest of her NDE account was fairly typical, as I remember. "I was relating this to a [skeptical] resident who in a mocking manner left. Apparently, he got a janitor to get him onto the roof. When I saw him later that day, he had a red shoe and he became a believer, too." (Interview with Kenneth Ring, Oct. 19, 1992).

Interestingly, this was not the only shoe story. In the book *After the Light* by Kimberly Clark Sharp an incident is recounted where a woman named Maria suffered a heart attack and was taken to Harborview Hospital in Seattle. In her NDE, she allegedly spotted a tennis shoe hanging from a rooftop ledge of the hospital, and as with Kathy Milne's story, medical staff investigated the occurrence and confirmed the shoe's existence[31].

Veridical perception has also been explored at length by Dr. Penny Sartori, former intensive care nurse and current UK NDE expert. Sartori found in her research that the OBE phenomenon of the NDE results in accurate descriptions by cardiac arrest survivors of the resuscitation process, including extremely specific details by comparison to inaccurate descriptions by control groups that did not experience the NDE. A 2007 paper by Sartori, Badham and Fenwick describes a particular patient profiled among Sartori's out-of-body experience investigatory work who experienced an NDE with strong veridical results[32].

The patient in question gave an "extremely accurate account of the events occurring during the OBE, and the events reported happened at a time when he was deeply unconscious with his eyes closed. These events were verified by the nurse and physiotherapist who were present, and they were also documented in the patient's medical notes by the consultant who reviewed him at the time of his experience." (Sartori, Badham, Fenwick 2007).

According to the case study, the patient was a 60 year-old man recovering from emergency surgery related to bowel cancer. Following the surgery he was very sick and developed sepsis and organ failure. Shortly afterwards, under the belief he was getting better, the physiotherapist encouraged him to move from his hospital bed, although because of his sudden attempt at movement he soon relapsed into severe symptoms, and required emergency assistance by Sartori (who was the active nurse) and fell into deep unconsciousness.

Three hours later, the patient's consciousness restored. Unable to speak as he was hooked up to ventilation, he was given a letter board, whereupon he spelled the words "I died and I watched it all from above". The patient recalled a traditional NDE, minus the more advanced stages such as a light or entering another realm. In this case, he reported leaving his body, dwelling above them in the air, encountering his deceased father and mother-in-law (who he said he'd never actually met before), and eventually being required to return to his body.

In the moments following his OBE and entering total unconsciousness, a series of specific events occurred in the ICU that the patient was able to recall seeing during his OBE state, as reported to Sartori in an interview she conducted just moments after the patient regained the ability to speak. Reportedly the patient was able to report the following information, all observed while he was inside his astral body

The doctor's consultant shining a light in his eyes:

Shortly after the patient stabilized, his pupils were examined with a light to ensure the eyes would react (dilate) to rule out brain death. The patient witnessed this. The patient further identified that it was the consultant who shined the light, and not one of the junior doctors. The patient had been familiar with the junior doctors, and not the consultant. There was, again, no consciousness present for him to be able to make this distinction, unless a complex process occurred where he had heard the consultant's voice earlier in the hospital and somehow created a mental model. But in this case, why didn't he create a mental model around a junior doctor who he had actually seen?

The nurse cleaning his mouth:

After the patient, then unconscious, was returned to bed care, he had been drooling from the side of his mouth, and so the nurse made a point to clean his mouth using two items: a pink sponge dipped in water, as well as the use of an oral suction catheter to clean his mouth's interior. Both of these objects and their usage on him were identified. It's possible he could have heard the nurse repeating her actions out-loud as she performed them for record-keeping purposes, but this is questionable given his unconscious state.

The physiotherapist poking her head around the curtains:

The physiotherapist originally suggested for the patient to leave his bedside and try some movements. This incited the rapid degradation of his condition, and it resulted in the physiotherapist becoming paranoid that it was her fault that his condition worsened. As a result, she began checking on the patient repeatedly, looking through the curtains to see check up on his condition. The patient reported that during his OBE he saw her "poking her head around the curtains, looking very nervous". Again, the patient had no consciousness during this time.

The conclusion of the report is that while it's possible some type of complex mental model may have been constructed by the patient between guess-work and information gathering before the incident, it does not account for the total breadth of highly detailed descriptions that occurred while the patient was verified to be unconscious.

Keep in mind, this was only a single example of veridical information reported during an OBE, specific to a study that was being conducted by Sartori. NDE literature is filled with even more impressive case studies than this one.

The Pam Reynolds case, for instance, involved a patient whose brain had entered complete "stand-still" during an experimental operation where her blood was completely drained from her brain; and her face outfitted with complex instruments that would have blocked all auditory senses. Despite these facts which virtually ruled out any type of semi-conscious information gathering, Pam reported similar veridical information as she observed the operation from the ceiling. Pam also reported a remarkable and interesting continuation of her NDE, involving reunions with the deceased.

Aside from these cases, there is a great deal of more information about OBE perception available. A good place to begin is the book *Mindsight*, which is available on Amazon.

Spontaneous Healing

Another very interesting element of the NDE is the tendency for the experiencer to undergo remarkable healing which may accompany being sent back to Earth. NDE literature is filled with stories of people returning to life with renewed health when they certainly should have died, or at least suffered brain damage and remained in a debilitative state. One famous story is that of George Rodonaia, a psychiatrist from the Soviet Union[33]. He was one of the few Soviet residents in the 1970s brave enough to be a vocal dissident of the regime. His subversive behavior caught the attention of the KGB, who ran him over in an assassination attempt in 1976. George was left in a cold morgue for three days before spontaneously reviving on an operating table (and reporting one of the most profound NDEs ever told). Although some have called into question whether George, despite being left in the morgue, was truly clinically dead or not—George did experience the remarkable effects of not dying from dehydration or any other number of issues that could have resulted from being presumed dead in a metal coffin. Not to mention recovery from the cardiac arrest which had led to the presumption that he had died.

Aside from recovery from the injuries or sicknesses that resulted in the NDE, an experiencer may also make sudden recoveries from preexisting conditions. As one example, the case study I referenced from the Penny Sartori paper (the 60 year-old man who had sepsis from cancer surgery) also involved an incident of spontaneous healing (which, in addition to out-of-body perception, was also a subject of investigation by Sartori and her colleagues). In that incident, the patient had his entire life suffered from a type of cerebral palsy, with his hand permanently stuck in a "claw" position, which required special care during his admittance to the hospital. However, after his NDE and subsequent recovery, the claw position of his hand mysteriously healed itself (Sartori, Badham, Fenwick 2007).

Increased Cognitive Awareness

Another element of the NDE that confounds critics is the contradictory nature of cognitive awareness. Skeptical assertions of oxygen deprivation leading to hallucinatory states can be easily refuted by the fact that if a damaged brain is deprived of oxygen, it will lead to an overall decrease of consciousness levels. The near-death experience, much like terminal lucidity accounts, involves a sudden *expansion* of consciousness just as the physical brain should be highly impaired or even non-functional. This is further evidence that suggests consciousness expands as its reliance on the physical instrument of the brain diminishes, and the mind begins operating from its natural astral state. It also shows how the oxygen deprivation debunking attempt has no merit.

In regard to just how expanded the mind becomes during "death", here is some research by Dr. Bruce Greyson[34]:

- 47% of experiencers report thinking clearer than usual.

- 38% thinking faster than usual.

- 29% thinking more logical than usual.

- 17% experiencing more control over their thoughts than usual.

Understand that these accounts are being reported at a time of cardiac arrest when the person is unconscious with brain activity turned off. At minimal, we'd expect muddled, dream-like visions. But this is not how NDEs occur.

Encounters Relate Specifically to the Deceased

The quickest way to stump a skeptic is to point out the dilemma of how NDEs always involve deceased loved ones. If it were a hallucination, we'd expect dream-like encounters. At the very least, the NDE would involve people who are close to us who we are familiar with—*living* parents, siblings, children, or our spouse. In addition, we'd expect the beings encountered to include some degree of abstract nonsense-characters cooked up by a brain under distress— much as we may hallucinate the Pillsbury Doughboy walking about our bedroom during a fever-induced nightmare (not that I have anything against the Pillsbury Doughboy).

However, this just doesn't happen in NDEs. I've read hundreds of archived NDEs at this point, chronicled on nderf.org and other sites, and I've never come across anything similar to this. And yet, I hear skeptics point out that NDErs encounter dream-like hallucinations of living relatives as one of their arguments against the NDE. But where? I've never read it. There may be one or two stories if you dig deep that were perhaps bedside hallucinations. The existence of NDEs does not preclude that people can't still have hallucinations, as well—but they're not NDEs. This argument that is proposed seems to just be an attempt at misdirection (intellectual sleight of hand).

An NDE is marked by specific characteristics, sometimes referred to as the Greyson scale. When the NDE begins to occur, starting with a sense of separation from the body, floating about the body, expanded awareness, and then perhaps a visitation by the deceased—at no point has there ever been a documented case where a clear hallucination occurs. There are no stories of Ronald McDonald bursting through to start selling hamburgers, and there are very few—if any—encounters with living relatives. In short, they're not hallucinations.

If this is not enough to prove there's something going on, then consider that these encounters with the deceased **often include veridical, objective information**. NDE research is filled with stories of people encountering deceased loved ones who they a.) had never met before (great aunt Helga) or b.) did not even know had died (great aunt Helga died? Geez, no one told me).

These confirmations of deceased loved ones occur after the NDE finishes and they find out the person had passed away. In other cases, they meet someone who was a distant relative or somebody they were separated by from birth, and it becomes a revelation afterward when they scour records to discover a confirmation about the person's existence through photographs. One of the most well-known incidences of this happened in the famous NDE account of neurosurgeon Eben Alexander (*Proof of Heaven*).

Penny Sartori's 2014 book *The Wisdom of Near-death experiences* recounts further cases of revelatory NDEs documented among the thousands of patients she witnessed die or come close to death during her nearly two decades as an intensive care nurse[35].

In the case of Fred Williams, a man admitted in his 70s dying of a heart condition, the staff were expecting him to soon pass away as he slipped into unconsciousness. To the surprise of the medical staff, he returned quite cognizant the next morning. He described how his mother, grandmother and sister visited him at his bedside and kept vigil until he made a recovery. He said, however, it was curious that his sister was there—as she was still alive and healthy. His family confided in private that his sister had suddenly passed away a week earlier, and they were hesitant to reveal the news to Fred as it might hurt his condition. Fred however still passed away a week later (and hopefully reunited with his sister).

Prominent NDE researcher Bruce Greyson reports a similar story by American pediatrician Dr. K.M. Dale. A nine year-old boy was admitted with severe meningitis, and was lingering between life and death, with his parents at close watch throughout the ordeal. Slowly, the boy began to recover, and recounted an NDE where he was met by many deceased relatives. Among them was his sister, Teresa, who told him that he had to return.

The parents, however, were confused by this report, because his sister was alive and well, attending university in another state. Troubled by their son's story, his parents immediately returned home and tried to contact Teresa, with no luck. They soon found out that college officials had been trying all night to reach them, as their daughter had just been killed in a car accident.

Another NDE researcher, Pim van Lommel, chronicled a story about a man who suffered cardiac arrest, and during his NDE he encountered an unfamiliar man who greeted him as a departed family member, before sending him back to his body. Years later, the experiencer's dying mother confessed that he had been adopted, and that his father was a different man of Jewish background who had been killed during the German invasion of Holland in WWII. He was shown a photo of his biological father, who he recognized as the man he encountered in the astral.

One of the best known stories of this nature would be Dr. Eben Alexander's encounter with a mysterious girl who he learned the origins of sometime after his recovery (I will not recount the whole story; to avoid spoiling the end of *Proof of Heaven*).

Experiencers Return With New Knowledge

An interesting, but rarer, phenomenon is that of an experiencer coming back from the brink with unexplained knowledge acquired while on "the other side". In Sartori's *The Wisdom of Near-death experiences*, she recalls her favorite case. In 2008, a woman named Rajaa Benamour from Morocco had an anaesthetic injection for minor surgery, which resulted in a bad (allergic) reaction. Rajaa recalled an NDE that she described as highly profound—which included a rapid overview of the creation of the universe and many other cosmic topics that were shown to her.

After she left the hospital, she started researching books by scientific authors to get a better understanding about what she was taught. Rajaa soon realized that she had been given an in-depth understanding of matters related to quantum physics, despite coming from a background with no scientific educational training.

She was then motivated to pursue an understanding of quantum physics on a university level. Her professors were amazed to find that she had entered the course with a very high level of understanding about their topics, which they claimed could not have come just from studying textbooks.

According to Sartori, this woman also presented quantum physics theories that, at the time, were unknown. In recent years, science has been able to catch up to her own understanding with new papers published that seem to include what she had written during her university studies.

NDE After-Effects

Near-death experience after-effects are markedly different from both close encounters with death that do not include an NDE, as well as hallucinatory experiences. The following after effects have been known to occur, according to the notes of researchers like Ring, Sartori, Moody, Long, and others:

- Experiencers tend to withdraw from normal, orthodox religions and begin following a more self-directed spiritual path. In other cases, however, former non-believers or atheists may take on a religious aspect of their lives, like becoming a priest or minister (such as with George Rodonaia).

- In most cases, the experiencer loses their fear of death.

- Some experiencers suffer depression as a result of longing to return to the world they experienced, or because they no longer find it easy to fit in among their previous social groups or even families.

- Many put less priority on material acquisition; caring more about charitable causes compared with previous career, status or money-related pursuits.

- According to Sartori's research, a lesser-known NDE after-effect is anomalous electrical powers. Experiencers have reported being unable to wear watches because they

105

constantly malfunction, light bulbs repeatedly going out, and creating large, even hazardous electrical fields around appliances.

- According to Sartori, some experiencers also report a sudden increase of psychic abilities such as precognition and mediumship capabilities, including abilities they may find disturbing and unpleasant, like knowing when people around them will die.

Materialist Explanations

The NDE is easily the strongest argument in support of the afterlife (although certainly not the only one). Attempting to refute the NDE has proven to be a great challenge. The oxygen deprivation explanation makes no sense, as it does not account for mind expanding experiences, the fact the brain is often non-functional during the NDEs, and that researchers like Sartori have actually tested blood oxygen levels on patients who subsequently had NDEs, and found them to be normal (please Google Sartori's reports and books or check my bibliography to learn about this research).

Another proposed explanation recently was that near the moment of death, rats who were killed for science displayed a sudden surge of electrical activity, which has been construed to suggest the entirety of the NDE might be just a brief surge of brain activity before "shut down". This explanation also suffers for a number of reasons:

- A dying surge of electrical function in the brain does not necessarily mean consciousness (many parts of the brain have no function related to consciousness)

- Electrical surges are brief whereas NDEs can last for a long time, NDEs can occur when there is no cardiac arrest and death pronouncement (therefore no surge).

- NDEs involve veridical knowledge and paranormal experiences that transcend this (and every other) reductionist point of view.

106

- We do not know if humans experience the same phenomenon in the way that rats do. A rat's brain is not the same as a person's brain.

- And finally NDEs do not have the characteristics of hallucinations—as I discussed earlier in this chapter. Experiences are clear and not hallucinatory.

In an attempt to clutch at straws, materialist explanations may then sway towards the cultural / delusional ramifications; or basically the "people are making things up" route. This is a low-blow and an insult to all NDE researchers. It's especially harmful when this attitude is adopted by medical professionals themselves; who will then try to medicate the experience away when they believe their patient is suffering from a mental health problem.

Some may argue against the NDE based on poor results from the major studies published in journals. This is incorrect, as both Lancet and AWARE studies returned with some very interesting NDEs and accounts of veridical perception. However, AWARE did not accomplish their original goal, which was to have an out-of-body patient identify a string of numbers placed cleverly in the operating room. However, among the out-of-body experiences reported in Parnia's study, they unfortunately occurred in hospital wards that did not have the displays set up. It's very possible if they had, then this aspect of the study would have been successful. Currently, a second AWARE experiment is underway, and the results could be published around the year 2021.

There is currently no adequate materialist explanation for the NDE. Therefore, the NDE becomes a matter of belief or disbelief. Those who, for cultural and personal reasons choose to not accept the evidence, a skeptical explanation (however poorly construed) will suffice as a method to push the subject away and consider the book closed. Anyone who is not predisposed to disbelief is likely to look at the evidence and come to a different conclusion. Some people may even accept that the evidence cannot be refuted, but they choose to not believe in it out of an inability to comprehend it. This choice has to be respected. The NDE, if taken literally, would prove the existence of the afterlife and all of its ramifications, as well as the countless, mind-boggling questions that accompany this possibility. If it's not a pill that someone is ready to swallow, who can blame them?

NDE Conclusions

According to researcher Kenneth Ring, simply learning about NDE stories has an effect on readers similar to those who have the NDE themselves (*Lessons from the Light*, 1998). This is because although NDEs vary greatly in the size, shape, length and style—the messages are often similar and universally positive in nature: we do not die, our loved ones are waiting for us after we die, we experience a great deal of love after we cross over, that separating from the body is not something to be feared, and perhaps most importantly of all—we retain our individualities and identities. This knowledge can have a very positive psychological effect on the students of NDE knowledge, often alleviating fear of death and providing a greater sense of purpose. The NDE paradigm is far less grim by comparison to what we are taught in school—that the cosmos is blind, life is an accident, and death is oblivion.

Learning about the afterlife through NDEs is definitely one of the best ways to go about it. However, it doesn't answer more complex questions. I notice that people who solely study NDEs do not realize that this topic can be explored with much greater detail by researching many similar areas of knowledge, to be able to paint a more accurate description of what *really* happens after we die; and not merely when we are at the gates of the astral.

As an example, in the next chapter we are going to explore some of the scientific progress that has been made into these metaphysical topics to help us better understand the conditions of the next world in a more literal, detailed sense. Let's get started.

V – Science Explores Realms Beyond

"I regard consciousness as fundamental, I regard matter as derivative of consciousness" – Max Planck

"Consciousness cannot be accounted for in physical terms" – Erwin Schrodinger

"The statistical evidence, at least for telepathy, is overwhelming. It is very difficult to rearrange one's ideas so as to fit these new facts in. Once one has accepted them it does not seem a very big step to believe in ghosts and bogies." – Alan Turing

Science is simply a method of inquiry. It's neither a philosophy nor a set of laws, and currently science has no opinion of whether the afterlife can (or should) be investigated (as it has no opinion on anything—it's not an institutional power). Although it would seem we have an eternity (or at least a very long time) ahead of us to explore these other planes where we seemingly end up, our initial explorations must begin right here in this world, using our existing tools and knowledge.

In this chapter, I will list some of the more interesting progress that is being made in this regard. Despite that much of this knowledge goes "under the radar", it's steadily advancing at its own pace. Doubt and skepticism pervade on the higher echelons of academia, but gradually research into the astral is progressing forward within its own avenues.

The Mind and Brain Problem

One of the biggest, hot button topic in science, and where fringe and mainstream clash most frequently, concerns the mind and brain dilemma. Our entire society is built around the premise that the hunk of meat inside our skulls is who we fundamentally are.

However, throughout this book you've learned reasons to suspect that this is not the case. From terminal lucidity to flat-lined patients going out of their bodies in the OR, the brain doesn't always act as the governor of consciousness. And yet, at the same time, it certainly does—as even alcohol changes our personalities by altering our brain chemistry.

Near the beginning of this book, I talked about how the evidence is ultimately of contradictory nature. The supernatural, for lack of a better term, really should not exist—and yet it does, anyway, in spite of conditions like Alzheimer's, dementia, aggressive tendencies from brain tumors, and many other subjects where it seems that biological matter and mind are fused. It appears that somewhere there is an "X" factor that unites these two worlds together, and explains how the mind functions within the body, but could somehow persist outside of it, as well.

It's a very complex subject because nobody even in our advanced modern society can define what "mind" is—which is why it is referred to as the hard problem of science. This is where materialism delves into some very murky waters, going into concepts of eliminative materialism that tries to rationalize that because mind shouldn't even exist out of a chunk of meat, then maybe it *doesn't* exist—there truly is no "self". In this view, awareness is an accidental property in a world inhabited by robots. Some well-known scientists subscribe to this belief, including Prof. Stephen Hawking.

This philosophy is only a step away from the official explanation of mind, as materialist science currently theorizes it. This is that mind is an "emergent" property of the brain. What this means is that all of the neurons and signals firing everywhere in your meat sack, when put together in enough quantities and in the right pattern, somehow creates this illusion of self-awareness. As this mysterious, undefined structure begins to break down and important parts stop working, then the self disappears. During anesthesia and dreamless sleep, this is experienced in terms of the sheer *lack* of experience.

As convincing as these theories are, we are still dealing with something that even the most trained neurologist doesn't really understand.

Where Emergence Breaks Down

Putting aside all of the out-of-body perceptions and other "para" subjects that defy the emergent mind theory, there are still serious holes in the "mind is meat" theory even in mainstream research, such as how...

We Are Dependent On Our Brains—Except When We're Not

Medical science is filled with baffling cases of people who have either severely underdeveloped or damaged brains, or even no brains at all— yet are still able to function normally. In the latter case, the only functional parts they may have is a brain stem (which is supposed to only regulate core behaviors) and a thin layer of neurons.

During a 1980 conference, pediatrician John Lorber addressed the crowd with a most unusual question: "Is the brain really necessary?"[36] This question was based on case studies he had been involved in for about 20 years up until that point. He had been researching children with a condition known as hydrocephalus, where the brain's cerebral spinal fluid overloads the brain. The condition, if untreated, can result in disability or death.

The severity of hydrocephalus can vary. In the worst instances, everything in the skull basically becomes "soup" and there is only minimal brain function left. Other cases are less severe, and some parts of the brain are replaced by fluid while leaving the most important areas intact, and these sufferers can often lead relatively normal lives.

There are, however, anomalies. Lorber recounts from the *Developmental Medicine and Child Neurology* journal two cases where infants aged 3 months and 12 months were born with hydrocephaly and had no cerebral cortexes[37]. The children did not live past these ages, however their developmental and cognitive function was no different from any other infants despite missing the parts of their brain that are most important.

While this was odd, it was not the most impactful study. Lorber continued to try to research, and document adults who had lived past their infancy with hydrocephalus. A young man from Sheffield University showed signs of the disease due to an enlarged head. This young man, with an IQ of 126, was an honor student in the mathematics program. Upon receiving a CAT scan, doctors were shocked to learn that his hydrocephalus resulted in a pool of liquid where his brain ought to be. All that was left, according to Lorber, was a thin layer of neurons about a millimeter thick.

Some critics argued that perhaps the CAT scan was misread, but Lorber stated that the brain's overall weight was somewhere between 50 grams and 150 grams, compared with the normal weight of a brain at 1.5 kilograms—and much of this weight was the spinal fluid. It's safe to conclude that this student had about 95% less brain matter than normal.

Lorber continued with a wide study of 600 hydrocephalus patients. Of this sample, 10% were victims of extreme versions of the disease with 95% of their brains missing. Of this group, half suffered severe retardation while the other half fit the profile of the student, with average IQs living normal lives. These patients, including the student, continued healthy lives, with the only difference being their new awareness that they didn't have brains.

Cases like those studied by Lorber continue to crop up in medical journals. Psychiatrist and consciousness researcher Bruce Greyson, in his 2014 lecture "*Is Consciousness Produced by the Brain?*" cites a case from 2007 that he researched:

"[A young woman] underwent surgery after she was injured and knocked unconscious in an automobile accident. An X-ray of her head just before surgery revealed that she had no cerebral cortex at all; she had just a brain stem inside her skull. And when the surgeon opened up her skull to operate, that is exactly what he found: just a brain stem with no cerebral cortex."

This brings up the question: just how many other people are currently living with most of their brains missing?

How This Phenomenon Breaks Down Emergence Theory

If consciousness is an emergent property of the brain, then it becomes an extremely confusing argument to uphold based on these facts. These studies show that leading a normal life, which includes both conscious action (thoughts) and unconscious mental action (our heartbeat, nervous system, etc) appears not to be dependent on the brain active in any particular area, or of there being any particular quantity of neurons present to enable overall mental / bodily stability. The official explanation of these cases is that the brain has the ability to reconfigure itself even if it's missing nearly all of itself. This explanation, however, raises many questions—namely, what is the physical trigger of consciousness if it appears consciousness can "move around" the brain and shrink itself to nearly any size without compromising the body that it's hosting? For all conscious activity to be able to shrink down to only 5% of its former physical shell without side-effects suggests that consciousness can transcend variables like size, location, orientation, mechanism, etc—which are all the factors required for consciousness to somehow be an emergent property.

Does a Non-Physical "Brain" Function as an Auxiliary Physical Brain?

A puzzling question remains: why is it that most die of hydrocephalus, while others lead normal lives? How come one person gets hit on the head with a baseball and loses half their memories with their personalities permanently altered, while others can be born with just a brain stem and a hollow shell for a skull—and lead perfectly normal lives?

This also calls into question the phenomenon of terminal lucidity discussed back in chapter two. Why is it that some die of Alzheimer's and lose every semblance of themselves along the way, while others suddenly see a complete return to their conscious functions corresponding to the rest of the brain shutting down?

An explanation for both terminal lucidity, and brainless accounts, is that if consciousness is not directly sourced in the brain, it can regain normal abilities as the brain's function is reduced—in *some cases*—by activating a type of "auxiliary" function from its primary source. This obviously doesn't occur in every instance, but this auxiliary source—when enabled—ensures that the mind and body has complete, normal functioning capabilities without any hindrances. This would account for terminal lucidity in particular. As the brain shuts down, suddenly the auxiliary source is enabled shortly before the patient dies, and they return to full operational consciousness again.

One theory about this auxiliary source is that it's our "duplicate body" activating. In almost every near death episode recounted that involves an out-of-body state, the patient leaves the body in what is sometimes called the *astral* body, or could be otherwise be referred to as a version of the physical body that is existing on some type alternate energetic wavelength compared with our own. Experiencers often recall that this body matches their normal body in many ways, but may have "spectral" elements—see-thru or covered in energy, for instance.

Further, this body is almost universally reported *coming out* of the physical body, sometimes attached by a string of energy (referred to by New Age books as the silver cord) which somehow tethers two bodies together. Over the millennia, experiences with this duplicate body have led to belief in the soul. Although, few until now have considered that this secondary body is, first and foremost, a *body*, not necessarily the *soul*. It exists in conjunction with your current body (as also described in ancient Egyptian, Tibetan and other teachings).

What if this secondary body is the seat of consciousness, and as your brain begins to shut down, or if you are born without a brain, the astral body assumes control? Scientists currently struggle to find where the mind is located within the brain. The reason is that it may be that the mind **exists outside of** the brain altogether, controlling it from a different energy frequency, like a puppeteer controls a marionette doll. However, it's a very convincing illusion as in many cases consciousness becomes more reliant on the physical brain than its auxiliary but primary counterpart, leading to severe changes as the brain is modified.

This is not a matter of spirituality so much as neurology and medicine. An important question to ask is: how is it possible that some people maintain consciousness through auxiliary methods, while others do not? Could the same function that allows a dying patient to regain consciousness in terminal lucidity, in some way, be activated in a patient that does not have this ability? If the amount of brain damage incurred by Alzheimer's is only a fraction of the amount by hydrocephaly patients and others who are living without brains, then theoretically if those same conditions were to apply to an Alzheimer's patient, their symptoms would disappear. How can we make that happen?

Has the Hard Problem Been Solved?

Whether or not you have an astral body inside of your sweaty Earth body, it still doesn't answer the question of "what is consciousness?" Today, a new theory has expanded on this question—one of the first solid attempts to place form and function around the hardest question science has had to tackle. The person who spearheaded this is anesthesiologist Dr. Stuart Hameroff, from my own University of Arizona, who works at University Medical Center.

Hameroff works explicitly with the subject of consciousness, namely the importance of shutting consciousness off in-order to perform surgeries on patients. Even anesthesiologists, however, are not completely certain how the process really works. Where exactly in the brain is the consciousness located—and how can you materially measure it in order to understand the process of anesthesia? These types of questions led Hameroff into the field of study of the "hard problem".

This has led to a very interesting theory that has gained a lot of traction in both fields of spirituality and also physics and biology. Hameroff believes that the actual units of consciousness processing is information that is contained within microtubules. A microtubule, also known as a microfilament, is a common biology term for protein structures of the cell's cytoplasm. Their primary function is the support and shape of cells. As far back as 1992, Hameroff began

115

speculating that the microtubules inside of brain cells were a good candidate for where consciousness may arise. Since then, in the *Physics of Life Reviews* journal, Hameroff as well as Sir Roger Penrose have published further findings. Researchers say these microtubules contain fine "quantum vibrations", which are responsible for EEG rhythms (brainwaves), the location of which had long been a mystery in science. Deep within these cellular structures, there is an energy pattern that is resonating, and in essence, that is our consciousness[38].

Locating this as a source of consciousness has many practical benefits. Firstly, it explains to a large degree how general anesthesia operates. If a cell's ability to communicate with this resonating energy is turned off, then it would make sense that unconsciousness would arise. Further, it means that aspects like the physical health and structure of these cytoskeletons could determine the rest of our synaptic activity. Advancements in this area would spell good news for memory, personality disorders, and other subjects. Not to mention the sustainment of life in general, as consciousness in essence is what life is, and locating the origin of consciousness is locating the origin of what animates us.

They have also introduced a method of measuring consciousness. According to the researchers, quantum bits—or qubits—seem to move in helical pathways through microtubule lattices. Future advancements may include finding ways to modify or amplify these pathways to manipulate how well the cells transfer this information.

Hameroff and Penrose then bring up the subject of spirituality versus biology. Biologists currently assert that consciousness arose (in an emergent way) from complex brain functions that evolved over time, became more complex, and led to the united property of consciousness we see now. On the other hand, spiritual thought suggests that consciousness is a fundamental thing that doesn't change. In the journal, Hameroff and Penrose say that these discoveries lend credence to both theories simultaneously:

"...our theory accommodates both views, suggesting consciousness derives from quantum vibrations in microtubules, protein polymers inside brain neurons, which both govern neuronal and synaptic function, and

116

connect brain processes to self-organizing processes in the fine scale, 'proto-conscious' quantum structure of reality." (Hameroff, Penrose 2014).

This statement is also part of a deeper view of physics and reality, one supported by famous scientists like Dr. Robert Lanza and shared by Hameroff and Penrose, which is that consciousness itself is both inherent in the universe, and that the universe is dependent upon it. This is based on much further quantum scientific studies that have shown that the very framework of reality requires observation, as the act of observation, as first described by Einstein's *spooky action at a distance*, actually affects the physical world around us on the quantum scale. It's consciousness that allows physical reality to organize itself. The answer to the famous question "If a tree falls in the woods, and no one is around to hear it, would it make a sound?" could in fact be "no"—the tree falling only exists as a potentiality in the universal "software code", before the act of conscious observation collapses all other possibilities and manifests the most likely occurrence (more on this later, in chapter 13). .

The greater implications of these views is that the same consciousness that is inside of you is part of the same that the universe may use on a much higher scale. If these "qubits" of consciousness can exist in a grimy chunk of meat, there is no reason to assume that they cannot exist inherently in nature, and as energy cannot be destroyed—then "non-existence" is a physical impossibility.

Where is the Quantum-Level Energy Coming From?

A major question that is brought to the surface from this research concerns how this energy even exists inside the brain to begin with. Initial skeptics of the quantum energy theory explained that the brain is too "warm, wet and noisy" for a sensitive energy pattern to exist in there at all (so how does it occur?). In addition, how does the quantum information get inside the cell? When a brain cell divides, and new microtubules are produced, when does the resonating energy go into it, why does it go into it, and where is it coming from?

This is where science, as we typically understand it, may finally start to integrate with spirituality (as we typically understand that concept, too). This is also where other topics discussed so far in this chapter may be integrated, as well.

Before I talked about the rather esoteric topic of astral bodies. One way to interpret this is to simply think of the astral body as an energy pattern, molded into a form. This would certainly explain the source of the energy that fuels these innermost sanctums of our brain cells. We could hypothesize that our consciousness is separating into bits of information, in the form of energy, and it's being leaked into our cells directly from this energy source on a different spectrum. Even the so-called "silver cord" reported often during out-of-body experiences could be the transmitter of information, in the form of an energy "plug", connected directly into our brain cells—thus powering our conscious mind. It would also explain how this astral body is linked in corresponding physical space to our existing body. It must exist in a multi-layered sense right on top of us to establish the energy transference dynamic. (As an additional note, further anecdotal accounts of out-of-body experiences and NDEs always observe the energy cord connecting the energetic body to the physical through an area around the back of the neck. This would make sense if it's the brain cells that the energy body is providing bits of power to.)

Another question is how this might integrate with accounts of brainless people, as well as accounts of terminal lucidity, as discussed earlier. The question we must then ask is how much of our cells are dependent on the quantum-level energy transfer to enable consciousness in the physical world. In the studies of hydrocephaly patients, it was discovered that their brains were reduced to thin layers of membrane. This suggests that the quantum microtubule interaction present was greatly reduced from a normal brain (by 95%). This means that either: an auxiliary source of consciousness was activated (as discussed before), or the actual amount of microtubule interaction required to allow consciousness is very small. The latter explanation is also highly indicative of consciousness beyond the brain, because it suggests that the energy patterns are a dominant force in the brain that requires bare minimal physical interaction to function, proving that consciousness is essentially completely energy—and not a physical manifestation in any shape or form.

118

Quantum Consciousness and Near-death experiences

Dr. Hameroff takes the phenomenon of NDEs quite seriously. He believes that it further demonstrates the power of the quantum energy consciousness in our brains. And that it nicely summarizes the natural existence of life after death.

According to Hameroff's model of death, the energy that is contained inside the microtubules simply dissipates when the physical brain is finally finished. In the bio-centric view of the universe as proposed by Lanza, consciousness is fundamental across not only this universe, but potentially infinite other universes. There is literally a never-ending supply of usages for the "qubits" of consciousness currently taking very temporary home inside your brain cells. This would explain how some NDEs are extremely "cosmic" in nature, where experiencers report sudden merging with the universe as a whole, and returning with complex knowledge about astronomical and quantum physics related information (as described in the NDE profiled by Sartori in the previous chapter).

Consciousness and the Nature of Energy

As I'll discuss in more detail later in this book, I think when looking at the Hameroff model for death and near-death experiences, we also need to take into consideration personal experiences, and raise questions about the nature of energy itself and the ability for energy to manifest in a physical, material way.

When we think of "energy", including these wavelengths inside the microfilaments of brain-cells, we think of radio waves or satellite signals bouncing around our planet. It's energy. It's amorphous, non-physical "stuff" with no substance.

We forget, however, that physical matter is simply a form of energy, too. Right now you are made of energy in a specific solid form. If that solid form were to suddenly be converted into its less-solid energetic counterpart, a nuclear explosion would occur.

Accounts of near-death experiences, and the many other "supernatural" phenomena, often involve varying fashions of this energy that composes our realities. A near-death experience may involve speeding through the universe and being provided extraordinary amounts of information, or it may involve waking up in a very physical world, similar to our own, in a new body that also matches many of our own qualities—but perhaps with certain enhancements (one can fly, communicate telepathically, and so forth). This shows there are varying levels of solidarity comprising the view of the universe (or more appropriately, *multiverse*) as argued in this book, which is that countless planes exist all around us, with different conditions and varying levels of aspects like physicality.

The reason I am mentioning this is because we don't want to make the mistake of limiting our understanding of what our experience may be when we die. The idea that our consciousness energy re-emerges with the collective whole may paint a picture that we join some type of infinite "soup" upon death, with no more individuality to speak of, until we merge into some other physical incarnation—which may not even have memories of its prior self.

However, this is not the nature of the experience that we learn from studying NDEs. If Hameroff's description is true, we must also factor in things like our human individuality, which by all accounts appears to stay intact. When we die, I think our experience depends a great deal on our desire and personal preference. Some consciousness patterns desire joining with a collective embodiment of the greater universe at large, while others simply want to see their dead parents and pet dog from childhood again, and will gravitate toward a *new* universe that may have earth-like elements. These human-like universes reported should not be considered some type of illusionary creation, either. They could very well be *older* than our own physical universe; which may simply be an interpretation of other more advanced realms. This notion that there are many possible neighboring universes that allow functional physical forms is the essence of multi-plane theory. It shows that not only is consciousness abundant in all universes, but there are most importantly other civilizations of intelligent beings, including humans who once died on our plane, and are now thriving in realms both similar yet vastly different from our own.

Perhaps it is this relationship between neighboring planes that comprises the great story of Earthly civilization, with all its philosophical battles and religions over the span of millennia, with the incorrect assumption that personalities from other planes are gods and deities that deserve worship. While the discovery of consciousness interacting through bits of energetic information in the brain may be the first step, I'd like to believe future steps involve establishing contact with other forms of life, also composed of energy, but living in spectrums just beyond our sight.

The Location of the Afterlife

Some theories have suggested that the afterlife as we know it is in fact a solid, detectable part of our own current universe, with its own laws of physics and very objective presence. Some believe that the physical location of it is literally *all around us*. And, we simply need to begin taking a harder look at other unseen universes that physicists and astronomers are already, in our mainstream scientific understanding, very aware exist.

Dark matter is said to encompass 95% of our universe. But what is "dark matter"? It's a higher spectrum aspect of our physical universe that we can detect, and that even creates an influence upon our matter, but we cannot seem to access. It is non-luminous, invisible, and the only component of it that scientists have been able to directly measure are neutrinos.

According to the Planck publications, dark matter also comes in both material and purely energetic forms[39]. These estimates theorize that 4.9% of the known universe is only our physical (baryonic) matter, compared with a 26.8% percentage of dark matter, and 68.3% of dark energy. Combined together, this consists of the sum of "stuff" inside our cosmos. The dark matter constitutes 84.5% of the total matter in the universe. This means that every rock you pick up has the equivalent of a handful of more rocks in the dark matter spectrum. The existence of these dark spectrum forces were determined through observation of gravity, and observing that something very large and unseen has an effect upon our universe that alters the measurements of how mass interacts with space. For instance, the kinetic energy of moving galaxies is completely disproportionate.

One thing we are certain of is that our physical universe is dwarfed in size by the "dark" spectrum. But just what is it? One of the more controversial—yet still widely accepted—theories comes courtesy of the CERN institute (the group responsible for the Large Hadron Collider currently spitting particles under the soil of West

Europe). This theory, based upon research conducted at the LHC and among other teams worldwide, states that a "Hidden Valley" exists all around us. In the words of CERN, this valley is: "a parallel world made of dark matter having very little in common with matter we know"[40]. Far from having no purpose, this dark matter could actually be responsible as the type of glue that holds our galaxies together.

What they are basically saying is a much larger universe exists all around us, on a different spectrum which can be observed through their instruments, and may even exist as a functional parallel universe (or universes) to our own, but we just don't have the scientific power to reach into that world. Does any of this sound familiar? Is it possible that mainstream science and quantum physics are now beginning to meet esoteric concepts face-to-face?

Some afterlife proponents believe what is known as dark matter could be the existence of other planes. Far from being some empty realm, these could be vast worlds teeming with civilizations and life—far more-so than our tiny corner known as the physical universe. In fact, this astral matter operates on an energetic level in conjunction with the very energy that composes consciousness (as described by Hameroff), Therefore, these are realms designed around the primary driving force of the universe (consciousness), and are even more suited for life than here. By contrast, our baryonic universe is much more rigid and requires special conditions to allow life-forms to exist. Really, we might be the cosmic anomaly, stuck in a very unnatural universe, like fish out of water for lack of a better term.

Sir Oliver Lodge

An early researcher who proposed that the so-called "spirit world" was hidden "in the cracks" was Sir Oliver Lodge. Lodge was one of the pioneers of radio technology—namely, the first person to ever send a radio message. His discoveries and research are readily apparent to all of us today simply by stepping out the door.

Before the discovery of dark matter, and long before the Large Hadron Collider was attempting to figure out what mysterious "glue" holds our universe together and affects it from an invisible spectrum; there was a different theory known as ether. Luminiferous either was a widely established idea, spanning back to the 15th century and earlier (as far back as Aristotle), which proposed that for light and other

122

waves to travel, it would need an all-encompassing substance which it could pass through. Ether was therefore another universe, out of our spectrum, that existed as a layer on top of every square inch of space, which accounted for quantum phenomena[41].

Ether was disproven by Einstein, and his relativity theory which showed that energy does not require this restriction to be able to operate. Today, it's obvious there is no ether binding every movement of energy particle. However, advancements in quantum physics have shown there are phenomena that are surprisingly similar to these early propositions of layered realities affecting our own universe, such as the aforementioned dark matter phenomenon.

In Lodge's day, he claimed to have been able to measure and make mathematical assessments about the "ether" layered over our world. The following is an excerpt from Lodge's 1933 article "The Mode of Future Existence"[42]:

"As the Ether is not matter in the ordinary sense of the term, our ordinary units of measurement are inappropriate ; but on the analogy of matter, the Ether is of the order a million million times as dense as water. All its properties are of supernormal magnitude. Its rate of vibration which enables us to see any ordinary object is five hundred million million per second : a number so great that to try to conceive such a number of vibrations per second simply dizzies us."

Lodge made no mistake about it; he believed that these unseen worlds (in his time, ether) were to account for all experiences with the so-called spirit world.

Today, it's been demonstrated that "ether' does not exist in the way it was once believed. There is no medium for energy to operate However, based on research into parallel universes and dark matter— one can't help but wonder if scientists like Lodge, Sir William Crookes, Charles Richet and others had some basis behind their assertions that an alternate universe was "superimposed" over our own, and that life-forms in that realm could interact with us in this universe, thus being responsible for all manner of so-called paranormal phenomena.

Ether is still supported by some contemporary researchers, like former mechanical engineering professor Ronald Pearson, who believes an etheric world (or i-theric) is a necessary result of the natural expansion of the cosmos.

So - Where is the Afterlife?

At the very least, quantum physics and cosmology have shown that there are extraordinarily large aspects of our universe that extend beyond baryonic matter. In fact, according to measurements by institutions like CERN, our universe is completely eclipsed by these other worlds that are undetectable to us. The science of the afterlife would simply take these discoveries one step further by postulating that these worlds also possess the energetic phenomenon of consciousness, and that there can exist particles functional in the same way as our material particles. The afterlife is just any number of other planes extremely close to us. These other universes are our neighbors, and they are filled with life.

The Consistency of the Afterlife

The afterlife is, by no means, a dream world, as is commonly misrepresented. This is a frequent mistake that people make, because for most of us our only personal experience with entering some kind of other universe is when we sleep, and explore our own mental projections and their faux solidarity. This is not an accurate comparison as the real afterlife is interpreted through the same consciousness that is inside those little microtubules right now, and therefore when you are in that plane—you have the same awareness that you have now, only typically greater, clearer amounts of it.

Another way that afterlife is thought of as dream-like is imagining a purely thought-based hodgepodge. While it seems our minds play a much greater function when solidarity is less forced as it is in the physical dimension, we should not prescribe the afterlife as an abstract dimension. Switching to another plane is simply a matter of changing frequencies, and while we might be leaving behind a dead shell on this side, we'll immediately be just as solid and aware on the other side—perhaps not even realizing we had died. (The 2002 movie

124

The Others starring Nicole Kidman comes to mind. I suggest to go watch it.)

For me, this notion of solidarity has brought on a lot of philosophical oddities. Namely, that of the function of physicality. What purpose would a brain, liver, skin, bones and so forth have in another Earth-like plane that is seemingly without the same restrictions of our current plane? In other words, what exactly is the nature of these astral bodies that are reported, as well as the physical worlds that we seem to find ourselves in after death?

Perhaps to understand this, we need to again consider the nature of energy. Everything is energy. Matter is energy, and energy is matter. All of it is just "stuff", and all "stuff" has the power to change in spectrum. And if consciousness is energy, too, then a case could be made for the notion that any "stuff" can exist on a gradient scale. As the frequency increases, it morphs into a more energetic state. By contrast, if it "thickens" into a material state, it then requires some type of physical apparatus to operate and interact with other physical materials. In our world, we are restricted entirely to physical form, whereas in the astral multiverse it would seem that forms, and their corresponding civilizations, range from physical in a mirrored sense to our own, to completely energy based in the sense of free-floating consciousness, as well as various gradients in-between these states.

Measuring the Physical Nature of the Astral and the Work of Alex Katsman

Alex Katsman, a senior researcher at the Israel Institute of Technology, created a series of formulations based on revised theories of the ether that were proposed by Ronald Pearson, as well as the early research of Crookes, Lodge and others. "The Physical Model of the Parallel Ethereal World", published in 2004, attempted to ascertain the physical nature of the "astral"[43].

According to Katsman, citing the work of Pearson, both our world and the mathematically determined parallel worlds are manifested by the same types of wave particle phenomena that exists here. As a result, at least much of the etheric world is in-fact a material realm just like ours is, with both similarities and differences to our own laws of physics. Nonetheless, it still operates based on the natural laws of our own universe, and shares both our same space and time (in other words, it is far from an alien realm).

Katsman's theories do not seem to account for the purely non-physical NDEs reported, which suggest there are further gradients of planes that defer from Earth-like conditions and become abstract or extra-dimensional in nature. However, based on his estimations, it makes perfect sense that at least one element of the afterlife, and perhaps the one that the majority of us reside in upon crossing over, bears many similarities to our own world, including the necessity to possess physical bodies as a means to interact with that environment. Katzman even believes that, based on similarities in particles, physical bodies in the second universe have complex internal structures (ie: organs) made from elementary wave-particles.

Through complex measurements, comparing the densities and properties of this higher vibrational matter with our regular (baryonic) matter, Katsman made the following conclusions about the exact conditions one would expect after your consciousness "crosses over" into the second dimension:

- The speed of light is much higher than in our world.

- Typical frequencies of elementary particles, like photons, electrons, protons and neutrinos, are much higher than corresponding particles in our world.

- Planck's constant is much smaller.

- Masses of elementary particles as well as atoms are much smaller.

- Elementary charge (the electrical charge carried by a single electron) is the same.

- The size, geometry, and energy spectrum of atoms are the same as in our world.

- Ethereal solid, liquid and gaseous matter can be formed from ethereal atoms in the same manner as in our world.

- Ethereal photons as well as the other ethereal elementary particles are invisible to us because of their high frequencies. This also includes any structure made from etheric matter.

- Gravitational forces in the secondary world are much weaker compared with our own. Energy no longer needs to be exerted to overcome gravitational forces.

- Therefore a need for our bodies to overcome gravitational forces and struggle to obtain a finite supply of energy is no longer necessary.

- Because there is no requirement to expend energy on gravitational forces; digestive, blood and respiratory systems are no longer required to maintain the body.

- However, Katsman states that our bodies in the secondary world are still analogous to our current ones (it is an exact clone represented by our body's equivalent higher-spectrum particles).

- Katsman believes our secondary body includes the presence of a functioning brain and nervous system. This part of the body's structure, unlike the digestive or respiratory systems, is necessary even in the etheric.

- I would personally conclude that while apparatuses like the digestive and respiratory systems are no longer a requirement of survival, they still exist as part of the general physiology of the body, adding structural integrity and allowing the option of food consumption and taste.

Further, Katsman suggests that the mysterious several grams of weight that decreases in the physical body immediately upon death is the release of the secondary body, and this may be evidence that this secondary body has the ability to interact with this world despite the differing density of the particles. It has a very light gravitational impact that can be detected.

He concludes that the reason the ethereal world is invisible to us is because the speed of light is faster, and Planck's constant is smaller. What this means is that the astral particles exist at a higher frequency. In particular because photons that precipitate electromagnetic interaction between atoms are moving at a different speed, it becomes impossible for our atoms to absorb etheric photons.

To read the entire paper written by Katsman that describes his methodology and mathematical theories, follow this URL: cfpf.org.uk/articles/rdp/physicalmodel.html.

The Author's Opinion

Katsman's work is very eye-opening to me, as a way to comprehend what some have claimed we can't even understand using our limited, mortal brains (I don't believe this is true). It also fits nearly one hundred percent with the accounts from credible spirit sources that have relayed information about their living conditions.

I think one of the most important take away points is to realize that it's a false assumption to believe the afterlife—rather alternate spectrum planes of existence—are "non-physical". This term is often used involuntarily as we compare other planes to our own, and call this one "the physical universe" or "the material universe" (I've probably done this quite a few times throughout this book already). Throughout my years nose-deep in this subject, I've encountered many who assume physicality versus non-physicality; which would mean that our world has solid objects you can touch and feel, whereas the afterlife planes are chaotic, dream-like, or spectral in consistency.

However, this is not the case. A term I prefer to use is **hyper-physical**. There are still rules of physics, but they are less strenuous as here. It's a different "version" of what you're experiencing right now. But it's not altogether different in the crucial areas. The idea of non-physicality could be panic inducing for some of us. Imagine, no nerve-endings so you cannot feel the touch of someone you love. Or, if you enjoy green tea, imagine trying to create a cup and bringing it to your spectral lips; only to find it all just dribbles down.

A ghost-like realm would not be compatible for anyone. Fortunately, the evidence suggests that such phantasmal existences are only the result of incompatible vibrations. As postulated by researchers like Katsman, it would be the result of your electrons spinning at a wrong rate in relation to your physical environment; causing you to become shadowy and inconsistent in nature. Once you rejoin with the proper vibration, then you are once again in a completely solid, completely physical universe—only with many more options for fun and exploration, and merely fewer limitations.

Spirits in the Laboratory

If there's another world all around us, filled with inhabitants, can't they be tested in some type of controlled condition? This is a common argument proposed by critics, and it's a valid one—where is the laboratory evidence that these entities exist?

The answer is that experiments have, indeed, been performed concerning this matter, through the Laboratory for Advances in Consciousness and Health at the Department of Psychology / University of Arizona, spearheaded by Gary Schwartz (author of *The Afterlife Experiments* and other related books). Schwartz has undertaken a very interesting line of experiments to compliment his research into mediumship. Schwartz designed an isolated area, blacked out from any sources of external light penetration, and then began implementation of a silicon photomultiplier which can detect the presence of photons even in extreme conditions. The concept behind the study was to see if spirits could make their presence known using the simple variable of generating the tiniest amount of light within the chamber, and making comparisons using control methods where 1) there is no scheduled spirit contact, and 2) the experimenters themselves try to influence the photon count (to test whether it is psi usage that is responsible).

The spirit contact in the experiment depended on the assurances of several experimental mediums that were working within the lab. Upon consultation with the four research mediums, they made the claims that spirits present were: committed to the research, and that they would listen to mentally directed requests from the experimenter. By the third experiment, the hypothetical spirits were asked to watch a computer monitor with instructions for carrying out the test. Further, the equipment was left running so that hypothesized spirits could, upon request, "play with the instruments" to learn about how they function and how they can be manipulated.

The sealed, light-proof chamber consisted of a set of box-like chambers triple stacked. The device itself, attached through Velcro and wiring, was further sealed off within its own containment unit, with its lens focused into the primary chamber. With the full coverings in place, and the unit attached, the photon detector would on average return 13 to 25 photons every 5 minute interval.

Before the experiments were carried out, baseline tests were established to control for any variables. Further, each experiment included three phases: the test with the hypothesized spirit, an intentioned experiment where the user attempts to use some form of psi to manipulate the readings, and an experiment with no intention. Baselines were also conducted for each individual test. After numerous trials, the first experiment produced the following results:

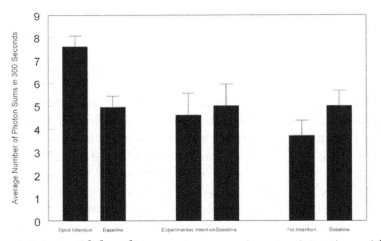

Far left: spirit test with baseline, center: experimenter intention with baseline, right: no intention with baseline.

As we can see from these initial results, the bar on the far left shows an increase of photons that is very noticeable compared with the others. The immediate baseline test, on the other hand, demonstrates the statistically predictable amount of photons. It is very hard to account for this mysterious photon increase.

Schwartz conducted two more experiments. For the second, he attempted to perform the experiments among two isolated, hypothetical spirits named Sophia and Harry. These tests were performed in a similar way as before, using baselines to control each test, separating the variables of regular photon detection with and without the influence of the supposed spirit communication. Below are the results, with the bars on the left sides indicating the test results from engaging with the spirit entity compared with the baselines:

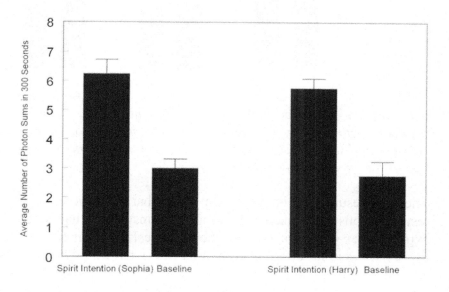

Left: Sophia + baseline, right: Harry + baseline.

A third experiment was then carried out, exploring the idea that this type of technology could be used as a binary communication device, using simple yes / no indications with the spirit team. They left the method of communication "up to the spirits" by not determining a variable to define the yes / no patterns for questions asked. It was discovered that photons were apparently generated in a way that was faster for "yes" answers compared with baseline trials, while the photon generation for "no" answers came more slowly compared with baseline trials. Results are shown below:

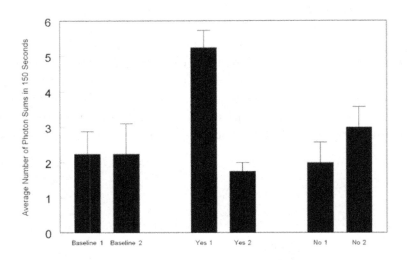

Left bars: baseline experiments for yes / no, middle bars: yes / no results for spirit entity, with very significant increase for "yes" answers and slight decrease for "no" answers, far right: yes / no results for experimenter influence (psi).

The final results of this experiment show that there were significant results. Constant baseline testing demonstrated that once the experimenter was engaged with the hypothesized spirit entities, then the results were far different compared with what would be ordinarily expected. Further, although the presence of psi (the experimenter's intentions) were not ruled out, we can still see that the results also vary significantly when compared with the experimenter's intentions.

This experiment, which was published in the journal *Explore*, has yet to be replicated, but it certainly shows that the "spirits really do exist hypothesis" is something to be taken seriously. This setup would not be able to, by itself, completely prove a subject as weighty as survival of consciousness, but it lends credence to the idea that spirits could be interacted with in a carefully controlled laboratory setting. It's hard to explain this data without considering some type of invisible, intelligent entity—unless the psi effect of the experimenter's intentions really is exceptionally subversive in its abilities to influence the quantum world.

The Future of Afterlife Science

Although it seems we are far away from the afterlife becoming a recognized part of science and physics, what many are noticing is that a lot of areas are converging together at a rapid pace. Subjects that would have been considered unthinkable to be taken seriously at an academic level 20 years ago, are now being studied to at least some extent.

The way that I predict the most headway will occur is through our continual advancement of our regular, physical sciences—biology, cosmology, physics and quantum physics. As I discussed in this chapter, our normal sciences are facing an increasing amount of "weirdness" which pokes holes into the materialist framework of reality. Simultaneously, as quantum physics and the work of institutes like CERN delve deeper and deeper into reality, we may find material science no longer able to ignore the idea that other universes are directly and intimately involved with our lives.

VI – Strange Tales

Interestingly, I've come to find that within most families are some version of "ghost stories" that get passed on. Even if these are not spoken of out in the open all of the time, usually everybody has had one or two experiences, whether by themselves or together with friends or family, to create a type of lore that may get told from one generation to the next. This is probably how an arm's-length interest in the paranormal is so deeply engrained in our culture. And also why general belief in some type of supernatural world is so common.

It seems like spooky tales are more culturally accepted to talk about compared with more in-depth "para" subjects. The reason is that everybody enjoys a good scare. Browsing Internet forums like Reddit.com and similar sites, I've noticed that ghost story threads are very popular—these are things everybody likes to share and talk about. The cultural taboo, however, takes effect as soon as you start trying to take the idea seriously beyond the campfire. Yes, you can have an experience with something spooky, but whatever you do— don't use science, logic, reason, physics and metaphysics to support the existence of some type of otherworldly encounter.

Exploring people's stories beyond the campfire is something that becomes very interesting when you get into the juicy details of paranormal investigatory work, and namely the science of survival of consciousness (as this book is about). An apparition may be a terrifying story to the uninformed, but a blessing to those who learn about it simply as a rare encounter with a human being living on a somewhat different physical wavelength than us.

For this chapter, I'd like to mention some of the eye-opening stories I grew up with, and which probably spurred my later interest. Anomalous experiences were always consistent tales in my family, but none I could personally relate to, as my conception of paranormal topics was, at the time, extremely limited. My parents—eclectic post-hippies raising us on a ranch in the Sonoran desert—had a long history of brushes with the "supernatural" which I learned about at an early age. To be perfectly honest, the problem with some of these stories is the problem that maligns all second-hand reporting; how much of it is exaggerated, distorted, or even made up? As is the nature of ghost stories—it's impossible to ever know for sure, and I suppose that adds to the mystery of such tales.

I recall a story my father told me about when he and his former girlfriend had experiences with a troubled spirit in their home. Somehow, my father claimed that the spirit had found residence inside of a male statue that was decorating the outside of their home, causing the statue to begin to "animate". My father did the only sensible thing which was he took a shotgun to it. I could never seem to probe him for more details about this story, as he was reluctant to talk about it. Ultimately, I decided it was, if nothing else, a great plotline for *Tales from the Crypt* or a similar show that was on TV at that time.

My mother did a great job of traumatizing me from an early age by recounting her experiences with her former roommate, a psychic medium, who she lived with in Boston. She and this roommate shared the same bedroom. The medium kept claiming that there was a troubled spirit of a dead sailor in their apartment, that she was trying to help to cross over.

One night, the roommate woke my mom up in a panic. She said there was "something" in the hall that had materialized into the physical world with them, and was coming toward their bedroom. My mom said, at that point, she immediately closed her eyes and refused to open them. As her eyes were tightly shut, her roommate became hysterical—screaming and crying and yelling at the "thing" to go away, which I assume it eventually did. The medium described what she saw as the sailor—covered in seaweed, mouth agape and staring straight ahead—floating back and forth, up and down the hall like some type of ghoul. My mom, coming from an orthodox background, interpreted the experience as a demon—and it inspired her to later take up Christianity.

Another sailor-related ghost story occurred many years later with my oldest brother (then around 25), when he used to stay with us at a medium-sized ranch house near Oro Valley, AZ which my parents had rented (I was perhaps 5 or 6 at the time). Everybody knew there was a "haunted" room in this house. It was a commonly known fact, whether it be friends of my parents, friends of my brothers, random contractors working in the home—it didn't matter, no one went near the place. The room in question was simply an empty bedroom. There was a window in the room looking out across the pool and recreation area. I remember one of my brother's friends making it a point to cover his eyes anytime he'd walk past the window—he didn't even want to accidentally catch a glimpse of the interior bedroom. People just knew to "stay away".

When my oldest brother stayed in the room, he recalled how he woke up one morning, and a sailor in full U.S. Navy attire was standing directly *over* him, with a broad smile on his face. He stared at the apparition wide-eyed for several seconds, until the sailor simply disappeared. He never slept in the haunted bedroom again.

Later, in the same home, my other brother (who was about 13 or 14 at the time) was swimming by himself in the pool. To this day, he becomes bug-eyed and unnerved when he describes what happened to him next. He said that an invisible figure, which he interpreted as a child, jumped into the pool with him, creating a sizable splash as it entered the water. The apparition then began swimming freestyle toward him at a rapid pace. Horrified, before the spirit reached him my brother jumped out and ran back into the home as fast as he could. He never went into that pool again.

We later learned that the house had, in the late 1970s, served as an orphanage. A few children had apparently died in the house of different causes—and at least one of them had drowned in that same pool.

I never had any experiences like these. And, growing up, I was grateful for this fact. These were not the only paranormal anomalies that occurred, and in many ways I was happy that they seemed to skip me. As a child, I had no understanding of esoteric concepts, nor even skeptical explanations. To me, "ghosts" were real—and it was an annoyance. I did not like the idea that phantoms could just decide to make a room "haunted" and then suddenly the place was off-limits. I had a reasonable amount of fear of them, and I did become paranoid that certain parts of our home were haunted. My closet was an immediate culprit—which was worrisome because it was in such close vicinity to where I slept.

My mother later explained to me that these invisible creatures that composed hauntings were damned, and were basically akin to demons, as they could not get into the Kingdom of Heaven. She told me the only real solution for dealing with hauntings in life is to pray to Jesus. Jesus, she explained, could keep you protected from any type of ghost, spirit, spook, phantasm, etc.

"Just imagine you are enveloped in light, and pray to Jesus. They will never hurt you."

This explanation sufficed pretty well, and that's exactly what I did, so ghosts and other spooks were never a problem. Of course, many years later into my adulthood, I'd actually be seeking these experiences out—with a very different mindset.

The Oasis Spirit

One of the more interesting strange tales from my childhood occurred in our primary home in the desert around the year 1990. As a precursor, I should point out that our main home was simply *ripe* for otherworldly tales, because it seemed like a place more fit for some surrealistic dimension than our own physical plane. My father acquired a large sum of money in the late 1980s through the 1990s. He used much of this money to create a vision born from his imagination—an oasis in the desert, seeable for miles across an otherwise barren expanse of southern Arizona. Unfortunately, my father has always suffered from a range of mental illnesses that have influenced his paths in life for the negative. Instead of merely making a suitable home for a family or even something legitimately imaginative and cool, he created a compound more akin to the infamous *Winchester* house. Now, unlike that well-known creepy house, our primary home was extremely small—a single-wide trailer fortified with some extra rooms and utilities. The trailer was placed there when he was poor, and as he earned his wealth, he never thought to remove the darned thing and build a proper house in its place.

The strangeness of this abode was therefore in all the areas *surrounding* the tiny home. Endless brick walkways, statues, grinning suns and moons staring down at you, adobe wall fortifications like that of a Spanish military outpost, bridges to nowhere, gazebos packed with disused furniture, and lots and *lots* of various trees, over-watered and unkempt, growing into a literal jungle that encompassed the entire compound. At its height, my father owned nearly 100 acres surrounding this oasis, installing stables and turning the place into a legitimate horse-ranch. A huge solar-powered gate was hooked up to the entrance, with the letters "K" for Kirkpatrick embossed on the front to greet our frequent guests. In its own odd way the place was indeed very beautiful, but also surrealistic, and clearly reflective of some of the strange happenings in my father's mind during those years.

It was in this environment that I grew up. And, if there was a single adjective I'd use to describe it, I'd say "boring". My brother and I did not go to public school. Friends our own age were rare, as most locals assumed my father to be some type of eccentric wizard (and they'd be correct) and warned their kids to stay away from the strange place. We did have our secondary rental home (mentioned earlier) in a more civilized suburban area surrounding Tucson. And, it was more enjoyable to be there, closer to the city. However, a great deal of time was still spent in the oasis, with very little to do (besides tend to the plants and bond with the sublime Sonoran desert, which was the one perk to the place).

Perhaps as a result of the general uneventfulness of life at the oasis, many of my memories from a very early age are foggy at best, which I think was because so many of my days just glossed over from one to the next— a consequence of not having things like grade-levels, school trips, sports, school plays or other "normal things" as highlights of one's young life. And so, given my vague memories of my early years, it's particularly interesting when there's one memory that stands out despite what was a very early age (I was about 3 or 4). Sleeping in the same room as my mom, I remember both my parents being in a panic one morning at about 4 AM; and me saying something to the effect of "Mama, go back to bed, what's the big deal?"

My mother was on her knees in-front of the open backdoor, gasping and praying to Jesus. My father, meanwhile, was standing next to her, wide-eyed like a little kid as he seemed to be talking to someone. My father then looked at my mother and scolded her. "Relax, it's not here to harm us," he said. "Everything's fine Sue, get up, it just wants to meet us. It's not dangerous," I remember him saying.

I also remember going back to bed. My parents were weird, I thought, and I honestly didn't care about whatever they were up to. It's interesting that I had these critical reasoning skills at such a young age.

The next morning, I remember my parents were explaining to my brother about what went on the night before, and they seemed uncomfortable talking about it—while my brother was trying to pry the information out of them after they had merely hinted that they had had some type of paranormal encounter. I'm happy to say that in this instance, my parents seemed concerned about disturbing their kids with any kind of outlandish tale. They talked about the experience for years to come between each other, but I had to really inquire to obtain any details about the incident.

Here is the story as relayed by my dad: every night my father liked to roam his oasis during the early hours, and who's to blame him?—it was a very peaceful place, with fresh desert air that would sweep down from the mountains, and the gardens, plants and trees he setup were quite tranquil. That evening, in the backyard area, he caught sight of a light hovering near one of the palm trees. Curious if it was some type of insect, he approached it. Suddenly, it swooped down and stopped directly in-front of him. He described it as a golf-ball sized orb of light, that was purely self-contained (not emitting a glow, yet it was bright). Most importantly, however, is that he said it behaved intelligently and seemed to have a desire to communicate with him.

My father said he remained in contact with it for a while, until it floated back up toward the trees. He then knew he had to contact his wife to keep from being thought of as a crazy person. So he went to her bedroom and tugged on her shoulder to wake her up (I remember this part, as well) and they both went to the backdoor together, at which point the light immediately returned, hovering not far from them and staring at them, as if waiting to be introduced. My mom (sadly) decided to flip out. As the more Christian-oriented of the two of them; she surmised all encounters with the other-side may be demonic. "If you're not with Jesus, begone!" she shouted as she knelt at the backdoor, at which point my dad got rather annoyed.

My mom decided she would have nothing more to do with the situation. Feeling embarrassed, my dad decided to go back out into the night to try and find it again. Not long after, he located the entity again, which he said swept around from the night sky, doing a "B line" to the front-yard to find him, and returned to hovering near him in a kind of playful way. Then, it flew off once more, but slow enough for him to follow. Across from the compound was a sizable gorge which opened into a large wash. He walked to the edge of the ravine, and watched as the entity disappeared into the night.

To this day, my father cites the experience as a life-changing event that he'll never forget. As for my mom, when the topic is brought up, she often boasts that she had the courage to make it "fess up to Jesus", at which point my dad rolls his eyes at her. Upon my cross examinations, my mom's description of the wisp matched my father's.

My brother (about 12 years-old at the time) was a junior paranormal investigator. After he found out what happened, he spent every night, in the early morning hours, wandering around the oasis instead of sleeping, hoping to make contact. Despite months of his doing this, the wisp of the desert never returned.

Many years later, around 2005, my father was away on business and it was just me and my mom in the house. One night she was out getting some fresh air, standing near the gorge, when she looked up and saw some lights in the sky. She said she then witnessed not one wisp but "dozens" that were filling up the air—all of varying sizes (some very small, some very big), dancing around the night sky. She watched in awe as the event unfolded, before all the orbs seemed to dissipate or travel away. Unfortunately, she said the sighting didn't last long enough for her to get back in time to wake me up. To this day, it is now her belief that these orbs are of extraterrestrial origin, while my father believes it was of the "spirit world". My opinion is: who can say? However, if my father's story occurred as it was told, it was certainly a benevolent, friendly entity.

By 2009, sadly my father's oasis—as well as every other property he owned—was lost in a series of foreclosures. Despite all the money he spent during his heyday, he made no plans to preserve what he had built, and he recklessly placed leans against all his properties in-order to maintain an extravagant lifestyle. Today, my parents live on meager Social Security checks—with all the riches of my youth long since gone.

If this hadn't happened, I would have loved to keep visiting the family home to look for sightings like these. The last time I drove out to this nook of the Sonoran desert, the oasis had fallen into ruin—every palm tree appeared dead, overgrowth consumed the edges, and the structures built by my father were beginning to crumble. Today, truly, it is a "haunted" part of my past.

When Out-of-Body Experiences Go Wrong

Even when I was quite young, and before I began studying supernatural topics, I knew there was some link between astral projection and these apparent ghost encounters that everybody was always talking about. My mom, despite the fact she possessed a kind of religious conviction against the supernatural, confirmed the existence of OBEs. She would sometimes boast about her experience in her 20s, when she was married to her first husband. She suspected he was cheating on her, and this bothered her constantly.

One night, as she was obsessing about this, she said she actually came out of her body and was transported to the location of her husband. She said she was standing outside of a sliding glass door in a type of casita, looking in at her husband cuddling with some blonde on a couch. Her husband suddenly looked up in shock, wide-eyed at my mother (in astral form) as she went into a fury, lunging through the wall and racing toward him—shortly before the experience ended and she was back in her body.

My mom recalled how her husband came home, trembling and unable to speak—as something traumatizing had happened, but he refused to talk about it. They later divorced, and my mom said he knew he was cheating on her as a result of that experience which confirmed all her suspicions. He never revealed what he saw that night, and presumably if it was an angry woman racing through the glass door to kill him—he didn't suspect that it was his own wife.

I pieced together how, in that case, my *mom* was the "ghost" despite the fact she was still alive and well. "Interesting" I thought, considering that this "ghostly world" could be accessed by living people under certain conditions.

Later, my brother's interest in the out-of-body experience served to both propel me into esoteric research, and also terrify me from ever going too deep into that realm by myself. The reason is that his experiences taught me that merely dabbling into that realm can be unwise unless it's performed with liberal amounts of both knowledge and caution.

For years, growing up, my brother lived on one side of our small home, and I on the other. My father lived in a much smaller bedroom in the middle, while my mother had her own camper out back, just past the main part of the oasis (my parents didn't always get along, to say the very least). My brother kept to himself a lot, and spent a lot of time studying various topics—including astronomy, physics, biology, and interestingly—the esoteric. He would sometimes talk about his forays into astral projection with me as well as his friends. It was very interesting to hear his accounts of entering a translucent, duplicate body and floating around the home.

One morning, I found myself having a weird experience. I sensed a strange sound, which I remember sounding like the "whirring" of a generator that reverberated into my mind, followed by weightlessness. My eyes remained closed the whole time, but I knew I had somehow moved "up" out of my body. I then "fell" back into it. I sat up in bed, wide-eyed and my heart beating fast. It was a rather frightening experience.

My brother, however, verified that it was an OBE. He told me the strange noise was telltale as the astral body disconnects. For some, it's whirring, or popping, or a dull sound. What's next, if you have the courage to open your astral eyes, is when things get really interesting. I, however, did not have the courage—and told myself I had NO interest in having the experience again, mentally assuring myself that I would not play around with any more strange consciousness states. The spirit world, it seemed to me, was something I needed more knowledge about before I went about exploring it. I don't always pat myself on the back about things, but this was one moment where I am today proud of my judgment.

The reason I consider this to have been sound judgment is because there were things my brother was not telling me. He was not telling me that his ventures out-of-body had turned dark and even unbearable. Years later, he would begin to open up to me and others about what was really going on. What started out as simple astral expeditions around our home began to change with the addition of what he described as "visitors". During his astral trips, he noticed other beings would come into the house with him. It should be noted at this point that encounters with sometimes frightening entities is not unheard of during OBEs. In fact, just Google "obe shadow people". It occurs so often that many teachers give instructions about how to deal with them and make them go away. According to OBE experts, like my friend Kensho (author of *Out-of-body experiences by Kensho*)— these entities are usually projections of your own mind, which have literally no power, at all. They are created by your own fear.

Unfortunately for my dear brother, I do not believe he was encountering normal "shadow people". These "visitors" were described as being unnervingly similar to the accounts in popular culture of the "grey alien". Small, greyish skin, big almond eyes. However, in my brother's words, they were a bit more "insect-like" than is commonly depicted.

What started out as these entities simply appearing in the home and being visible during his astral states progressed into the same entities appearing in his bedroom and violating him. His attempts to stop the experiences yielded no results, as he was now entering an OBE-like sleep-paralysis state against his will on a nightly basis. And so nightly, the creatures materialized into his bedroom, and could do whatever they wanted to his sleeping form—which ranged from merely hovering over him and inspecting him, to other things my brother refuses to talk about. It was the alien abduction phenomenon in the truest sense.

It also sheds some light onto other abduction reports, as these things were operating in an astral level. He was never being taken to any kind of space-ship in a material sense. However, if you're wondering how something can be manipulating you in a physical way while you are in an astral state—please recall my previous chapter where I explored the physical nature of the astral body. Dealing with an entity in your astral body may feel exactly the same as dealing with something in your Earth body.

My brother did not tell me these stories at the time. It was so horrifying and traumatizing to him, he spoke of it to nobody. I can only imagine what it's like to be attacked by monsters every night.

And truly, based on his descriptions, that's exactly what was happening to him. I feel immensely bad that anybody—let alone my flesh and blood—should have to deal with something so horrifying.

By around 1999, when I was 13, my brother met a girl on America Online and then drove to California to elope with her. And so, I inherited his larger bedroom. He left behind many of his things, including the information he studied to learn about OBEs. They were books and cassettes from the Monroe institute—the renowned consciousness exploration research center. I began to read these books, and my mind started to open to the nature of the supernatural, and the possibilities that some of it may actually be real (I was still rather skeptical though, even of the experiences reported by family members). This led to further research on the internet, where I began studying near-death experiences and many of the other topics I would go on to acquire a permanent interest in.

Some years later the revelations about what went on during my brother's astral experiments were revealed. By around 2002, when I was 16 years-old, I spent my days playing computer games, shoveling horse manure, talking to my girlfriend whom I also met on AOL (but never eloped with), and studying for my not-too-distant college exams. And, of course, I also maintained my interest in esoteric matters, reading interesting books on the subject and subscribing to Victor Zammit's (still very active) "A Lawyer Presents the Case for the Afterlife" weekly report.

On top of this rudimentary schedule, sometimes my father would also schedule trips to our other home. He had been in the process of building his second crazy oasis, but this time in the forests of New Mexico, as a summer getaway. Compared with our tiny home in the desert it was a palace—an impressive three-story log cabin, with the beginnings of my dad's unusual design touches (gazebos and walkways to nowhere). Due to faulty internet at the place, however, I had no great enthusiasm about going there. Nonetheless, I didn't have much choice in the matter.

So that summer, my parents and I left for New Mexico for a few weeks, but we needed caretakers for the ranch. And so, my brother and his new wife agreed to do it. They stayed together inside my bedroom (which was previously his room growing up) while we were gone.

It was the last time they'd ever do caretaking. In fact, it was really the last time I ever saw my brother coming around our old home for any extended period of time.

One morning during his caretaking, he woke up early to feed the horses as his wife lay asleep in bed. He marched to the stables to take care of his business, and as he was returning to the trailer; he heard the sound of his wife screaming, and saw her through the window running clear across the room.

He raced inside to console her. She was terrified out of her wits.

"I woke up, but I was experiencing the sleep paralysis thing that's happened to me many times before. But this time, there was something else in the room with me, I was able to look over at the mirror by the bed, and there was a monster in the room," she said.

What she described, of course, was one of the same entities that had haunted my brother for years.

"I remember looking at it and thinking 'oh my god, this is so cliché' because it looked just like some representation of an alien you'd see in a movie. It was short, with big eyes, but something about it almost reminded me of a termite. I think it's because its skin was thin and partially see-thru."

She managed to escape their clutches by snapping out of the paralysis state, at which point she bolted out of the bedroom in terror just as my brother was returning from the stables.

Let me tell you something: I did *not like* hearing this story. This was also when my brother finally revealed his years of traumatizing experiences at the hands of the entities. At this point, I was still confusing astral for physical states. I had simply assumed that most of these experiences were occurring in the Earthly plane, and that these aliens were literally sharing the same physical space as I was. And so, for months after, I began sleeping with a .22 rifle next to my bed.

Now it is important to point out that at the oasis we had a neighbor—an elderly gentleman named Carl, who lived about a half-mile away and would sometimes visit us. Much to my dismay, he had reported similar experiences with the same creatures. Most of us didn't believe him at the time, but given my brother's new testimony it was now all making sense. His descriptions sounded very physical in nature—including his claim that he saw an "alien" in his drive-way one night, and that on another occasion one of them "melted through his wall" and into his bedroom. The driveway experience, which occurred around the year 2000, was so unnerving to Carl he called in the middle of the night to chat about it after it happened. No one was awake that night, so I had taken the call and got to listen to his whole account.

"He's probably on some new medication," was my thought at the time.

Suddenly, I was no longer so skeptical.

"I'm going to kill one of these motherfuckers as soon as I see one," I resolved. "I won't let them get to me. In fact, I'll donate one of their bodies to the University of Arizona and become famous."

From casting Wiccan spells of protection to praying again to old J.C.—I tried various techniques in addition to good old fashioned bullets on standby. I would not allow my mind to be visually raped even by accidentally catching sight of one of these astral-alien-demons, let alone would I allow them to touch me or experiment on me. That was my resolution.

A little later on, my brother proposed a new theory about the entities.

"I think what happened," he said "Is that because I was going out-of-body so much, they could detect that I had evolved to a certain point where I could enter into their dimension. What would you do if you saw an ant scribbling messages in the sand? You'd investigate it. When a human starts learning how to enter other dimensions, it greatly fascinates them, because that's not something humans are able to normally do."

He seemed oddly forgiving of them, attributing his traumatizing encounters to the aliens having curiosity, versus exhibiting pure malevolence.

Gradually, I began to realize that whatever these things were, their abilities in our own plane were greatly limited, just like our abilities in their plane are limited, as well. If I was not going out-of-body, I would not become the metaphorical "ant writing messages in the sand", and I would never attract the attention of the termite demons.

And it was true. I never did. I put the .22 rifle away. This incident also pushed me toward learning about more spiritual topics, instead of just researching the nuts-and-bolts of esoteric concepts. I started reading about how your "vibration" will determine what can—and cannot—contact you beyond the veil. If your thoughts are on a more positive, loving wavelength—then it's impossible for a creature—whether alien, ghost, demon or any other spook—that does not possess those attributes to have any control over you.

Although only technically of token significance, any kind of "ritual", whether praying to Jesus or imagining you are surrounded by light, has an actual effect by programming your mind to enter a positive framework. I believe now if my brother had been practicing some type of positivity prayer from the beginning, he would have never experienced what he did. Now, I am not saying that these entities were evil, or even negative, however his experiences were certainly dark and horrifying to him, and what he was not properly educated about is that in the astral our thoughts have final jurisdiction. His consciousness was simply not trained to the high enough point where he could have control over such creatures. Instead, the creatures and the experiences they generated were in control of him. This type of illusion, that the alien is the dominant creature and the human is powerless, occurs frequently because of a lack of understanding of these topics. Once the human realizes that he or she is also multi-dimensional by nature, and that he or she exists on a lighter, more spiritual and loving wavelength that would never tolerate rubbing shoulders with any creature that would horrify innocent lives, then that person becomes invincible to such entities.

It took some years for me to realize these facts, which is why for over the next decade I would purposefully resist any kind of out-of-body experience. "Better safe than sorry," I'd say.

It wasn't until 2014 that I felt confident enough to venture into the same types of astral experiences that my brother once practiced—which is what we will delve into next.

VII – My Forays into the Astral

Our understanding of a universe beyond our normal physical senses is very difficult to conceptualize without a first-hand experience, regardless of how many books you read about the topic. And while having a ghostly experience, like those I recounted in the last chapter, can have an effect—these too are limited to typically brief encounters.

The most powerful brush with the beyond are probably near-death experiences, followed by the out-of-body experience as a close second. The NDE, however, is the truest experience with another plane—when boundaries are fully removed and the experiencer recounts touching, tasting, and breathing the air of a parallel universe, including communion with inhabitants and the deceased.

Out-of-body experiences, on the other hand, are a rougher version of this. While organizations like the Monroe institute help to train people to perfect this ability, we are very much still "tethered" to our bodies. OBEs are also often induced during states that are in-between waking and sleeping, and so initial experiences may involve dealing with dream-like hallucinations and the effort to separate what may be a real experience of projection into another plane—and a mundane lucid dream.

This is not to say the OBE is dream-like. What occurs is what I can only describe as a period of "wrestling" between sleep-consciousness and astral consciousness. When I first began exploring the OBE state in 2013 and 2014, I would begin to experience the initial phases and I was shocked by how my consciousness was the same as waking—immediately clarifying that I was not asleep. What began occurring is a state no different from wakeful consciousness, indistinguishable in most ways. I'd do what I typically do when I wake up which is to lean over my bed and grab my phone to check what time it is. However, I would find that there was something "wrong" about my hand—it was often mildly translucent. I would try to grab my phone only to find my fingers went straight through it.

Realizing I was in an astral body, I would attempt to mentally chronicle every moment. I'd perform tests—can I feel my fingers? Am I able to breath? (the answer is yes, but the instinct to breath does not exist), and most importantly—can I leave my bed and look around? I would even conduct experiments like licking things with my astral tongue to see if there was taste present. I remember licking the wall at the head of my bed. I started to find that almost everything my tongue contacted had this distinct metallic flavor. And yes, it left coats of saliva just like as it normally would. These details were all very important to me, and so I'd take careful notes in my log.

I soon learned, however, that the OBE state still means I am tethered to my body, and that concentration was absolutely required to keep from falling into a dream state. This always occurred upon trying to leave my bed. I would get up and try to pull my astral body out of my physical body, but then inevitably my consciousness levels would break down, and the environment would turn into a dream-world. I may begin to experience dreaming, and then resist the dreams and return to an out-of-body vantage from my bed, just like before.

This happened continuously until I was able to remain in focus long enough to leave the bed without losing consciousness. The first time I did, I fell out of my body onto the floor, and found it was like swimming in zero-gravity. I didn't know what I was doing, and I fell straight *through* the floorboards into the very dark crevices beneath the house I was renting near Hollywood, CA. But as soon as I started to panic or lose concentration, I'd "snap" back to my body, and often return to a dream state, or simply wake up.

I consulted with my friend Kensho, an out-of-body trainer from Mexico who I met in Los Angeles. He explained to me that when you are skilled enough at the out-of-body state to where you can take journeys around the house, if you are living with others you can see what it looks like to witness people dreaming. According to him, dreams are purely mental hallucinations, but they occur inside the astral bodies. The astral body typically leaves the physical body while asleep, and so what you witness are people in their astral bodies, talking to themselves and floating around the room as if they were intoxicated. According to him, these people are behaving much like sleepwalkers, and it's very hard to rouse them. However, joint experiences are possible if a sleeper regains astral consciousness at the same time that you are observing them. He claims that in this case, they will be able to see you in your astral body and you can communicate to them—and then confirm the experience with each other upon waking. According to Kensho, he practices tandem out-of-body experiences with his mentor (Master Dharmapa) in Mexico all the time.

This of course sounded outstanding to me. It would prove the existence of the out-of-body state in an objective way. As a result, I became more interested in continuing my practice. I would set goals to travel further and further from my bed. I wanted to find my roommate and harass him while he was asleep. He was also aware of the OBE phenomenon and trying to practice it as well, and so I figured if there was even a remote chance of making contact with him, it was worth the effort. After weeks of practice, I could only ever float just through his doorway of his bedroom, before losing concentration. I came to find the task was extremely hard.

All the while I was practicing these out-of-body ventures, I was also taking careful note of my mood and my "protective abilities"—imagining white light, making sure that I felt "loving" and not angry or in any other negative mood. This lesson was a direct result of the traumatizing experiences that my brother incurred by carelessly not paying attention to his mental states before the OBE. I knew that if I was sloppy with this, I'd begin experiencing projections of shadow people, up to even the horrifying creatures my brother and his wife used to deal with.

What I did not know at the time is that my OBE practice was leading to some experiences that I would have never have even imagined were possible. I was on the threshold of some rather extraordinary things.

My First Experience Entering Another Plane

The conceptual ideas of an afterlife came head-to-head with reality the morning that my out-of-body practices were suddenly taken to the next level.

One morning I had fallen back to sleep around 11 AM. I immediately entered a lucid dream state. I have no memory of the initial dream, except I returned to a normal "waking" level of consciousness during it. As I enjoyed the dream, I began to feel the familiar electrical sensations in my body, along with "whirring" feeling which is always the prelude to disconnection from the body. Suddenly, the dream "melted" away, and I was back in my bedroom spinning.

At this point, my consciousness was only slightly better than the normal lucid dream state. However, I could sense a gradual increase in my consciousness levels. I glanced to my left and looked in the mirror, and noticed I was a few feet above my body, flailing my arms around as I awkwardly floated in the air. In this form, I was wearing cotton pants and a red T-shirt. In bed, I was in just my underwear, but on the head of the bed were the same two pieces of clothing that I was planning to wear after I awoke. Somehow, my astral body had duplicated them, which I found odd (why not just go OBE in my underwear? This is one of many interesting phenomena I've taken note of).

Regardless, I then sensed I was traveling "upward." I thought I was in the attic of the rental house. But it seemed "different," like someone else's home. My consciousness came in and out of focus, switching between what felt like a regular lucid dream, and something more vivid. It was a scrambled sensation, and my environment seemed to fluctuate, until finally I was in a place that felt very "solid". I knew right away that this was different.

I was on a stone walkway, and there were trees lining a kind of veranda that was attached to a bigger stone structure like a temple. I realized immediately that I was either experiencing one HELL of a lucid dream, or I was not in Kansas anymore. And so, I wanted to experience as much detail as I could before I woke up. I went to a tree and inspected it. It was then I discovered the tree was a really amazing specimen. Every single leaf on it would fluctuate in color, and the

151

colors seemed to respond to my touch or my thoughts. The leaves flashed between blue, magenta, purple, green, etc.

As the reality dawned that I was not only astral projecting, but I was in another realm in the truest sense, I began performing tests on my environment. I held my arm out and focused hard, attempting to create an object (in this case, an apple). From my experience with lucid dreaming, such mental states are extremely fickle, and you can shape and alter the environment through your willpower alone. I wanted to test if I was in a solid realm, or some figment of my mind.

No such luck making the apple appear; nothing could be manifested or changed in my environment. The place was solid and felt "real". This was an indication to me that I was in an objective world that was not tied to my own mental activity. I was seemingly in the "real world"—just a new version of it.

However, at the same time it's like I could sense my body lying comfortably on the bed, asleep. It was like I was in two places at once, wedged in-between worlds. While the environment felt like a real place, it was my presence which was not entirely solid. I was the anomaly.

I decided to just start trying to explore as much as I could. So I headed in a random direction away from the temple, and found myself in the foliage. I was pushing through brush, sticks, and twigs as I left the path behind. At some point, the foliage cleared away and there was a well maintained dirt road. The road was actually the path to the temple I had just visited. So, I started marching the opposite direction.

As I walked down this road, I saw two people coming my way. A man and a woman. When they saw me, they both stopped their conversation together and stared straight ahead at me, almost shocked to see me. I stared back at them. Suddenly, the man started waving his arm in the air. What he said I still find amusing. "Hello over there! You're in the afterlife now, what do you think of it?"

At a loss for words, I approached closer. I immediately identified them as Eastern Indian. The man wore a traditional brown and gold colored outfit common among Hindu men, with what I identified as a very fancy looking turban. He appeared maybe 30 years old and he reminded me of a very well-groomed Bollywood star. The woman was wearing a white and blue sari dress, and her arm was hooked around the man's arm.

At this point, something hit me. It was the weight of the experience. I tend to be a very calm and non-reactive person by nature. I like maintaining calm even in drastic circumstances. Moments in my life of severe injury or panic I've always been able to cope with.

However, this particular experience was too much for even me to bear. I started to have a panic attack. I landed on my knees and I was hyperventilating and, to an extent, crying. I'm not entirely proud of this fact, but it was an emotional overload. The couple rushed over and they both put their arms around me and tried to talk to me. Finally, I mustered up what was wrong, and why I was so distraught.

"This is my problem," I explained. "I've spent much of my life studying these alleged other planes. Now that I think I'm in one, it's like I can't tell if you're real, or if this is some type of illusion created by my brain. In fact, that's the big question I've spent so long trying to answer, and now I'm just even more confused. You see part of this is still very dreamlike, I can still feel my other body lying on my bed sleeping. But all of this also seems completely real, at the same time. I hate to imagine that when I someday die, I'm going to be in a confused state like this, stuck in-between a dream and reality."

"Look," he answered. "I actually know what you're saying. You have to understand that the borders between the dream world, and our world, are extremely confusing. It might not feel like you're entirely physically here right now. But let me assure you of something." He stood up and started stomping his feet on the ground, kicking up dirt with his shoes. "See that? I'm here, I'm really here, and it's completely physical and real to me. When you actually cross over to my side, you'll discover it's the greatest feeling you can imagine to wake up and really be here."

I started to wipe the tears off my face. "OK, well I'll take your word for it that you're not in my brain."

He knelt next to me again. "You have to remember something, the key to going between these worlds lies in what you're doing right now, which is called astral projection. That's how you can come here at will."

"OK, but how do I do that?"

"You have to learn to embrace the fear. When you feel frightened as you are going out-of-body, you have to push past it. OK? When you are ready you'll be able to come back here."

"OK."

Then, suddenly, a shift occurred. Everything turned hazy, and in a flash I was awake again in my bedroom, saying out loud "Holy shit, holy shit, holy shit." It was now 11:30 AM. The whole experience did, in fact, feel to be about half an hour, so there was no time discrepancy.

The first thing I did was grab my laptop and began dictating, word for word, as much of the experience and my dialogue as I could remember. This was not hard because the memory did not feel dreamlike, but it was more like something I had physically done, no different than the memory of having just been outside the house, visiting the grocery store, or any other "real' event.

What this man told me is the only way I've been able to make any sense in my mind of these discrepancies between dreams and supposed other planes of reality. That unless we are completely disconnected, as in the case of certain near-death experiences, our minds must process these worlds through a mental state that is often sub-par in terms of true physical awareness.

As our awareness increases, the dreamlike elements subside, and we are brought closer and closer to a "vibration" that matches what residents on these astral planes experience.

The way the Hindu couple looked at me with shock when they first saw me gave me the impression that I was a phantom in their world. Maybe I was partially translucent, or some abnormality gave away the fact that I was not supposed to be on their side. Their response of "Welcome to the afterlife" could be because they believed I was a recently deceased person, who had just landed on their side. Perhaps this is how the newly departed commonly arrive on this particular patch of astral real estate—lost, confused, coming out of the bushes and questioning reality.

In the end, the most convincing part of this was my interaction with the couple. When I communicate in dreams, it's like some part of me understands that the people I interact with are figments of my own consciousness, which is distinct from talking to people in real life. Communicating with this man, however, felt like a real conversation, with a real person, complete with all the tiny details that occur when really talking to somebody—including the minutia of body-language and social cues.

Further, I found his exotic outfit to be unusual, as I had never seen it before. Later, after browsing Google image search for traditional Indian clothing, I identified the exact style of dress he wore.

For me, this trip was like the astronomer peering through a telescope and confirming research through observation. The only problem is that the telescope isn't available for just anybody to look through.

I am not extremely proud of the fact I did not maintain my composure. In retrospect, the way I was "summoned" to this plane makes me feel that it was a privilege granted to me by some higher power. It's possible I botched the opportunity for further exploration. This would be my only experience with what I felt was a "higher" and very beautiful realm. However, it would be far from my only venture into the astral.

The Strange Case of Aleister Crowley

(Warning: There is a bit of harsh language usage later in this section. Get your black magic marker out if you think your kid might pick up this book.)

My next remarkable—and far more unusual—experience occurred a couple of months after my illuminating projection into the afterlife. This story began with a conversation on Skype.

A friend of mine, also an astral practitioner, began talking to me at length about a man named Aleister Crowley. Known once as the "most wicked man alive", Crowley was also a father of the occult movements of the early 20th century. Over the years, various Spiritualist groups have claimed to be in touch with the powerful magician from "beyond the veil". My friend, who is far more mystically than scientifically minded (unlike myself) told me of his desire to personally contact Crowley. His belief was that Crowley had great powers that he could learn from. My opinion was eye-rolling. I thought he was wasting his time. Further, from what I understood about this occult figure, he wasn't necessarily the healthiest spirit to try to contact.

"Ok, if you want," I said. "I heard Crowley was a pretty dark character, so I personally don't think that's a good idea."

I knew very little about Crowley at the time. The conversation with my friend, however, spurred me to learn a bit more about him and his beliefs, his work in ancient Egyptology, and his practices with the occult. I thought little of the subject afterward. It was interesting but not of any immediate relevance to my current areas of research.

Not long after, I went to bed, and fell into a most unusual dream. Within that dream, I encountered a woman, middle-aged, with short-black hair and wearing what I would best describe as period clothing. The location of this dream was unmistakable; it was a rather luxurious mansion with a huge chandelier and spiraling staircase. She told me that "Mr. Crowley" was aware that I was researching him, and that Crowley was fascinated by all the work I had been doing for many years into the subject of life after death—and so he wanted to meet me.

"Where am I?" I asked her.

"You're in the Hollywood Hills, and this is Mr. Crowley's home." (I was already living a stones-throw from the Hollywood Hills in the material side. Was this the astral equivalent?)

"Ok, then."

"If you're ready, Mr. Crowley will meet with you now," she said.

Suddenly, the dream melted away, and I was fully awake in my bedroom. However, I knew something was different—I felt the familiar electrical tingling sensation that always occurs as my body separates. I was now about two or three inches above my body. It almost felt like I was being gently pulled out of it, versus the struggle that usually occurs as I try to disconnect.

Suddenly, a presence entered the bedroom with me. Up and to the left in my room, a blackness appeared—what I could only describe as "dark electricity" that absorbed much of the light in the room. I knew right away it was Crowley. He possessed no physical shape, but took the form of this blackness which I sensed was a reflection of his aura.

And then, just like that, the communication switched to "on" and the words "Hello there!" in a thick British accent echoed out of this blackness. I sensed Crowley's presence, but he was not fully there with me, either; as the apparition was more like his own kind-of astral projection. The communication, however, was not purely mental. While it seemed to be occurring telepathically, I could hear his voice as clear as day, and it reminded me a great deal of a normal phone-call.

"Well, hello Mr. Crowley. I am pleased to be of acquaintance with you." I said. I was not using my vocal cords to talk, but the sound of my voice, projected through my thoughts, was no less crisp than how I normally sound. If anything, it was even sharper and clearer. It was astral physics at work.

"I am aware that you were researching me, and your friend was trying to reach me, and all that. I just thought I would pop in and say hello, as I've been interested in the work that you've been doing."

"Thank you. It's true, I spend a lot of my time now researching and trying to understand your side of existence. There is unfortunately a great deal of ignorance currently in our world, and a lot of damage that is caused by this lack of understanding."

And so began our conversation which lasted approximately twenty minutes. We discussed the afterlife, but we also discussed a number of other issues—namely mental health. I brought up the topic of spirits lacking in awareness, crossing to his side confused and uncertain, and Crowley confirmed the severity of this issue.

As our conversation wrapped up, the spirit claiming to be Crowley offered a generous compliment. "You know, Cyrus, there's something different about you. The way you think, the way you talk, it's not the same as most people on your side who I encounter. It is far more similar to the people on my side, in the etheric."

"Well, I think it's because of all the time I've spent researching this topic. I'd like to create some piece of work to really help people gain knowledge and understanding of your world, so we can remove so much confusion over here. If necessary, I should act as a type of ambassador between my realm and yours."

"Now this is where I wholeheartedly disagree with you," Crowley retorted. The exact words that followed are hard to recall, but Crowley was not approving of any attempts to "enlighten" mankind, in any shape or form. To him, it is a matter of personal choice and discovery. And that in some ways, humans are supposed to be in the darkness, confused about their true nature, as this is part of our developmental process. Unfortunately, as this conversation continued, just like a dropped phone-call, I lost connection.

"Mr. Crowley, are you there? Hello? Hello?"

And it was done.

157

Still out of my body, I tried to gather my thoughts. When I realized he wasn't coming back, I reconnected, reopened my physical eyes, and immediately grabbed my laptop to jot down as much of our dialogue as I could before I'd forget any of it.

Later, I Googled Crowley and tried to get as much additional information about him, looking for any further clues to confirm my experience. Interestingly, I discovered a photo of Crowley with his second wife, Maria de Miramar.

I have no doubt that this was the woman I spoke to during the dream part of my experience.

Further, due to my limited knowledge of Crowley from before, I wasn't even aware that he was British until the visitation occurred, and then I confirmed this fact. Communicating with him; he reminded me of some other older British folks I've known, articulate smart-asses.

I later contacted my friend on Skype, who had been taking trips out-of-body in an attempt to make his own contact with the old magician. He, however, was not so lucky.

"I focused in on Crowley, and astral projected. I ended up in what I can only describe as a room full of Crowley's servants or followers. Lots of guys were sitting around in this waiting area, and when I appeared and asked if I could meet Crowley, they told me something to the effect of 'Get in line, then. We're all waiting to be ass-fucked by Crowley, too.' They were basically a bunch of losers, so I got out of there quickly and returned to my body."

This lewd account did not surprise me. Crowley, a kind of astral rock-star and cult leader, I believe takes some dark pleasure from followers and admirers. It would not even surprise me at all if his attempt to reach out to people on Earth from through the astral was quite routine for him, in his attempt to gather new disciples. In some ways, I think Crowley is aiming to be a God, by appearing in that dark, spectral form to gain the reverence of new followers. I, however, had no interest in worshipping him; and I communicated with him in the way that all people should truly think of one another in the sense of equity and fairness under God—as equals.

While I don't think Crowley is truly so "dark" as he presents himself, and I believe he's always been concerned with the spiritual advancement of mankind in the most benevolent sense, I would still be concerned about maintaining a long-term apprenticeship with someone whose intentions may be also quite self-serving. However, if this spirit truly was Crowley (and I sense it was), then I'm more than happy to consider him as a friend of mine—so long as that friendship remains at arm's-length.

I later learned how this spirit claiming to be Crowley has been influential among developing mediumship circles, as well. Crowley, it seems, remains quite busy in the affairs of the Earth. And, it was certainly an honor to be among those he's chosen to visit.

This experience was, in my estimation, quite simply not a dream. The incident in the manor with the woman was certainly dream-like, but it was markedly different from the point when the dream ended and I was leaving my body to begin my communication. The only other incident in my life that's even come close to the lucidity of this spirit communication was the prior experience a couple of months earlier with the Hindu couple.

My take-away point from this incident involves the nature of dreaming and projection. Lucid dreams are some type of link to other planes, but they're markedly different from the literal experience of disconnection from the body. When we do successfully appear in their world, it is inconsistent and unstable; and so it is ultimately an imperfect method of travel, compared with when the consciousness is in unity with the body (form to match function) as we experience right now during our waking lives, or how we will experience it when we finally die. Truly, upon death, we will obtain the ability to enter these worlds in fully realized forms—something that we seem to be denied from fully appreciating when we must rely on projecting our consciousness as our only method of travel.

Nonetheless, even as astral projectors, we can still explore these realms and interact with people in them to a high capacity, especially as we practice and train. Further, it creates a personal connection to the other side that enables us to experience the mystery of the afterlife without ever having to have a cardiac arrest.

Seeking the Veridical

While my experiences in the heavenly plane and with Crowley were very significant to me—they are not very significant in the grand scheme of things. Stories of spiritual contact are a dime a dozen, and they don't bring us any closer to the main objective, which is to separate this subject from the "occult" and the "paranormal" and into the light of day—under the guidance of reason, science and socially accepted research.

For this reason, I put more weight on experiences that, in some way, can be verified by others. Although such experiences are still anecdotal, after such an incident I would at least personally ensure that whatever was experienced was objective and not within my mind.

It has been difficult to obtain veridical information while out-of-body, but it's not unheard of. Earlier in this book, I mentioned the experiments of Tart and "Miss Z" that yielded some success. After experimenting with the OBE, I've come to understand more clearly why it's hard to obtain the results that critics demand. I estimate it would take years of practice to perfect the OBE. The most stability occurs for me when I am just barely poking out of the body. However, once I attempt to leave the body—it's as if I'm subject to all kinds of chaotic unpredictability that makes the phenomenon a nightmare for scientific control. Very often, I'll simply end up somewhere else entirely.

As a recent example, I felt myself leaving my body one morning, and then I made my best effort to pull myself out using the "rope technique" made famous by the Monroe institute—which is when I imagine I am grabbing on to a rope with my astral hands and pushing myself up and out.

Upon doing this, I ended up in a kind of country cottage, with big cobblestone floors. I started walking around and trying to make sense of my environment. I went into the next room and encountered two very blue-collar individuals on a couch ("rednecks" as I would call them), chain-smoking cigarettes. They asked me how the heck I was in their home. I told them I was astral projecting. One said "So you mean to tell me you're back on Earth, lying on some couch somewhere, but you're here at the same time? That's some crazy stuff." Both of these individuals appeared to be quite aware that they were deceased.

That's just one example. I have no idea why or how I ended up in what appeared to be a random person's house in what I assumed was an astral environment. There appears to be some higher force involved in our subconscious mind that sends us to places like this. The less trained you are and the flimsier your concentration, the less control that you have over this phenomenon.

And so it has remained a goal to "stabilize" during the OBE and to remain in the immediate, unaffected physical environment surrounding where I sleep, in an effort to glean information. I have, so far, had one successful experiment in this regard.

In spring of 2015 I was traveling in central Europe. I found myself in the beautiful city of Prague. Needing a place to stay, I made contact with a friend who happened to also be the same out-of-body practitioner from Mexico who I had met in Los Angeles the year before—Kensho. He had setup a meditation workshop out of his apartment in the pastel-colored baroque streets of Praha 2 just past the historic old town. Together with his guru—the Buddhist esoteric leader known as Dharmapa—he had been working on setting up Prana meditation centers in different places around the world. And so, for a

161

while, I took on the not-very-glamorous position of sleeping on a mattress in a cleared out corner of his apartment-slash-workshop.

Making the most of this situation, I figured that with Kensho's frequency of OBEs, if I began practicing my own abilities as I slept on his little mattress, there was a possibility that I could catch Kensho projecting at the same time—and experience the elusive shared OBE.

And so, I began attempting my techniques every morning when I seemed to have the highest probability of going OB. Kensho, at the same time, gave it a good effort, as well. One morning, Kensho told me he managed to project into his living room, and caught me in my astral body, standing around mumbling to myself. "That means you were dreaming," he explained. "I tried to yell at you to get your attention, but you were lost in your dream hallucinations."

Unsure if a breakthrough would happen or not, I kept trying. One morning at about 7 AM, I felt the familiar electrical tingles, and knew I was disconnecting. Now floating gravity-free in the apartment, I realized I had to make something work before I lost concentration. So, I pushed myself straight towards Kensho's bedroom.

Upon entering, I encountered something unusual. Kensho, instead of being asleep in his bed, was sitting down on the floor, in his bathrobe, staring straight ahead as if in a trance. I assumed maybe I was dreaming, because this was unusual behavior. I yelled at him to get his attention, and no luck. Soon, my concentration broke and the OBE was over.

After we were both awake, I pried him for information.

"What were you doing at 7 AM? Were you sleeping" I asked.

"No, this morning at 7 I was on my meditation futon, meditating."

"What were you wearing?"

"My bathrobe."

I had no idea beforehand that Kensho meditated on the floor every morning. I put this down as a verified account, and I was very excited about this fact. It was truly veridical. As good as any account in the lore of parapsychology.

During my time at Kensho's in Prague, I would hear second-hand reports from him about his OBEs with his guru, Dharmapa, back in Mexico.

"You won't believe what happened last night," he said excitedly one morning. "I went out-of-body. Soon, I drifted through the walls of the apartment and found myself in an old castle with my guru. I met a well-built man in traditional Bohemian attire who identified himself as the God Poseidon from Atlantis."

"Okay," I replied. "Can you verify any of this with Dharmapa?"

"I am going to try now," he said, as he loaded up his Facebook account. He sent his guru a message, and about an hour later he got back to him.

"Yes, precisely. We were astral traveling together last night," Dharmapa said.

"Who were we with?" Kensho asked.

"One of the old masters of Atlantis."

Whether "Poseidon" was real, a mental projection, or some astral resident who's taken it upon himself to role-play an identity, it seemed likely this was a real veridical account. According to Kensho, however, such experiences are of no great surprise to him, and he only inquired about the details to his master for my sake, as a demonstration of the validity of the shared OBE.

"This happens to me all the time. Dharmapa and I constantly astral project together," Kensho explained. He recounted a story of when he was astral projecting in his house in Mexico (which he had shared with Dharmapa) and floated into the living-room.

"That's when I saw my guru and a team of scientists in white lab coats. They were operating some type of machinery."

"What was he doing?"

"Well, the next morning I asked Dharmapa what he was doing in the astral, without mentioning what I had seen. He explained to me that he was working with some scientists, who were astral projecting also, to teach them some important technological concepts that will have benefit for the Earth plane. They would not remember their experiences the next morning, but it would stay in their subconscious mind and would influence their work."

According to Kensho, plenty of Earth masters are working diligently to help mankind progress out of some very dark, ignorant conditions. This can be done through scientific advancements, as well as artistic ones. He said that masters, both on Earth and in the astral, may use their abilities to positively influence popular filmmakers in the same way that they influence scientists. This occurs among some movies or TV shows that have strong underlying themes about the nature of life, death, and worlds beyond (one movie that I was told was allegedly "directly inspired" by spiritual intention was *The Matrix*. However, when the otherworldly influence ended, the quality of the Wachowski's work dropped, which probably explains *Speed Racer*).

This experience in Prague was certainly eye-opening. The part of my mind that makes rationalizations about incredible experiences could not dismiss the veridical perception I received. And as the true potential of astral projection dawned on me, Kensho's stories became a bit more plausible.

This is important because if there is a major turning point in the science versus spirituality front, it may occur from veridical OBE perception. This phenomenon, as it occurs during the near-death experience (NDE), is still being studied extensively with the second part of the AWARE study currently underway. However, through my personal experiences, I've learned how difficult it can be to get right. The OBE requires a great deal of concentration, and it's like learning any skilled art form, from singing to playing the piano—it takes years of practice. I believe the key is to work with skilled OBErs who have been doing it for many years, have a complete education on the topic, and can maintain prolonged out-of-body episodes in the near-earth astral plane surrounding the projector's body. If such highly talented people were to be extensively studied, we'd see some remarkable results.

How long must we wait before a study like this happens?

Out-of-Body Conclusions

Aside from my one veridical "hit", the most amazing aspects of my journey into the OBE have been my communications with "spirits". Before these incidences, everything I studied was far-away and inaccessible from my ordinary life. I quickly realized that communication beyond the veil is surprisingly ordinary once you actually do it. Before then, my only attempts at communication beyond the waking world would be with dream constructs. These are the personalities that your mind builds while you sleep, maybe representing parts of your subconscious. We've all encountered constructs before. As an example, the last time you were sleeping, and dreamt you were sailing on a boat with John Travolta, this was a dream construct. Trying to communicate with them has always been a waste of time—because it's essentially talking to yourself. During my incidences out-of-body, it's markedly different. These are people who talk like you and I do. They answer real questions, provide information you did not know before, and they may be just as curious about you as you are of them—asking questions about what it's like to be astral projecting from Earth.

I also came a long way from my childhood fear. That fear was spurred on from the negative experiences of my brother. And, it took a long time—over a decade—to get past those anxieties. Today, my brother says that he may always have difficulty going out-of-body for the rest of his life due to those traumatizing years he experienced on the ranch. This highlights the great importance of approaching this world with enough understanding of one's state of mind beforehand. Unless you are in a more-or-less happy frame of mind, I would never risk going out-of-body as anxieties, fear and / or depression can all be made manifest into physical form in the astral. Or worse, those emotions can draw creatures to you that exist on that particular wavelength—as what happened to my brother.

Benefits of Astral Projection and How You Can Start

Despite some of the dangers of the OBE if you are untrained, I am a sincere advocate for the experience as learning how to leave your body opens up communication channels that can be very important to us. That includes the ability to speak to deceased loved ones. This is a line of communication that is far more direct than mediumship. Instead of going through a third-party, you are going partway there by entering, at least partially, into their world. Even if you are merely above your body, within your own bedroom, you've still entered astral space and can then be contacted by those on the other side who possess the ability to meet you, or who can contact you telepathically. I've experienced this phenomenon already to an extent. If I were suffering from the grief of a close friend or family member who died, I may be inspired to try to reach them this way.

And now you may be wondering how concept can become reality. The following is the basic technique for how I am able to enter this state. It tends to differ between people, so a fair amount of personal experimentation may be necessary.

- The first step is to gain awareness while you are asleep. When your body is asleep, but your mind turns "on", this is when the astral body can separate.

- I will sometimes transition to an OBE through a lucid dream. To enter a lucid dream state, try asking yourself throughout the day the question: "Am I dreaming?" Make this into a habit. The point is to habituate it until you ask the question *while you really are dreaming.*

- Once you ask yourself this question as you sleep, it will reactivate the rest of your consciousness, regaining your access to logical and linguistic centers of your brain that are usually lost during sleep. What follows may then be a lucid dream. These are often fun, because you obtain the ability to manipulate your dream hallucinations however you see fit.

- The purpose is not to stay in the lucid dream. The next step is to switch out of the dream and begin moving your astral body.

- What occurs for me is that while I am lucid dreaming, I simply shift my consciousness back to my body, and attempt to move my limbs as normal.

- However, your body has released chemicals to immobilize you (sleep paralysis) which prevents the ability to move your limbs (this is so that we don't thrash around and hurt ourselves as we sleep). So, if during this state you feel the ability to physically move, you'll discover that it's your astral body instead.

- Sometimes, sleep paralysis will occur as you experiment doing this. This is where you will be unable to move either astral or physical bodies; and you will feel "stuck". If this happens, just relax. You'll very shortly either return to a dream-state, wake up, or obtain astral access (go OBE). If you panic, the fear may create a negative hallucination, as you're still partially dreaming.

- The next common thing you'll find is that as you try to move your astral body you will experience a very noticeable sensation. I typically feel an electrical pulse that moves up my entire body. Sometimes it is uncomfortable, but it's fortunately brief. Popping or whirring sounds are also reported.

- You will then find yourself moving your arms around. However, you are moving them *out of* your regular arms. Sometimes your astral limbs are translucent, and other times they seem just as physical.

- Most of my OBEs occur in this state. I will move no further than my nightstand, leaning over my bed. At times, this state **has been indistinguishable** from regular waking consciousness; to where I've even been uncertain if I was out of my body or not, only realizing it after my hand passes through objects on the nightstand.

- For me personally, I find it hard to get past this step. What has taken practice is the ability to launch off my bed, at which point I'll find myself in a kind of low-gravity environment that is hard to "steer".

- The further away I get from my body, I also notice the harder it is to maintain concentration. If I lose focus, I will end up back in my body again, as if I am invisibly tethered and constantly being sucked back.

- Generally, more elaborate OBEs occur when I find that my astral body was already outside of my physical body as I regain lucidity (and this has been confirmed by Kensho and other teachers I know as something that occurs during sleep). It is like we are wandering the astral plane, chasing after dream images—and once we regain consciousness, we realize that we are in some strange, random location.

- A good example of this was the story I cited earlier, when I ended up in a cottage with a couple of blue-collared guys intrigued by my presence. My dream ended, I felt a vibration as something disconnected, and realized I was in this other very unusual environment and not connected to my bed.

- When this occurs, I appear to be in a condition that's already adapted to my astral body. So no low-gravity axis to get used to like when I am coming out of my physical body normally. This is when I notice my astral body is very "solid" without translucency or other issues. This is probably because there's no vibrational difference in the environment to contend with.

- The biggest challenge then becomes maintaining my conscious state in the astral. I find that I am being constantly assaulted by the sensation of wanting to return to dream-consciousness, and to begin chasing hallucinations again. If I don't maintain pristine levels of focus and concentration, my experience in the other plane will end. That being said, I try to get as much information as possible before my concentration breaks. This includes communication with anyone around me, I also put emphasis on examining my physical astral body; as I am endlessly curious about the nature of physical existence in a duplicate body (there is no desire to blink, no desire to breath, but so far I have identified all the same physical apparatuses work the same as ever, including the ability to breath and smell things—but only if I choose to do it. I have also experienced strong physical sensations like cold and heat that are no less painful than in my normal body).

- My experience in the first astral plane with the Hindu couple, and my other experience with Crowley, were distinct. Both these experiences, I feel, were arbitrated by "guides" or some other power. In the first instance, whoever was the arbitrator was unseen to me; while in the second it was clearly the spirit claiming to be Crowley himself who helped me to leave my body.

- In these cases, under the influence of a helper, I had distinctly less need to concentrate to maintain the experience. In other words, even if I stopped focusing on maintaining lucid awareness, the experience would not end, and is therefore more similar to our normal waking experiences. This creates what could be described as a profound spiritual experience.

- What this means for you is that you should try to ask for help from a guide (or whatever positive, good-natured entity might be listening) to help you along. This could very well initiate a more profound experience than your typical OBE.

- Finally, a major development of mine has been the timing of my OBEs. I no longer have OBEs during normal sleeping hours. This was on purpose. OBEs are intense. I will often wake up so excited by the experience, I won't get another wink of sleep, and this became disruptive to my rest. So, I actually told myself "no more astral projection during normal sleep hours". As a result, without fail every time I take a daytime nap, I will have an OBE. This means if you encounter a similar problem, you can also train your subconscious to work with you the same as I did.

Objectivity is All That Matters

Finally, I want to mention some parting lessons I've learned. The most important is that the objective world is what matters. Life itself is just a giant shared dream. But it's the "shared" part which is critical. When we dream as when we are asleep, we enter realms of the mind. These are useful for gleaning information from our subconscious. But they are subjective and disconnected from the meaningfulness that comes with sharing experiences with other souls.

Exploring the OBE state would not be interesting if we were limited to a dream-environment. Most skeptics of the OBE assume that all experiences are some type of dream-state. I can confirm that this is not so, and I would have no interest in the subject if it were all merely dreams; as dreams themselves in many ways do not interest me. What I desire is the true and the objective. As it's only in the ability to share our experiences with others that reality itself even takes any sort of meaning.

From My Notes Concerning Dreams

July 12th – 2015 (Location: Sarajevo, Bosnia)

I've always been puzzled by the dream phenomenon. Although it's easy to dismiss them with the word "hallucination", I cannot help but think dreams are still linked to our astral experiences in some way. After practicing going out-of-body earlier this afternoon, this begins to seem more likely.

I fell asleep and found myself dreaming that I was at a bar in a restaurant. It seemed an underground venue, with old brick walls, only a couple of patrons, and several waitresses who I was talking to. As is often the case with dreams, there was an ample amount of what I could only describe as "dream nonsense". In this case, it took the form of video game characters that were, at one point, occupying the bar with me. Later, my dad came stumbling forward, intoxicated. Buried in my subconscious is a general apprehension of going to restaurants with him, because he'd always have a tendency to get drunk, stumble into the kitchen and begin giving everyone money. While the restaurant staff certainly liked this, growing up I would generally roll my eyes and cower away in embarrassment by my dad's "generosity".

At one point, the waitresses looked at me confused as I grabbed a roll of paper towels and attempted to put it on top of my head. It made sense to me at the time.

So it can be said with confidence that these were all mental projections in typical dream form, conjured up out of my mind. Shortly afterward, I woke up. Then, I decided I would close my eyes, go back to sleep, and try to create an OBE. As I drifted to sleep, I concentrated part of my mind to stay conscious and awake during the process of falling asleep. Within moments, I felt the electrical tingling sensation and then—boom! I knew I was out-of-body and projecting somewhere.

I was lying down on a small mattress as if I were sleeping. However, it wasn't my own bed. I got up and realized I was in a totally foreign environment. The open doorway led outside of the little bedroom and down a hallway made of old brick and dimly lit. I turned a right and realized I was in a bar and kitchen area. As I looked across the counter, it was clear I was in the same environment I was dreaming about earlier. Except I got the sense it was "late" and all the wait-staff had finished their work. I wanted to test the physicality of my experience, so I picked up a frying pan and played with it. I then inspected myself. To my embarrassment, I was wearing a long sweater—but no pants—including no underwear. Shocked that I'd be spotted with my genitals hanging out, I realized I needed to scramble back to my bedroom. Some of this panic broke my concentration and the experience faded, I was back in my regular bed.

I went OBE again 2 more times and found myself back in the foreign bed each time, but I couldn't keep the experience going long enough to get out of that bed and explore the place again. I found myself shifting between both bedrooms until I couldn't seem to go OBE anymore.

I recall many spirit sources repeating the same thing; that often during what we view as sleep, we are in actuality traveling into other realms. Spirits from the Flint séances and many other communications have often said things to sitters such as, "Yes, I saw you recently, you came to us while you were sleeping. But I reckon you'd have no memory of the experience back in your physical body."

This is also a concept I've had a difficult time grasping. However, based on today's experience, I have a theory that may shed some light on this:

What if dreams are imprints of real experiences we are having in another plane, but they are being "filtered' through our physical brain? What if they are like an echo of something that is really happening elsewhere at that very moment in time, but our brain-consciousness is muddying the whole thing up?

As an example, let's pretend you dream that you are in a big, golden field. Now, maybe at that moment on the astral side you are traveling in a big, golden field somewhere. Suddenly, King Kong appears in the field and is swatting at fighter jets attacking him, and you run and hide. This is obviously a projection of your subconscious mind. So on the astral side, the golden field part might be real, but through your dream impression of it, you've placed some nonsense from inside your head there. If you were to follow this dream by immediately having an OBE, you may find that you're still in that big field, but certainly King Kong isn't there anymore.

This also suggests that maybe we have lives happening concurrently in the astral without even realizing it. Dreams bridge our two bodies only slightly, while the OBE completes that bridge—merging both spheres of consciousness temporarily together. In this case, it would seem I had been traveling somewhere, and I was staying at a type of inn with a restaurant attached to it. The waitresses were likely real people, and the dream included some bits and impressions of real conversations I was having with them. By the time I had started going out-of-body on Earth, I had already retired to my bed in the astral.

The one thing that seems inaccessible are full memories from the astral side. When these spheres of consciousness merge, I only have my Earthly memories. So, I will appear in another realm and have no idea where I am. This makes sense if our astral memories are being stored somewhere else (my astral equivalent neurons, I would assume). So this is one link we may not be able to easily bridge.

Spirits say we are only in the astral at the time of sleep. So while we sleep normally, we "appear" in the astral to continue our journey from wherever we were at last-time. This would mean that the $1/3^{rd}$ of our lives that are spent seemingly with no activity as we slumber may in-fact be a time that is spent leading a dual-life in other planes. It would seem for me personally, I spend a lot of time traveling and staying at Inns for weary astral travelers! Not entirely unlike my life on Earth as I hop from pension to hostel as I wander the world.

The next time you have a dream, especially when it seems a strange foreign environment, consider you might be experiencing an impression of somewhere that you've really been to while in astral form. This provides a whole new meaning behind keeping a dream journal.

VIII – To Exist Between Planes

The following story is contributed by my friend who is a suicide-survivor, Amy Kristine.

Never in my wildest imagination would I have thought one day I'd be sharing my NDE testimony. As a fervent atheist, the concept of consciousness existing after physical death seemed like a fairy tale for people who couldn't "handle" reality. And yet, nearly 9 years after my near-death experience, I feel compelled to share my story with friends and strangers often at the expense of ridicule and disbelief. Over social media or over grocery carts, I recant the tragic spectacle that was my life prior to death at age 26. I was a wife, a mother—and hopelessly addicted to prescription drugs. My life ended on a stormy night in December of 2006, and two weeks later when I woke from the coma, my real and eternal life finally began.

To tell you the truth, I remember very little from the night I overdosed. It was nearing Christmas, and I frantically wrapped presents while family and friends gathered over pots of soup during a region-wide power outage. At some point I wandered upstairs to the bathroom where my pills were kept hidden. The day prior my month's supply of methadone was refilled—a lethal and legal opiate painkiller responsible for 1 out of every 3 opiate-related deaths. Before the night was over, I had taken all 80 pills, or the entire bottle. When my husband found me unconscious on the bathroom floor, he carefully put me to bed and listened to my breath which he described as someone trying to "breathe underwater."

The next morning he called from work to have my mother check on me—but by then I was blue and had stopped breathing entirely. 911—swamped from the previous-day's storm—was unable to respond, and so my parents took my limp body to the hospital in their car. By the time we arrived, my heart had stopped. It would be defibrillated twice that day—my blood pressure barely registering on the machines. My family was led into a private grieving room where they prepared themselves for the worst. A less-than 10% chance of survival was the prognosis given to them. Two collapsed lungs, liver failure, kidney failure, and sepsis so widespread I would require an almost complete blood transfusion. With Christmas just weeks away, the holidays had suddenly been shattered.

While all of this chaos and terror was enveloping my family on Earth, my near-death experience was set to begin. I remember waking up from what felt like an impossibly deep sleep. I opened my eyes to see the night sky and there were brilliant white stars flying by. With me was a woman seated to my left. The cold was one of the first things to register, and as I continued to wake up, I could see we were on a mountain road, climbing towards the summit. The road seemed very treacherous, and even though I was chilled by the cold, I saw no snow outside, just that dark night sky and all the stars. I turned my mind towards the woman next to me and asked her where we were going, barely realizing I was telepathically using my mind to communicate. She told me I was on a journey, and that I just needed to rest. She indicated that the two of us had never met on Earth, but that she was a friend of my brother-in-law, Gabriel and here to take me on my journey. It was so cold and my eyelids felt so heavy that I had no choice but to fade back into sleep while we climbed toward the mountain.

When my eyes opened again, I was surprised to find myself in the loft of a wooden cabin. I was nestled in a warm bed of exquisite white linens, and cured meats and cheeses hung from the overhead rafters. A stairwell to the right of the bed descended into a room filled with party-goers—the tinkling of glassware and sounds of laughter and conversation wafted noisily into the loft. Suddenly, I felt overcome with sickness. Within moments the woman who had taken me on the mountain road was by my side, a cup of tea in her hands.

"That's the methadone in your body," she said. "Take this, it will help." Confused, I sipped the tea, the nausea and sickness melting away as I settled back into the bed.

"Who is the party for?"

"It's for you, "she replied. "Everyone is so happy to see you." Overcome by exhaustion, the last thing I remember asking before drifting back to sleep was me saying, "If the party is for me, could you please turn the music down a little? I'm so tired."

An incredible rushing noise was what woke me up next, and my brain could not register where the sound was coming from. It was as loud as a jet engine, and I concluded that I must be on an airplane. Everything was dark. I couldn't tell if I was laying down or standing up. It was all darkness and rushing noises. And then I saw her—or, more specifically—I saw me. My body was on a stainless steel hospital gurney, dressed in a hospital gown with a ventilator sticking out of my mouth. In horror, I approached my dead body realizing something was terribly wrong. My hair was greasy, and I was disgusted by this carcass I had left behind. The shock of that moment is hard to describe, and I was having a hard time piecing together what was happening. Struggling to understand, gazing at the bloated body in front of me, a man suddenly appeared.

The first thing I noticed about him was his hair. It was styled in an old-fashioned way, shiny with carefully sculpted waves. He was dressed in a khaki-green flight suit with a series of ribbons across the chest. His presence felt very calming as the panic of realizing the truth was starting to surface: I was dead. The shock wave of that knowledge was horrifying.

The man introduced himself as a friend of my grandfather—a former fighter pilot in World War II. He also communicated telepathically, letting me know of the respect he still carried for my grandfather, who was still alive at this time. Bewildered, I let the man in the flight-suit lead me out of the sight of my body and into "The Observatory."

The Observatory was on top of this great mountain, and there were no walls and no ceiling. It was just pristine blue sky. The floor was white and there was a white podium, but everything else was radiant blue sky. At this time I wondered where my family was and *INSTANTLY* I found myself standing in the rose garden outside my parent's family room window. Staring back at me through the glass was my father, holding my two year old son in his arms. "Dad!!!!! DAD!!!!! I'M RIGHT HERE!!!" I started shouting and waving my arms, frantic to get his attention. Instead, my son pointed out the window right at me. "Birdie, birdie" I heard my Dad repeat. Frustrated, I yelled and yelled to no avail. The flight-suit guy gave me a compassionate smile and said, "They can't hear you or see you anymore. But they can FEEL you. You see, love is like a tether that connects both worlds. They will always be able to feel your love."

Struck with the pain of this realization, and saddened by my father's eyes laced with grief and worry, I had no choice but to turn away. His pain radiated from him, and to be right in-front of him was nearly unbearable when he couldn't see how close I still was to him. As I left the garden, the bird my son was pointing at flew away.

We returned to the Observatory and its sapphire sky, when suddenly an all-encompassing Light began to illuminate everything around me. The sensation is nearly indescribable. The Light radiated peace and love and comfort. It enveloped me like a mother would wrap her arms around her child. Softly, it lifted me. My gaze turned from the Light back down to Earth, which was slowly disappearing. In this moment, I could see in explicit detail a forest below me. It was filled with evergreen trees, pure and lush. As my eyes took in the details of every needle on every tree, it began to rain. Huge droplets cascaded from the sky around me, hitting the pine needles and funneling the water like shimmering diamonds to the forest floor. I watched the rain run together, collecting in rivulets and forming a stream. At the stream stood a doe and her two speckled fawns, drinking from the rainwater. It was all so beautiful and perfect. And now I was saying goodbye to its beauty. My heart wrenched at how easily I had taken all of this gloriousness for granted. How I failed to recognize the intricate perfection of nature and life and us. I had lost it all by not recognizing the beauty of what it means to live. I turned back towards the Light, and let it hold me in total peace, love and tranquility. Out of nowhere, the loud rushing noise began again. The man in the flight-suit turned towards what looked like an instrument panel. The deafening sound was only cut by the voice of the man telling me that I'd been chosen to see the Council. Figuring he was referred to my dead body, I wondered if this Council were the doctors who could heal me. I closed my eyes and the rushing noise took over.

The next thing I remember was waking up in Hell. Of course, I didn't immediately know I was in a hospital bed in suburban Seattle, but to me it felt like Hell. A hissing, rasping entity had been shoved inside my throat, perpetually choking me. My tongue and lips were dry and cracked, seeping blood into my mouth as the only respite from the thirst. My eyelids were taped shut. In a white-hot panic, I struggled to pull this unknown intruder from my throat, only to find my hands bound to metal rails.

"I'm in Hell, I'm in Hell, what have I done, I'm in Hell…" I kept repeating to myself. Hot slippers cooked my feet under what felt like pounds of blankets. The thirst was unbearable. Wrestling against my restraints, a cacophony of bells pealed and footsteps rushed in to silence the alarm and tighten my restraints. I heard a man's voice talk about "involuntary muscle spasms." I tried to scream and couldn't. The alarm bells sounded again. "I'm in Hell. I'm in Hell. And I put myself here. What have I done, what have I done?" The agony of that thought gave way to blackness as unconsciousness blissfully overtook me.

Coming out of my coma was a hazy existence of terror and exhaustion. The periods of consciousness were pure torture. The family and friends who visited looked haggard by grief and worry, aging their faces by decades over what seemed to be overnight. Staff members, unaware their patient was listening to every word for clues, would talk about when it was best to "pull the plug" with consideration of the holiday season and my mother's profound grief.

A male voice called me a "vegetable." Voices would discuss my prognosis—extensive brain damage from the lack of oxygen, kidney failure, liver failure, collapsed lungs. Slowly I realized I could no longer move my legs. My sobs and screams came out in chokes and bells. The voices of the hospital staff were kinder with their language around my family. Ice clinked in my mother's glass as she poured herself a soda. My parched tongue ached for a drink, and all I could taste was the salt from the tears boiling down my cheeks. My mother, holding my cuffed and weakened hand, felt it squeeze as I mustered up everything in me to move my hands that I could no longer feel. "Muscle spasm," she was told. Remembering the freedom, peace and glory of the Light, I tightened my eyes and wished myself to die.

It was Christmas morning and the voices of the hospital staff discussed the unusually cold and stormy weather as they stood around

179

the nurse's station in ICU. My fluttering eyes had been un-taped to find a room walled in green glass with the curtains drawn back, giving me an unobstructed view of the hospital's hallway. A door at the end crept open, and a woman wearing spike heels began her business-like 'click, click, click' as she marched towards the nurse's station. She carried a black leather attaché and wore a rich, gray tweed business suit with a tailored pencil skirt. Her heels stopped their 'click, click, click' at my bedside. She was of Asian descent, her raven-black hair glossy and long, her black eyes cold and hard. The attaché opened and with a quick glance, she said to me "The Council will see you at 3 o'clock." She spun around on her heel and walked out, her heels tapping past the nurse's station outside my door. The hospital staff never turned to greet her, unaware it seemed of her presence. The beautiful woman with ivory skin, black hair, and those trademark heels walked out of the ICU as my eyes turned to watch the clock.

The hours, minutes and seconds ticked away in slow-motion as I grew close to hysteria in wait for my "appointment." I didn't know who this Council was, but assumed it was a group of doctors summoned to heal my dying, broken body. It struck me as odd that this appointment was on Christmas, but with a ventilator in my mouth and hands that didn't work to write, I couldn't ask questions of the nurses who were busy adjusting my tubes or silencing the ventilator alarm. Instead I just watched the second hand on the clock tick by, my eyes wide with anticipation, listening for the sound of those high heels. The doors to ICU pushed open, and instead of a visiting family member or a housekeeper in scrubs, it was the beautiful woman in the gray tweed dress. With her were two young Asian women, both wearing white kimono-like robes. The "assistant," as I called her in my mind, proceeded with diligence to my bedside, and the attendants surrounding me on either side. The hospital staff who had been in my room left without acknowledging the three women who now stood quietly by my bed. She breezed by them and out the door without a word.

"You need to be clean to see the Council," the assistant said. She nodded to the other young ladies, and towels with warm, sweet smelling water were suddenly produced. My blankets were pulled back and I cringed at my pallid, hairy legs. The attendants bathed me softly, and as they did, I felt myself lift from my body and the bed. Standing up, the attendants wrapped an ivory-colored linen robe around me. It was simple and beautiful. I felt pure and clean and healthy. Finally on my feet again, and walking so easily, I felt like I was floating. We walked out of the hospital room and into a black hallway, the primary beautiful woman leading the way.

The hallway ended at a shoji screen, and I stood in my robe with the attendants as it slid open. The Council chamber was stunning. Sapphire blue sky and glistening sunlight poured through its non-existent ceiling and the room seemed to have no walls. At my feet was a brilliant-blue stream of the purest water, and it flowed around the room in a perfect square. Hovering above this bubbling square river was a golden, seamless floor of bamboo. I stepped barefoot out onto the bamboo platform, shocked at what I considered to be an obviously Buddhist room at a Catholic hospital. Around the room, standing on individual small squares of bamboo flooring were individuals in brightly colored robes. An Asian woman wearing a liquid, fiery magenta robe looked at me with her soft, loving eyes. You could feel her aura and love radiating, reassuring me in my confusion and bafflement. Other men and women were also present, all of the same ethnic descent, and draped in robes of green and gold and orange.

And then there was the man in the middle square, seated on his bamboo plank with his legs folded under him, his blue robe pooled around his legs as he hovered above the iridescent blue water. Instantly I knew that was the man I was here to see. The shoji screen closed behind me and the assistant and attendants vanished. It was time to begin.

As I looked into the crystal blue water, I remembered a trip with my family to the Athabasca glacier where we drank from a blue spring bubbling through the ice, and suddenly it dawned on me that I was no longer thirsty. As I went to gasp for breath, in delightful realization found I no longer needed to breathe. My body felt lithe and radiant as I sat down on the bamboo floor across from the bald, sun-kissed elderly man. He spoke to me kindly, without moving his lips—his soul talking to mine without the clumsy use of words.

"Are you ready to go back?" he asked.

My head instinctually shook. "No, I'm afraid of the pain."

A united compassion formed from the group of robed individuals, all with the knowledge that Earth was indeed a place of great pain and suffering at times. Looking deep into my eyes, the man in the blue robe smiled and said, "I promise that it won't hurt."

With that I let him take my right arm, where he grabbed me directly above the elbow. His thumb touched the crook of my arm and in a split second I was back in my body, being wheeled into my room in the ICU after a surgical emergency. While my soul was in the Council chambers, my body's blood pressure had given out. A team of doctors had been forced to implant a pit catheter to restart my heart.

It's been almost nine years since I got out of the hospital. There is no simple way to explain the excruciating pain of recovery. Having my lungs re-inflated was a horror worth enduring to be free of that wretched ventilator. Learning to walk again made my first few steps feel more hard-earned than my college degree. Tired of relying on annoyed nursing staff to give me small sips of delicious water—I trained my hands to work again through sheer will and determination. Learning to move my fingers again meant I could change the channel on my television. Training my wrists to move and hands to grasp a pencil meant I could communicate again by writing. And the ultimate goal would be to train my arms to work. Over 48 hours and endless marathons of shows like COPS on TV, I could finally pour myself a glass of water. I spilled and drank several pitchers of water that night, ecstatic for this new freedom and the thirst-quenching beauty of pure water and not caring how many times my blankets were soaked by the spilled liquid.

The lesson I found hardest to learn was taking responsibility for my choice to come back. It was my decision and it was my responsibility to do the work to find health and happiness again in life. No blaming God or my parents, no crutches or cop-outs for not giving it my best effort. I came back for the chance at living again, allowing myself to love wholly and without reservation and take risks and opportunities without imposing limits on what I can or can't accomplish. My soul became capable of showing itself in its most raw and beautiful state.

After a month of intense recovery in the hospital, I was released to go home on a clear morning in January. Wheeled out to the car, the fresh air was intoxicating and the scary freedom of my unknown future loomed open like an unwritten book. When my ventilator was removed, the first question I could scratch out of my beleaguered throat was, "Who were all the people in the robes?" Naturally, I was met with blank stares and concerned faces. Over the years, I've gotten quite used to the multitude of responses I get when sharing my near-death experience. Like I said before, I never expected to grow up and be the kind of person with a spiritual "testimony." Sometimes a response will be blasé about the tale, calling it a trick of the brain or maybe a dream. Sometimes the response is more cruel by calling me crazy or brain-damaged.

And that's ok, because we all learn our own way and are able to follow our own paths to understanding. But more often than not, my NDE brings comfort to the grieving and eases fear in the sick or the dying. My habits changed, my body changed having lost 80 pounds since those days in the hospital. My first marriage ended giving way to new love and a second, beautiful son. In an ironic twist of fate, my new husband earns our family's income by caring for ventilator-dependent patients as well as many who transition from this world to the next. I'm grateful for this second chance. And every day is beautiful, even the difficult ones. Every breath is sacred. Every moment savored. It's all so incredibly beautiful.

IX – Leslie Flint

"...People have got funny ideas, they think that because you kick the bucket, you suddenly become very angelic, well how boring we'd all be if we were all that angelic. We wouldn't want to be here, we'd want to be somewhere else. The point is there are different levels according to one's evolution and consciousness. People have got funny ideas, they really have about us, we're real people, we're not conjured up and made from imaginary things." - Mickey, Leslie Flint's Spirit Guide (Mickey, died age 11, in the 1900s), Direct Voice Recording.

These days, I now give more leniency to the controversial topic of physical mediumship than most; I personally know people who perform this gift, and I understand how the "they're all hoaxers" conspiracy theory is absurd. Some of them are as awe-struck by the phenomena produced during their séances as the sitters themselves. At the same time, due to the spectacular claims, and a murky history of deceptive behavior by early 20th century physical mediums, I can understand why many people—skeptics and parapsychologists alike—dismiss the phenomenon entirely.

There is, however, one physical medium from history on whom I place the most weight on. You've heard his name elsewhere in this book—Leslie Flint.

For me to consider a physical medium (whom I don't know personally) to be "genuine" requires no small degree of their worth being proven and demonstrated. History is on the side of Flint, and if his over 50 years of séance communications are therefore legitimate, then what we have is hundreds upon hundreds of hours of first-hand reports by ethereal humans of the exact conditions of the afterlife and what each of us can expect upon discarding our rotting old physical bodies.

Flint's communications were of greater interest to me after I had already studied countless reports from near-death experiences, mental mediums and spirit visitations. Flint's communicating entities provided the information to fit together the missing pieces of the jigsaw puzzle that I could not obtain just by studying NDEs, OBEs or other experiences. They allow a researcher to begin taking the afterlife hypothesis outside of the conceptual and into a realm that feels more literal—into something we can actually imagine with our Earthly minds. And as with other areas of afterlife study—what is communicated in the Flint séances fits nicely with everything else that is studied. There is an amazing amount of consistency in this field of research.

The Flint séances began around the 1930s, while documentation started in the early 1950s, with recorded sessions that would last until at least the late 1980s. Flint (1911-1994) was born in a Salvation Army home in Hackney, England, and he was later raised by his grandmother. According to Flint's autobiography *Voices in the Dark* (1971), he began to have psychic experiences as young as 8, when he encountered his deceased uncle who popped into his grandmother's home for a visit. He could see him, while no one else could, and his claims led to punishment by his grandmother who thought he was causing mischief with outlandish tales of spotting ghosts.

As a young man struggling amidst rampant unemployment in 1920s Britain, Flint worked for a number of years as a grave-digger, just trying to earn enough pence to keep him and his grandmother afloat. After hearing his boss at the cemetery preach about Darwinism and how spirituality was not real, Flint began to question matters of

185

life and death. He was drawn to the 1900s Spiritualist movements in England. He appeared like a fish-out-of-water as a young, uneducated laborer at a posh séance circle. Watching a medium allegedly relay messages from beyond was unimpressive to Flint. Until, the same medium singled him out in the audience and began delivering messages from the spirit of an influential school teacher of Flint's who had passed away when Flint was young, providing information that no one could have known about.

The most unusual happening, however, was when Flint began receiving letters from a medium from Germany. The letters were allegedly written by the recently deceased film star Rudolph Valentino, who Flint had admired during his life. According to the letters, the entity claiming to be Valentino had supplied a particular medium with Flint's home address, and that Valentino had, for some time, been trying to reach Flint with the message that Flint is to develop his mediumship abilities to be of service to mankind. Although skeptical, the young Flint realized that it was beyond bizarre that some woman he'd never met in Germany would have the mailing address of a totally unimportant young man living in England.

Flint soon began attending a private home circle with a local reputed medium and a new group of Spiritualists. With trepidation but encouragement by the other sitters, he attempted to follow the mysterious calling, and see if he could act as a medium himself. To his embarrassment, he found that he had "fallen asleep" in the medium's chair. When he woke up, the circle was clapping— apparently, a whole host of voices came through Flint, including deceased relatives of the sitters; yet he never even realized that it happened.

Flint later incurred a falling-out with the Spiritualists, and decided to put that area of his life behind him. Years would pass, however, and by his mid-20s he returned to the calling after reluctantly joining a new home circle upon being contacted by some of the Spiritualists he knew from before. Now the early 1930s, he would continue to develop his own Spiritualist church with his partner, where he would begin holding regular séances. His reputation gradually built itself as locals began reporting that the voices that came through Flint were unmistakably those of personal, deceased relations.

The Flint séances became immortalized by the work of researchers George Woods and Betty Greene, who began recording Flint and his discarnate voices shortly after tape-recording was first invented. Woods, a WWI veteran, had long been trying to find answers to the question of life beyond death after some especially traumatic experiences during the Battle of Ypres, when the Kaiser's army decimated the British Expeditionary Forces. A mortally wounded soldier clutched Woods' hand and whispered "is there an afterlife? What is going to happen to me?" Woods, seeking to console him, answered "yes"—but he was not entirely sure himself. This spurred a lifelong quest to get to the bottom of the subject. This led to Woods attending a Leslie Flint séance in 1945. From there onward Woods—and later his friend Betty Greene—would become the foremost investigators of the Flint séances.

Woods and Greene began a disciplined practice of questioning the voices that materialized through Flint. Their goal was to obtain a clear understanding of the afterlife, down to its tiniest details—so that we on Earth can gain some conceptualization of its existence.

Their research picked up in 1955 when an elegant female voice appeared in the séance room. The woman identified herself as Madame Ellen Terry—a stage actress of great renown who died in 1928. The voice spoke directly to Woods and Greene:

> "You are going to have some remarkable communications, And I suggest you keep these contacts going regularly to build up the power and to make possible this link which has been deliberately arranged for your tapes ... There are souls on this side who have a great desire to make use of these opportunities to pass through messages and information regarding the mechanics of communication between our world and yours."

And so, the communications became more than just a passing hobby into the parapsychological. It became a life-long ambition to record as much as they could and become record-keepers of afterlife information.

187

Analysis of the Flint Mediumship

So, what makes the Flint tapes something to take seriously? Flint, more-so than any other physical medium, placed himself on the chopping-block for analysis by researchers and investigators. Flint passed away in 1994, and his séances were his life's work; the impact they made is still felt as Flint continues to be a popular figure now in the early 21st century. Awareness of the Flint séances have been spread through the Woods / Greene recordings that were made available online for anyone to hear (follow this URL: https://www.youtube.com/user/LeslieFlintTrust?feature=mhee).

    Flint did not shy away from testing. There were scientifically orchestrated investigations carried out by researchers from the Society for Psychical Research, like Roy Firebrace and Drayton Thomas, who concluded Flint was an authentic medium, creating anomalous voices belonging to unseen entities. This was the result of many protocols, including the gagging and tying of Flint (pictured) designed to rule out fraud.

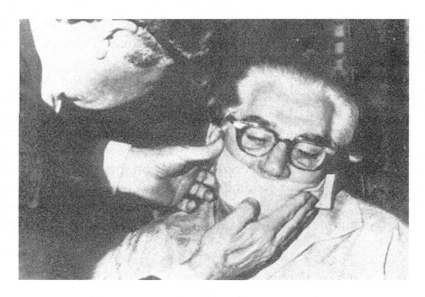

Other experiments further reinforced Flint's credibility. One such was carried out by Dr. Louis Young, a former partner of Thomas Edison and a reputed skeptic who considered exposing phony mediums to be a hobby. Young prepared a mixture of colored water and asked Flint to hold the water in his mouth for the duration of the séance. The lights were shut off, the voices materialized, and when everything was finished—Flint spat out the colored water back into a glass.

Investigators also employed the use of infrared technology and a wired, amplified microphone attached to Flint's throat to detect vibrations. Flint, again, passed these tests—the voices were not coming from his throat. Flint was then observed through the infrared scope, whereupon they witnessed the materialization of the so-called ectoplasmic voice box about two feet from Flint's head; which was the origin of the voices.

On the other hand, some SPR researchers attended Flint séances and immediately concluded they were fake. In the 1970s, William Rauscher and Allen Spraggett made these accusations, and their negative report is often cited by skeptics to disprove Flint's authenticity. Another negative investigation was carried out by Donald West, who also concluded Flint was a faker.

While the Woods / Greene recordings provide what could be some of the best evidence of any mediumship event to date—such positive hits are still challenged by the negative suppositions fostered by skeptics. In order to arrive at any kind of educated opinion about Flint's authenticity, it's therefore important to explore these skeptical arguments and analyze them in an objective manner.

As I have researched the criticism against Flint, I discovered a host of counter-claims to his mediumship proposed by one of the founders of the website Bad Psychics, which attempts to claim that *all* reputed mediums are hoaxers. Jon Donnis' arguments are often cited as reasons to maintain suspicion of Flint's work. The points of view of *Bad Psychics* are, unsurprisingly, approved without second thought to Flint's Wikipedia page—which claims without allowance for counter-argument that Flint was an elaborate magician (not the first, nor the last victim of the Wikipedia censorship campaign).

The following are the arguments I've encountered that are used against Flint, proposed by Jon Donnis and other skeptics on various popular parapsychology internet forums. Let's explore them:

Argument #1: An incident occurred where Flint's mouth was taped shut. Later, when the séance was completed, Flint was caught without the tape on.

189

Donnis, Wikipedia's skeptical biography of Flint, and the *Bad Psychics* team uses an account by the aforementioned negative SPR investigation as a damning report of Flint being caught cheating. "Flint was caught removing tape during an investigation," is a common accusation I've heard.

The truth, however, is that this incident was quite minor. The previously mentioned research officer with the Society for Psychical Research, Dr. Donald West, was sent to investigate Flint. He applied tape and Elastoplast to Flint's mouth and traced it with a pencil so that if it were moved, it would be detected[44]. The séance was successful, voices manifested, and carried on conversations with the sitters. Afterwards, West inspected Flint and reported the gag had been moved and was not lined up with the tracing (which is hardly the same as being caught removing it).

Flint's side of the story is that the experiment that day resulted in difficulty breathing. Personally, as someone with a deviated septum, I can understand how on some days I can breathe easily through my nostrils, and on other days it's very hard. Flint managed to free part of his mouth in a desperate attempt to breathe. He reportedly canceled further séances that week to recover from the dangerous experience.

Dr. West was also just one SPR investigator. A handful of other investigators concluded that Flint was an authentic medium after performing the same rigged mouth-taping and gagging protocol. It's unfair to use this one incident as proof of trickery by Flint when there is a very reasonable explanation for it, plus subsequent and prior investigations that confirmed validity and not fraud.

Argument #2: The voices are not how they should sound.

"Every single one of the voices has an English accent," Donnis and other critics argue. Indeed, if you listen to Flint's recordings, you'll find many of the male voices sound very similar—throaty, deep English voices. The female voices are pleasantly soft spoken and do not resemble the male voices; however, some of the female voices sound similar to one another, too. The main "spirit control", Mickey, does sound like a child's voice, but such a voice can be easily produced by anyone with voice talent.

This argument is critiquing the mechanism of the supposed physical mediumship without understanding how that mechanism even works. The voices purported are not claimed to be the real voices of the communicators. The claim used by Flint and the sitters was that an "ectoplasmic voice box" would be produced, usually hanging over Flint's shoulder. The existence of the voice box was confirmed by SPR investigators using infrared technology. The communicators, using some type of unseen methodology, were able to stick themselves into that box and talk through it; as somehow ectoplasm has a physical effect on both the Earth and astral worlds simultaneously. The box is basically a reproduction of a human body's vocal cords, trying to turn their thoughts into sound.

Ectoplasm itself is biological matter collected from the medium. It's essentially a piece of the medium himself, being manipulated by unseen forces. When a communicator would appear in a Flint seance, **they were not using their own astral vocal cords**. Rather, they were each pushing their voices through a single mold. Imagine for a moment that several different people of different accents were trying to communicate through a single machine that retranslated their speech patterns based on the design of that machine—would it be any surprise they'd sound the same? Based on this model, it's amazing that any of the communicators sounded different, at all.

However, while some of the voices do sound similar in terms of being deep and throaty, one phenomenon that researchers came to find was that the Flint voices matched the intonations and speech styles of the deceased identities. Woods and Greene attempted to match numerous recordings of the deceased with those who knew the communicators when they were alive. For instance, the taped voice of Archbishop Cosmo Land was presented to one of Lang's acquaintances, Mr. Conan Shaw, who was a chorister in York Minster from 1908-1915. Shaw's reaction was:

"His slow style of speech comes out very well in the tape, as do also his mannerisms. Both hands would clasp the top of his stole, then he would build up to a climax, to one word or one phrase as he does on the tape...Yes, I have every confidence that it is the communicator Dr Cosmo Lang whom he claims to be on the tape." (Neville-Randall, 196)

Similar positive reactions were expressed from other investigations. Further testimonials from sitters who were reunited with their deceased family members also maintain that the voice inflections, intonations and speech styles were always seemingly consistent with those personalities when they were on the Earth.

What this means is that for Flint to be a magician, he would have had to also be researching and mimicking the speech styles of his subjects, often without any practical method to study these things ahead of time. This alone would be a supernatural feat.

Finally, consider that some of the voices really are quite different. I am generally the most impressed by the female voices, because they are so clear and distinct from anything that one could imagine being conjured from the vocal cords of a man. For instance, I suggest to take a listen to this communication with the aviator Amy Johnson. The séance can be listened to at the following addresses: https://www.youtube.com/watch?v=Sx4Qra4H7V4 and https://www.youtube.com/watch?v=iPNxUvzVBpw for the second part (the audio quality seems to be improved quite a bit in the second recording).

Argument # 3: Chopin speaks perfect English, but he was Polish. How could this be?

This argument was raised by Jon Donnis (or someone purporting to be Jon, see bottom addendum) and it afforded a good chuckle. He is suggesting that a spirit cannot learn the English language in the astral after centuries with all the free time in the universe.

Argument # 4: Gandhi's real voice sounds different from the séance.

See argument # 2.

Argument # 5: Physical mediumship requires dark rooms, which perpetuates fraud.

Traditionally, all physical séances are held in the dark. The reason that's claimed is that light, no matter what, interferes with ectoplasm production and makes it very hard for spirits to make an appearance. This does pose some challenges (please see the prior section in this book about physical mediumship and the dark). A very skilled, Houdini-like magician might have been able to break out of the Elastoplast and other binding techniques used on Flint by taking advantage of the dark. However, this does not account for the fact that many of the séances led to veridical information, reunions and other credible experiences. The dark is simply the protocol that's needed, and it does not discount the existing evidence, even if the possibility of replicating certain feats fraudulently is not 100% ruled out.

And, as mentioned previously, Flint passed strict tests by the SPR, including infrared filming where Flint was observed by credible scientists who witnessed the séance taking place and the ectoplasmic voice box materializing. Flint also passed the colored water test—further demonstrating despite their usage of the dark, Flint had nothing to hide.

Argument # 6: Rauscher and Spraggett in the 1970s said Flint was a fraud.

And now to address the two skeptical researchers who attended a Flint séance and accused Flint of ventriloquism. It's very important to consider what Rauscher and Spraggett actually wrote in their report. Their argument was that the voices sounded too similar. They did not catch Flint cheating or anything of that sort. Instead, they presented argument # 2 about the voice issue. As mentioned before many (but not all) of the voices have similarities—they are deep and throaty sounding. However, the voices all seem to retain their intonations and styles of speech which were proven to be accurate. To use the voice argument to claim that nothing paranormal was occurring would fly in the face of all the other accumulated evidence.

Although their opinion was fraud, there was nothing conclusive about their investigation. They also complained that the characters did not know enough details about the sitter's lives. This is based on an incorrect assumption that astral residents know all and see all. It's repeatedly said by the communicators that they are not God-like beings or omniscient psychics but are merely regular humans in most respects. So, this is another weak argument.

There was no substantial argument presented by these researchers that Flint was a hoax. They attended a séance, had a negative feeling about it, but Flint was never caught cheating or anything of that sort. To say this negative SPR investigation was damning of Flint is quite silly. They simply chose to have a different opinion compared with some of their SPR colleagues who felt differently. In essence, the SPR was divided about Flint. Historically, the SPR are known to be "tough nuts" and almost simply out of the SPR modus operandi some of the researchers have to adopt skeptical positions.

Argument #7: Leslie Flint was exposed using cheesecloth to create the so-called voice box.

At first, this seemed the most devastating of arguments against Flint that I came across, until I bothered to scratch beneath the surface instead of simply taking a skeptic's argument at face-value. What I learned was an important lesson in critical thinking as it applies to anything in life (and especially this subject).

The reason some of these internet skeptics are commonly referred to as pseudo-skeptics is because they do not fairly debate; nor do they engage the information directly. Rather, they begin at a particular conclusion, and then piece together a prosecutorial argument however they can—whether by stretching facts or just plain making things up.

The cheesecloth rumor surrounding Flint turned out to be almost impossible to verify. The source I came to find was actually two internet forum characters with suspiciously similar writing styles: Darryl Forests and someone named "Tyler Snotgern" who uses stock photos for his forum profile images. "Snotgern" claims he had participated in Flint séances in the 1960s and discovered the whole thing was a hoax and that Flint uses cheesecloth to fake his voice box. Simultaneously, "Forests" began posting on paranormal forums and citing Snotgern's claim of cheesecloth usage.

Regardless of whether you decide Flint was real or not; it's never wise to use internet rumors to sway your opinions. So often, we take things at face-value without performing a fact checking operation as simple as Googling a name. The pseudo-skeptic movement, much like the charlatan psychics, often rely on this lack of diligence to get their way. In the end, Snotgern, otherwise known as Forests, appeared to be a forum "troll" trying to ruffle feathers and also make a name for himself in the skeptic-debunker community through tall tales. In summary, this character completely made up the accusation in an effort to win some debates. Other skeptics then read the phony account and claimed it was true, and began citing it as evidence against Flint.

Addendum: Some of these arguments I found came from the comments of "Randi's Prize" author Robert McLuhan's blog *Paranormaia*, by a poster identifying himself as Jon Donnis. However, on the *Bad Psychics* website, Jon Donnis has a message on the front-page that he does not post on ANY forums or social media sites other than his own. Why would someone pretend to be Mr. Donnis while representing his same opinions? The paranormal world is certainly a confusing place—and it seems the skeptical camp is often filled with just as much mischief as those who claim to be psychic!

Anni Nanji: The Most Convincing Evidence

When we investigate Flint, our minds often turn to all the alleged famous personalities that manifested—Rudolph Valentino, Sir Winston Churchill, Arthur Conan Doyle, and so forth. We may forget something that is perhaps more convincing to the outsider—which is the communications of a personal nature between sitters and former intimate companions who were not public figures.

There were multiple instances occurring over many years of sitters reuniting with their husbands, wives, fathers, mothers, and so forth. One of the most striking incidences, which could very well be the confirmation of Flint's authenticity to anyone but the most closed-minded, was that of the communication received by a woman named Anni Nanji. Researcher Victor Zammit, on his weekly report, once stated that the Nanji tapes are among the best evidence for the afterlife of all time.

Here's what's known about these recordings: Dina Nanji was a doctor from Bombay who moved to Sweden and married a Swedish (and believed to be French) woman named Anni, who tragically died of cancer at age 53. The full story of how Dr. Nanji found Flint's circle is not entirely known. Based on context inferred from the recordings, it would seem that Dr. Nanji had been experiencing some type of after death communication upon her death, and he knew she was trying to get through to him, which is possibly what spurred him to look for a séance circle, and which led him to Flint.

Shortly after he began attendance with the circle, a whispery, highly emotional voice entered the room which identified itself as Anni, crying out for him "Dina! Dina! Dina!"

This first séance included a lot of struggle to communicate. Among Anni's very first words to Dina included information of a personal nature that would not have been known to Flint:

"You keep the apartment very much the same," Anni said. "I come to you every night".

"I know darling" Dr. Nanji replied.

"I listen to the music," Anni said.

"I know," Dr. Nanji replied. Referring to music that Dr. Nanji would play in the house, with her in mind.

"What about the painting?" Anni asked.

Dr. Nanji explained he would put the paintings at the head of his bed.

"I am so happy about the pictures," Anni responded.

As the séance continued, an emotional Anni had to take a rest, while Mickey (Flint's organizer in the astral, whose voice seems to replicate that of a cockney boy) explained that numerous other relations were crowding around, specifically from Delhi, India, who wanted to make contact with Dr. Nanji. Mickey explained that Dr. Nanji's brother (who also passed away) was trying to make contact with his former wife, but she refused to believe it.

"(He) thinks she now has interest in another man, but he quite understands because she's been lonely," Mickey said.

"Yes, that's right," Dr. Nanji replied. Mickey continued to relay various bits of information about some of the doctor's relatives who seemed anxious to communicate a thing or two.

After the intermission ended, Anni's voice returned.

"Thank you for the roses," she said.

"Don't mention it, you know I love flowers," Dr. Nanji replied.

Anni cuts off, and Mickey returns to the voicebox.

"Your wife is very interested in what appears to be a painting of herself," Mickey said.

"Yes," Dr. Nanji confirmed.

"But I don't somehow think it's the one you're thinking about," Mickey continues. "Have you got a large painting of your wife in color?"

"Yes," Dr. Nanji went on to explain that he had had a full color painting completed recently by a psychic artist.

Mickey goes on to report that some of the differences in the painting compared with how Anni used to look were justified, however it wasn't an entirely accurate portrayal. For instance, Dr. Nanji found it strange that his wife's portrait included long hair. Mickey explains that the painting was indeed accurate in at least that way since upon entering the astral, Anni began growing her hair longer.

Further along, Mickey then reports that Anni is curious about whether or not her husband has memory of visiting her. According to Anni, Dina frequently visits her in his astral body after he goes to sleep. She finds it confusing that he is not able to fully remember these visits when he wakes up. Dina responded that he had some memory, nonetheless.

"There's a very special anniversary that comes in a few weeks time," Mickey says.

"Yes, that is her birthday,"

"She's laughing about when—November—is it? The 19th?"

"Yes, the 19th"

"She says that November the 19th is her birthday, but the years come and go, there is no age here, and she's now as young as she was when she was 20."

"Yes, yes,"

"And that's another thing about that picture," Mickey continued. "She says that she's younger."

Not long after this, the recording of the first séance between Dr. Nanji and his dead wife came to an end. By the second recording,

Dr. Nanji expressed continued concern about how much time he had left before his own departure from the physical. Anni reassured him it would not be that much longer—perhaps only a year or two—before they were reunited, but it would seem her prediction was not accurate. Dr. Nanji continued communicating with his wife, through Flint, from 1971 all the way until 1983—twelve full years of contact, allowing him to continue his relationship with her long past the boundaries of death.

And, most striking, many hours of their twelve years of contact were recorded and archived. These recordings are available at the following URL through the official Leslie Flint page: http://www.leslieflint.com/recordingsnanji.html.

In the field of afterlife research, the proof is *always in the details*, and this is what makes these recordings so impressive. As you sit through them, you can take note of such tidbits like Anni mentioning to her husband that he has a hole in his trouser pocket that should be fixed, or that he has been putting his bed-covers on the wrong way. This is information that would be completely unknown to anyone. Not to mention the host of private, intimate details related to their marriage and her passing.

Dr. Nanji was asked about the phenomena shortly after the first communications began. "This wasn't someone impersonating my wife, it was my dead wife who knew so many things unknown to the medium, Leslie Flint."

Let's just think about this *rationally*: Flint would be the greatest magician in history to have been able to hoax this successfully for twelve years. That's twelve years of personal communication between a man and his wife. The parts I've cited from the tapes reveal the personal nature of their conversations together, and it becomes obvious that for Flint to fake this, it would require the following effort:

- Flint would have to have employed a spy in Dr. Nanji's life who was close to him.

- This spy, for instance a maid, would have to be aware of his life in great detail and be relaying this information back to Flint.

- The spy would have to be an expert at the trade; able to manipulate people into revealing details of their personal lives and relationships. Undoubtedly, she would cost some money to hire—probably far more than whatever pocket-change that sitters were donating to Flint at the time.

- As revealed on the tapes, Dr. Nanji was only visiting England (although he may have moved there later to be closer to Anni). This means the spy would have needed to be employed in Sweden, and still be able to relay the information back to Flint in a timely fashion.

- Flint would need a sophisticated communication infrastructure to be aware that Dr. Nanji was interested in his work and planning to go to England to attend one of his séances. Dr. Nanji would have had to make it public his intention to visit Flint. There was no record if Nanji had any prior acquaintances from within the circle or not. If he did, and the information was passed on to Flint, then Flint would have had to immediately begin preparations to hire his spy in Sweden to start gathering information about the doctor before his arrival.

- Flint would have needed to keep this charade going for twelve years.

The extraordinary effort to fool one man for this long could only be conceived of if Flint operated within a branch of the British intelligence (MI6). This level of surveillance would have only been possible during the height of cold war drama with the investigation of potential Soviet plants. And it would require a sizable budget to spare.

The alternative to this wild conspiracy theory is that Flint was a legitimate medium. As Sherlock Holmes would say, when all other options are ruled out—the final conclusion, no matter how absurd, must be true. And given the enormous amount of evidence for the afterlife that's already been covered in this book, just how absurd of a theory is it?

Throughout the Nanji recordings, it was indicated to Dina that he needed to write a book about his experiences as part of his spiritual work. Unfortunately, it would seem this book was never finished—or it was never picked up by a publisher. It would be fortunate if someday the entire story of the remarkable communication was told for the first time in its entirety. Maybe somebody will discover his manuscript?

The Power of the Messages

Debating with those on the fence about the topic of the afterlife, I realize that the subjective is usually of no apparent value. Veridical experiences, objective information, scientific studies—these are the gems that make this subject recognized, scientifically valid, and admissible in a court of law.

However, there's something still to be said about a subjective interpretation if it really does show something remarkable. One's opinions of the messages relayed by Flint are simply interpretations—and a skeptic can always say any message, no matter how profound, is just a person's imagination. But if you take some time to really study what these communicators say—this becomes a new type of evidence.

If Flint were a hoaxer, then for over half a century he would have had to come up with profound, imaginative, inspiring and politically acute messages—while mimicking the personalities, words and styles of the deceased. I've come to find these communications sound as good as any great radio show or podcast. Although much of the topics concern the lives of the communicators in the astral world, a lot of time is also dedicated to matters of morality, life, politics, and many more topics.

And nothing less should really be expected, given the intellectual strength of the purported communicators—like Mahatma Gandhi, Oscar Wilde, Frederick Chopin, and Churchill. Among some communicators, like the playwright Wilde, they have all the hallmarks that one would expect of them in life, such as in Wilde's case; being very clever and certainly funny, as well.

Although not a type of nuts-and-bolts evidence, listening to these dialogues can create quite an impression. Flint, in addition to having a government level communication and spying network to account for incidences like the Nanji tapes, would also need to be a genius impersonator and intellectual heavy-weight of the highest caliber. How much more super-villain level cunning can we attribute to a working-class man who used to dig holes for a living?

And finally, while it might be possible to stretch one's imagination to believe that a man can impersonate famous personalities, like Churchill, who all English folk had heard on the radio or seen on TV, it's another thing entirely to have the ability to also impersonate the deceased relatives of sitters. It's important to point out that Anni Nanji was not the only loved one who manifested; but over the decades many more husbands, wives, siblings and parents made appearances.

Flint in Conclusion

All arguments against Flint eventually return to the conclusion that because quite a few of the voices sound similar to one another—then the whole thing must be fake. This is what we would call a knee-jerk reaction. Upon closer look, we discover instances like the Nanji tapes that show beyond all reasonable doubt that something extraordinary was happening in those dark rooms every weekend. And, this was only further reinforced by scientific investigations performed by diligent SPR research scientists.

We've seen how for Flint to have enabled this séance as a hoax, it would have required extraordinary talent that even Houdini would have struggled his life to perfect. And all of it was being done on modest means.

Finally, the voice argument itself breaks down when one researches many different examples and discovers that some of the voices—the female ones in particular—are extremely crisp and distinctly female; hardly reminiscent of a man trying to create an impersonation. The explanation that Flint's voice-box as the mechanism to manifest the voices creates similar pitch tones against the will of the communicators no longer seems unreasonable.

If we are to take Flint seriously and consider that he was legitimately channeling communicators from the spirit through his spongy ectoplasmic voice box, then we must also take seriously those messages received about the conditions of the astral plane. And these messages are provided in abundance, with the underlying goal to help people understand that death is simply a transition to an alternate world—a mere confirmation of so many other areas of evidence that also demonstrate this.

And so, for the next chapter, we are going to explore just what these communicators have to say, as we begin to narrow down our education in matters of the afterlife from broad, scientific theories and phenomena, to specific accounts that we can use to crystallize our understanding of the world unseen.

X – What Happens When You Die

The following chapter includes transcripts made available for use by the Leslie Flint Trust, which were also used by Neville-Randall's 1980 book *Life After Death* which I reference for these archives. Based on the strong case for Flint's authenticity as outlined in the prior chapter, we can use the information from the Flint seances as an accurate portrayal of the afterlife. By exploring the information received from beyond the veil, we can begin to understand the exact details of what death will be like for us. When combined with knowledge obtained from other areas of evidence, then an even clearer understanding is created.

The Out-of-Body State

The OBE is the first thing that occurs upon death or near-death. Sometimes, the OBE manifests simply as unexplained consciousness while in an operating room, which is the most common form of near death awareness according to the AWARE studies. At other times, the experiencer detaches from the sick or injured body altogether.

Upon detachment, for some this OBE state is shadowy, non-solid, even dream-like; similar to the OBEs we may have through sleep-states. Or, the experiencer discovers their consciousness has suddenly increased, they are floating, but do not exist in any type of physical body. Other times, the OBE involves an immediate transition to a duplicate body, and the experiencer is unaware that anything happened and that they had even died at all.

The latter is how it went for Alf Pritchett. One of Leslie Flint's communicators, Pritchett was identified by a subsequent investigation as Private 9023 A. Pritchett of the Machine Gun Corps of the British military, who died in 1917, along with so many others, at the horrendous trenches stretching across France during World War I.

The grisly life of a soldier in the Great War meant weeks huddled in one of the countless miles of trenches that spanned the front-line against Germany. Soldiers slept alongside excrement, dead bodies, giant corpse-eating rats, and endured various diseases like dysentery as they waited for the battle commands to go "over the top".

And going "over" was bad news. Charging out from the trench was when the highest number of fatalities occurred. These forward-assaults were often part of ill-fated attempts to end the perpetual stalemate that was WWI. As hundreds or even thousands at once would rush out of the trench in an attempt to secure the German lines—so too would hundreds of troops get decimated by artillery.

Alf Pritchett recalls the experience in his own words, using the artificial voice box during a Flint session in the early 1960s.

"It must have been 1917 - or 18. I'm not sure myself now. It's such a long time ago. We had been under a heavy bombardment practically all day. I thought to myself at the time, if we come through this lot we'll be lucky. Then, in the early morning we were given the command to go over the top.

Well, I thought. 'This is it, boy.' And I must admit it took all I'd got to really get myself over the top.

I was running forward. Some of the Germans were coming towards me. They rushed straight past me as if they didn't see me! I thought, 'God, this is it.'

But instead of them attacking me or in any way taking any interest in me, they were rushing past me!

I thought, 'Well, Good Lord! I can't make this out at all.'

I went on. I can remember running and running and I thought 'Well, if they're not going to see me I'm certainly not going to bother about them. I'm going to get into a little cubby hole somewhere and get out of it.

I remember getting into a hole in the ground created by a bomb I expect at some time. I got into this hole, and just crouched down, and thought 'Well, I'll wait till this shindy's over, and hope for the best, I might get taken prisoner. Who knows?"

In Pritchett's case, at some point after going over the trench, he was hit by artillery fire and killed. However, he simply kept running without awareness that he had left his old body behind him. He found himself in the same ghostlike environment of all who transition and are caught between worlds; where he could not interact with the physical space around him. Nonetheless, it was still close enough to his prior state that he believed he was still alive.

For people who undergo NDEs, you may read accounts of riding along in an ambulance, watching the body get worked on with a curious sense of disconnection. Other times, one may leave the body in a more "spectral" state—translucent, or even without a physical form at all.

The Light, and the Transition

As we study the near-death experience, many are familiar with "going toward the light", so much so the phrase has become a joke in popular culture ("Don't go toward the light!"). It is also one of the first stages of the death process, often preceded by the out-of-body state.

In fact, it is perhaps this step that is the defining moment of "real death" versus a recreational or temporary out-of-body episode. Although light takes many forms, from a simple otherworldly light indicating a tunnel or wormhole that has opened to another realm, to a light that seems to have a divine presence and power of its own. Regardless, it always exists to accompany some type of a portal to a new plane of existence. Often, the light is included with a tunnel-like wormhole, as well as the presence of a welcoming party—usually, in the form of deceased relations or family members.

Curiously, in many post-death descriptions from communicators, there is no mention of "the Light" to the same extent as we read about from NDEs. In many NDE accounts, the light possesses an interactive quality, and may even be the defining part of the experience; sometimes providing a tour of the universe, creation, and other cosmic concepts.

Perhaps these more advanced encounters are limited to highly developed NDEs. We are told there are many types of planes that one may traverse, and the cosmic descriptions of certain NDEs likely involve a different, more advanced plane where encounters with extremely powerful entities may take place who assume the form of pure light or energy. More often, I believe that people are typically taken to "human" like planes where these types of experiences may not occur.

Such would be the case for Private Pritchett, hiding in a foxhole shortly after getting killed; who experienced the same otherworldly light seen by so many, but it was merely a beacon of the next world to come.

"I don't know how long I must have been there. Anyway I must have fallen asleep or something, because the next thing I knew was that I remember I was seeing a bright light in front of me.

I couldn't make this out at all. It was a sort of light I'd never seen before, just as if the whole place was illuminated, and it was so dazzling that, for a moment, I could sort of hardly look at it. I had to keep closing my eyes and having a look. And I thought, 'Well, it's a trick of the light.' I got a bit windy.

Then, all of a sudden it was just as if I saw an outline - shape or figure appearing. It was the outline of a human being, and it was full of luminosity, and gradually it seemed to take shape.

I was in an absolute sweat. It was an old friend of mine who I knew had been killed some months before, named Smart. Billy Smart! We used to call him 'Ole Bill'. He was looking at me and I was looking at him.

After a bit I felt myself getting up, and that struck me as odd that I should be conscious of myself getting up. In a strange sort of way I thought well, here's me been lying here probably all night - all night and day. I ought to be feeling stiff and awkward and uncomfortable. But I didn't. I felt as light as a feather. I thought 'Well, something's gone to my head. Perhaps I've got a crack or something.'

Anyway I went towards him as if I was a magnet drawn to him. As I got closer I could see that he was, well, full of vitality, full of life. Wonderful sort of color in his face. And then, as I got near to him, it dawned on me that he was dead!

When I first saw him, I didn't think of him being dead, although I must have remembered and realized in a way that he had been killed some months before. Anyway, I was drawn to him. He smiled at me, and I suppose I must have smiled back.

'I could hear him speak and he says, 'All right, nothing to worry about. You're all right, mate. Come on.'"

During a near-death experience, this is usually the point that the experiencer would return to their body. The greeter may explain to the reluctant astral traveler that he or she must return to the body, as an opportunity has occurred for second-chances. Or, occasionally, the experiencer may even bargain with the welcoming team; and profess a desire to return for the sake of one's children or unfulfilled duties.

In Pritchett's case, there were no second chances as likely his body was torn apart and beyond saving. He was dead, fully. And so, through this personal account, we have an opportunity to learn about what happens next—something that by definition a story of a *near-death experience* cannot fulfill.

Arriving in Another World

Let us be thankful that what awaits us upon disconnection of the physical body is *not* the spectral existence of the near-Earth astral, as reported during OBEs and preliminary death experiences. What occurs next is access to the rest of the greater planar universe. And, this is most certainly always facilitated by others. One is never alone in this process. Immediately upon death one would otherwise enter a jungle without a map. We humans are always available to guide new arrivals so that nobody falls through the cracks in this way.

In the hundreds of hours of transmissions that occurred during the Flint experiments, it would seem the vast majority of the deceased entered a similar *plane* that I assume corresponded in some way to England. It is logical to say that astral civilizations coalesce around similar preferences, and create fitting countries for themselves. This English *Summerland* was specifically tailored as the opposite of the rainy, foggy and often grey landscapes of the United Kingdom. Instead, a realm of perpetual daylight and warmth, with luscious countrysides and beautiful but otherworldly cities. I suppose Londonites in particular have no desire to die and end up having yet more foggy and cold afternoons to deal with.

Similar lands as this English "heaven" have been reported during many advanced NDEs. One that comes to mind was that of Betty Eadie, author of *Embraced by the Light,* who entered a rather glorious astral city of similar description. Astral civilizations in general appear to be fashioned based on some commonalities of pleasantness or beauty as preferred by their immortal, albeit human, inhabitants. And given the billions of humans who have passed on before us, the human planes must therefore be greatly populated by countless hundreds of different cities and different types of realms, perhaps with corresponding cultures from their respective countries on Earth.

We do not know the styles of all the different planes. So, we must not assume all of these human habitats must match our own limited concepts or those descriptions we hear about the most. It is commonly reported that astral civilization exists on a spectrum: *closer* to Earth and *further* from Earth. In essence, that which is closer more resembles our physics and style. This means planes that feel almost identical to our world as we experience it right now.

On the other hand, a habitat that stretches far *past* Earthly or human mindedness may be altogether *alien* to what we currently understand. We can try to imagine bodies of pure energy, consciousness of extreme power, little or no barrier between thought and reality (you think it, and it becomes real), and architecture or style of environment with no relation to anything we are used to.

For excellent descriptions of realms ranging on both ends of this spectrum, I encourage to take a look at Jurgen Ziewe's book *Multidimensional Man*.

Let's look at what Pritchett experienced:

"The next thing I remember was sort of gradually coming in sight of what appeared to be a big city. It was luminous. It's the only way I can describe it. The buildings had a sort of glow about them.

Anyway to cut a long story short, I suddenly felt my feet touching the ground again. Most peculiar. It felt solid. I remember walking along what appeared to be a long avenue, and on each side were beautiful trees, and between every other tree or so there was what appeared to be a sort of statue. And on the sidewalk - I suppose what you'd call it would be: path or pavement - people were going about in a most peculiar sort of dress.

They were looking as if they might have been Romans or Greeks or something you see in pictures. And there were beautiful buildings with pillars, and beautiful steps leading up to them. Mostly flat-roofed, by the way. I don't remember seeing any roofs or gables like one sees in England. They seemed to be in Continental style. And this sort of glow coming from them. All sorts of people there were, and horses.

Bill was talking away to me. 'Of course,' he says: 'You know what's happened to you?'

What's happened to me? All I know is that I am having a good time here. It's better than being down there in that lot. I shall be sorry to wake up.

He says, 'Don't worry. You aren't going to wake up.' "What do you mean, I'm not going to wake up?' "You've had it, chum.'

"What do you mean had it?'

'You're dead.'

'Don't be silly,' I says. 'How can I be dead? I'm here. I can see all that's going on around me. I can see you. But I know you died some months ago. You got a packet. But how is that ... I don't know. You may be dead, but I'm dreaming.'

'No you aren't,' he says. 'You really are dead. You got a packet in that charge.'

'Never,' I says. 'How can I have? I wouldn't be here like this would I?'

'That's just it,' he says. 'You are here. You're dead.' "What,' I says. 'You don't mean to tell me this is heaven?'

'Well not exactly,' he says. 'But it's an aspect.'"

There's not always the same type of transition. Some appear on the other side immediately without being consciously guided. They simply "wake up" there, as with Mr. Higgins, a blue-collar worker from Brighton who died in a hospital after falling off a ladder.

Ms. Greene asks the new voice, Mr. Higgins, how he felt when he first passed over:

"Well, when I first had any sort of realization or consciousness of what was happening to me, I was lying on a sort of bank overlooking a river. I couldn't make head or tail of it. I couldn't make out where I was. I didn't recognize the spot and I couldn't think how I got there. Then I saw someone coming towards me dressed in what looked to me as if he was a monk. But I realized of course later that it wasn't. But he'd got a sort of long habit on, and he looked to be a benevolent gentleman, and quite young. I thought he's a young person to be a monk. As a matter of fact, quite frankly, I thought at the time that he looked just like Jesus. At least what I'd seen pictures of Jesus. But I realized of course it wasn't afterwards. He came and stood beside me and spoke to me: 'Ah, you've arrived.'

I says: 'Arrived? I don't quite know what you mean?' 'He says: 'You don't realize then that you're here, where you are?'

"No,' I says. 'All I know is I don't recognize this place. It's very beautiful.'

'You're dead, you know.'

'What?'

'Yes. You're dead.'

'I'm not dead. How can I be dead? I wouldn't be able to see.'

I felt myself.

'Look,' I says. 'I'm not dead. I'm solid.'

'Ah,' he says. 'There are a lot of people seem to think that when they're dead they're either nothing at all, or if they're dead that they go up to heaven, or they go to some place as hell. You are in a condition of life which is as real, as you can see for yourself, as anything you've ever known before. Life beyond what you call death is a state of mind. Your condition at the moment is perhaps a little bewildered. But you're not unhappy, and certainly you seem, as far as I can tell, quite at ease. You seem quite calm and placid. You're not over anxious about anything in particular are you?'

'No,' I says. 'But now I'm beginning to realize that what you say is so. I must admit I'm a bit concerned about my people. It must be a terrible shock for them, you know. I've no recollection of dying. I don't remember anything bar falling. At least I had a feeling I was falling, and then I don't remember no more.'

'Well of course,' he says. 'You died in hospital.'

'Oh, did I?'"

Particularly Nasty Religious Ideas Are Definitely Garbage

There are plenty of gospel related myths that clearly have no room in the human planes. One such myth is that animals are soulless creatures. George Wilmot, a divorced laborer, crosses over and discovers himself face-to-face with his guide, Michael, and his old horse that he always loved, Jenny.

211

''My name is Michael,' the figure tells George, shortly after George awakens in a foreign landscape. 'Do you realize you are dead?'

'Well. I don't know what to think.'

'You've just had that realization, didn't you, that vision of your body,' he says. 'You know you died in that hospital.'

'Well I recollect now I was very ill. How can I be dead when I'm here and talking to you, and I've got Jenny?' [George's horse, who he discovered alongside him].

'Well isn't Jenny some evidence to you that you're dead?'

'Well, it seems very strange. Then again,' I said, 'if I'm in heaven if that's it, you don't expect to find horses there. They haven't got any souls, have they?'

'Ah, that's what they tell you when you're on Earth,' he says. 'That they haven't got any sort of other life, only just the old material sort of life as you call it. That horse, because of its nearness to you and the love and affection you showered on it, has given it something which helps it to extend its life span.'

'I didn't quite get all 'this lark 'extend its life span' and all the rest of it.

'But while you have love and affection for that horse,' he said, 'that horse will have an existence. Human beings don't know their responsibility to animals. Ever since I've been here, which is hundreds of years ...'

'Of course I looked at him when he said that. I thought, well, this is a bit much you know, looking so young and spruce and nice looking after hundreds of years. I thought well anyway it didn't do to interrupt this gentleman. After all I felt a bit lost and I thought I'll have to mind my ps and qs.

'Oh,' he says, 'time is nothing, you see. I've been here for hundreds of years, and part of my responsibility and my job is to see and care for animals. I often go down into the pits.'

I wondered what the hell he meant when he said pits, and I thought he meant hell or something.

'No,' he said. 'Pits where they have animals down the mines. I tend to them and try to help them, but there's not a great deal you can do. Over here we have great plains where animals congregate and where there is love and affection, and they can be cared for. People have this stupid idea that because they are human beings they're the only ones that have got any right to a future existence, should there be one. Then you get the religious ones who think there must be. There is, but they haven't much of a conception of it either.'"

Other Flint visitors describe how some animals have the ability to telepathically communicate or even talk to people, as well.

Time and Space Are Limited or Non-Existent

The worlds described so far seem surprisingly terrestrial. However, don't be mistaken—every individual, at least in the planes that Flint had contacted, possess abilities that define the astral planes as a thought-based reality compared to the strictly physical reality of the Earth.

One of the hardest concepts for we Earth-based life-forms to understand is that "time doesn't exist". This is frequently reported in the Flint tapes as well as those who undergo trips through the beyond during NDEs.

We know that time is the sequential order of events. One thing precedes the next thing. As new events are created, they become stored as memory. Philosophers can argue that we only live in the moment, as the memory is not a true thing. This is certainly a truism that cannot be argued with. And perhaps in the astral planes, this is merely more apparent.

No information I've come across however suggests that time is non-existent in the literal sense, or that actions no longer precede other actions. Or that life exists on some type of cosmological constant, with no awareness of individual actions as everything just exists simultaneously in some incomprehensible multi-dimensional way.

Fortunately for our sanity, the way time's lack of meaning is described is that there's no time-keeping apparatuses or scheduling. With no day and night cycle, there is no requirement to sleep, pressure to eat, perform other actions to stay alive, or any other Earthly measurement that keeps us stressed and rushed. What we experience instead is a type of "flow-state" where people are highly centered in the present moment and have little or no conception of keeping track of sequences.

In the tapes, we hear communicators explain that they become re-familiar with time when they peer into the Earth plane and again recognize things like dates based on holidays or other schedules.

And it's reasonable to assume that certain planes are more familiar with time-keeping. While Flint's communicators came from the plane that seemed to have no seasonal differences, by contrast I have also heard of planes that do, in fact, have seasons. This would then naturally be used as a way to keep record of one's "age". As seasons can be kept track of, it becomes easy to mention one winter ago, two winters ago, and so forth.

Perhaps these qualities are largely a matter of preference. Being distant from the existence of time may just be what some people like over others. Especially if, on Earth, you led a hectic life of constant stress and worry about the clock.

The next topic is that of space. Typically, we hear "time and space" as a joint terminology. The notion that the astral has no space could also be confusing. Space "exists" in the astral—you can move from one place to the next. It is not some alien existence where there's no such thing as a geographic radius. The difference is that there is no longer a physical barrier of any sort for movement along any spatial plane. Travel by foot, carriage, car or whatever methods people may use in the other planes would be purely for enjoyment or cosmetic appeal. Locomotion, at least in many of the planes, can be undertaken entirely by thought.

Let's switch to what communicator Rose has to say about the matter. Rose was a flower-seller from London who died in the 1900s who also became one of Flint's contacts.

"What do you do with your flowers, Rose? Do you use them to beautify places?" Ms. Greene asks.

"Well, of course you can if you want to. You can cut the flowers, and you can use them in your homes but very few people do that after a time. It's usually people who haven't been here long. They see the flowers and think it would be nice to have a few indoors and so on. But the point is that you begin to realize it's not necessary, and it isn't perhaps a good thing. The flowers are natural. They have life. And it's not the right thing because you can have all the beauty of nature and the flowers without cutting them and taking them inside. And if you're sitting in your house and you want to see the flowers outside, you don't necessarily have to go outside and see them. You can just sort of think about them, and you can see them. I don't know whether that makes sense to you?"

"Well, we would open doors or windows."

"Well we don't even have to do that if we don't want to. I mean I can sit in my chair and I can think to myself that I would like to go to Flint's circle, so I just - er think and I close my eyes, and the next minute, you might say, I'm here with you. It may sound a bit farcical, a bit odd, but I can't help that. It's true. Time and space don't mean anything.' "

These reports are fairly universal in nature. There are two takeaway points to consider in relation to differences of space:

- The mind is not confined to the physical astral body. Although in some sense "tethered", the mind can project itself to any area of space just through thought. If you want to look at your face from any angle, you can do that (making mirrors unnecessary). If you want to see who's at your door, you can do that. If you want to go to another country, you can do that too. We can perform such feats in this world, but it requires a great amount of practice (out-of-body experiences or remote viewing). In the etheric, it's a natural muscle.

- The physical astral body, in addition, can go anywhere, too. It must require some difference in concentration. Physical teleportation does seem dependent on factors of practice (how long you've been in the afterlife, new arrivals may need training) and your plane (it's been suggested planes nearer to Earth-like conditions may be too dense to allow this type of transportation).

Our Appearance Changes; Most of Us Regress to Youthful, Beautiful Forms

When have we ever heard of an apparition of a loved one appearing who was older and disheveled? Unanimous afterlife sources agree that our appearances revert backward from old age, and seem to hover in one's 20s or 30s. I'd assume this is also a matter of choice. One who desires to maintain their appearance of older age as when on Earth would be able to do so.

It also seems that children age as normal, but may finish aging around the period of their peak physical beauty. Although, some may also choose to stay in the form of a child despite being an adult, like in the case of Flint's spiritual guide and arbitrator "Mickey" who died in the 1900s but remained as an 11 year-old boy.

Some of these points can be illustrated by Alf Pritchett's encounter with his baby sister who had died before he had been able to remember her.

WWI casualty Pritchett was taken to a town square in his particular astral city shortly after arriving, whereupon there was a bench to sit, and music playing around him:

"I sat there with my eyes closed listening to the music. Then, all of a sudden, I had a feeling there was someone sitting next to me. I opened my eyes and looked and there was a beautiful lady. Beautiful blonde hair she had and looked about nineteen or twenty. I was really taken aback.

216

'She called me by my name. I thought, 'Well, that's funny, she knows my name, but I don't know hers!'

'Are you finding it nice here?' she asks.

Very nice,' I says. 'Thank-you-er-miss.'

'You don't have to call me miss. Don't you know me?'

'No. I don't know you.'

'My name is Lilly.'

'Lilly? I don't know any Lilly.'

'That's not surprising in a way. I'm your sister. I died when I was an infant.'

'Golly,' I says. 'I remember my mother talking about a little girl who died when she was only a few days old. But you can't be her. You're grown up.'

'That's right,' she says. 'I'm your sister. I died when I was an infant and I've grown up over here. I'm going to look after you now that you are here. I'm going to take you home.'"

The Astral is Physical and Normal Unless Your Vibratory State Does Not Match

This is something I've been able to confirm through my own OBE explorations, as well. We don't have to worry about becoming phantasms or spectres. Nor do we have to worry that the afterlife is some semi-conscious, dream-like, impermanent state.

These types of oddities only occur when you're in the wrong physical dimension to match your body. Recall from chapter five that this is likely related to the speed to which electrons spin around corresponding atoms. Your astral body, made of non-baryonic (or dark) matter, is simply not compatible around physical matter. It sometimes has an effect on this world, but it's rare and requires skill and dedication by the entity trying to make contact (when it does occur, those rare incidences of poltergeists are recorded).

Ted Butler was rescued by a woman after hanging around the near-Earth in a phantasmal state; haunting around his wife's house,

217

where he was unable to make any contact with the world around him. At the woman's home in the astral, he was prepared a cup of tea:

> "I thought, 'That's funny. I wonder if I'm going to taste it. When I used to go to my wife's place and they were having a cup of tea, I used to think I'd like a cup of tea, but of course I couldn't pick up the cups, and I suppose I wouldn't have tasted it.'
>
> "Oh you will here,' she said, 'because you are in an entirely different atmosphere. You are in your natural conditions now, so everything around you will be natural and real. Now when you put out your hand you'll feel things is real, not like when you was going back to your wife. You have this cup of tea dear, and you'll taste it. It'll taste just the same as tea you have on Earth.'"

A takeaway point is that we can't make judgments about the afterlife based on reports of ghosts or people stuck in-between worlds. There's a reason every death almost seems like a rescue operation, with a tunnel and a light that opens and a welcoming party. If it weren't for this, we'd be bobbing around as specters, lost in an incompatible physical environment where no-one can see us and no idea of how to escape.

There is a Connection Between Thought and Matter

A prevailing theme as we learn about the astral planes is that what we think about has the potential to become physical, tangible objects. However, there are both limitations and variables to consider.

In the 1950s, radio owner Robert Monroe began dedicating the rest of his life to exploring out-of-body conditions after he realized he could travel above his bed at night. As he attempted to compile the nature of different planes; he named the Earth-like "heavenly" realms "Focus 27". The notable feature of this area of the afterlife is that "what you think becomes real". According to the Monroe Institute, if you decide you want a fine Cuban cigar, then you just imagine it and it will form in your hand.

Further information can be found in the book *Life in the World Unseen*, an alleged account transcribed through the medium Anthony Borgia and written by a deceased priest, Monsieur Hugh Benson. Within this detailed book about life in the astral planes, it's explained that the more knowledgeable you are about a subject, or the more you are passionate about the item, the higher quality of an object you can materialize. This creates a natural type of barter system where some may exchange goods with those created by experts or artists and are therefore of a higher quality.

Out-of-body explorer Jurgen Ziewe, in his memoirs, found that he, too, could create objects. However, he would often wonder about the substantiality of these items—were they real or imitations of sorts? He later learned that if one were to imagine a Ferrari sports car and create it out of thought-space, he could lift the hood and discover a fully working F136 engine, even if he had no awareness of the workings of this device. This led Jurgen to believe that objects materialized are brought forward from a type of universal database of information where seemingly all knowledge is stored. The job of the materializer is simply to use memory to access that stored knowledge. Elements like the details of the object are already taken care of by the "source code".

Desiring something on a subconscious level could therefore create objects, as well. Communicator Rose explains that she still drinks tea even though it's not "necessary" to have to eat or drink. She explains that because she is so attached to her cups of tea, they just seem to appear without her doing anything to cause it:

> "But I was one for my cup of tea, and I still like it and have it. Now I suppose people will say where do you get your tea from? Do you get it from some place on your side? Well, of course it must come from some place on this side, so it must be grown and it must be sort of made, mustn't it?"
>
> "How do you get it?' asked Woods. "Do you sort of think you want a cup of tea, and you get it?"
>
> "Well, it's a funny thing, you know. I'm not conscious ... I don't go into a kitchen and put a kettle on, and make myself a cup of tea in that sense. But if I feel

the need for a cup of tea, now all I can say is that it's there."

"Well, that's very nice."

"Of course, Some people say, and even people over here, they've said that it's not a reality. It's only because I think it's necessary I have it, and [so] it's made possible. But when I lose the desire for a cup of tea which I've been used to having all my life, it will no longer exist for me. I'll tell you the honest truth. That's one of the reasons why I'm afraid of going far [leaving her cottage or moving on to a new plane]."

This is one of the stranger elements of the astral planes that I can imagine. Rose's cups of tea are not a conscious intention but a strong subconscious desire that causes them to simply appear in her home without going through the process of actually creating the tea.

In some ways, it would be fair to say that this process is very much a trick of the mind. She's so committed to an old habit that now it's become a physical fixture in her life. Rose is obviously in a nicer environment, but we can only imagine how this phenomena could manifest in a very negative or dark way in other conditions among disturbed, angry souls whose subconscious minds are poisoned.

Physicality Still Exists

My early impressions of the astral, based on accounts like Rose's tea, made me think that everything is always manifested by direct thought-creation. If your mind wanders, you may begin seeing the ramifications of your loose thoughts appearing in real-time in-front of you; as well as dealing with the curious, unpredictable projections of other souls constantly.

Reading further accounts, plus deductive reasoning, has allowed me to conclude that this is not the case. These types of subconscious projections, like in Rose's case, may be related to the fact it's in her own home which could be deeply connected to her subconscious which manipulates that environment.

The idea that everything is thought-generated, to be perfectly frank, is something I always found distasteful. If I make a cup of tea,

I care about who made the leaves, I care about the process of boiling the water, and procuring the milk and sweetener. A complete lack of physicality means no more challenge, artisan skill, and no more being pushed outside of your comfort zone. Instead we are to be seduced into an endless universe of everything you want or desire just being handed to you.

However, from what I can deduce, materializing objects may not be the only standard of creation. In addition, they may pose the risk of disappearing when the mind no longer desires it, making materialization less practical when solid structures must be created for the long-term. Rose feels an urge for tea, the tea appears, but the cup and its contents vanish when she's done.

On the flipside, in contrast to these odd phenomena, there is also a physicality where objects, homes, monuments, or anything else you can think of are permanent (or at least semi-permanent) additions to that particular plane.

The following are some more Flint excerpts by Rose that allude to this:

> "Do you live in a house, Rose?" Woods asks.
>
> "Well, I do live in a house, but you don't have to. But I've never seen anyone who didn't."
>
> "What sort of houses are there? Like here?"
>
> "All types of houses, dear. Some are small little cottages like you'd see in a little country hamlet, and some are quite big places where whole families live. The point is that it's a matter of your choice of archi ... architecture, and all that sort of thing. Of course the houses are very real. I mean they are built by people over here. They don't just happen you know. You don't just think of a country cottage and you've got it."
>
> "No, no," Woods said.
>
> "I mean over here you've got architects and designers and so on, and they create and they build. It isn't hard labour like it is on your side, but it's a real formation that goes on."
>
> "They don't use money over there, do they, or anything like that?"

"Money! You can't buy nothing here with money, mate. The only thing you can get here is by character, and the way you've lived your life, and the way you think and act."

"But I was wondering,' asked Woods, 'how they - you know - you say you've got architects to do your work?"

"Well, you don't pay him. He does it because he loves to do it. He loves to design houses. He loves to do that kind of work, and he does it. The same as the musician loves to play the violin. He's happy to entertain his friends and people, and people who like music they form orchestras and choirs."

A communicator named Elizabeth Fry, purporting to even be from an advanced plane, confirms during a separate séance:

"You must not think we just think of a thing, and there it is," she said. "All kind and manner of work go on here. People make articles, create designs. Great artists paint great pictures still, because it is their joy to do it, but with a greater variety of hue and color. Great musicians compose great music ..."

Next, on this topic, we have George Harris. A builder in life, Harris explains his continued work:

"I was in the building trade, and I'm very interested in building and I liked my job, but here it's rather different. You do build. You do build of materials and things that are real and solid and all that, but of course you don't do it for money. You don't do it because you've got to do it. You do it because you like doing it, because you get some pleasure and happiness out of it.

Of course I've been told by some of the people where I am it's very sort of - well, I suppose you'd call it early stages you know - and that's why we have to build. But they do say, you know, on the higher planes as they call it, that everything's created by thought.

Where I am it's real as can be. You have materials, and you work with materials. I've seen practically a replica of, oh so many things which were common on your side. People don't just sit and think about something and there it is. Wouldn't be much pleasure in that. I should think that's a lousy way of carrying on. I think unless you've to make some effort towards it, and build for it, work for it, that's the only real pleasure and happiness as far as I can see."

"George," asked Betty Greene, "how do you get your bricks for building?"

"Oh, they're produced. Places where they supply them, and you can collect them and use them and build with them."

"Do you build houses for special people," asked Woods, "or everybody, or who do you decide should have the houses?"

"Well that depends on the individuals. I mean there's no business firms or anything like that. But everyone who comes over here - I'm talking about where I am - If they had a trade or something rather special, and they enjoyed it and it made them happy, they have the same thing here. You get carpenters, you get decorators and all that, and I suppose whatever you enjoyed doing on Earth, you can still carry on doing it here. They say as how over here that you can do whatever you want to do, until such time as you begin to think a different way.

I'm quite happy building, helping others, who you know were also in the building trade when they were on Earth, and we build and work together, and our houses are as real and solid as yours, and some of them are really beautiful. Of course the people that we build for are people that we like, people we're fond of, people who are anxious for something of their own, and their own way of thinking and idea, and it's all worked out.

There are people who create here. There are what you call architects and all that. They rough out things, you know, work out things. We follow it out."

Some interesting philosophical points could be made from Harris' account. It's implied that building things by hand is an element of the "early" planes; or ones that are nearer to Earth. Harris expresses some level of annoyance at visitors from less solid planes who tell him that what he does is not necessary because in their worlds, all things are made by thought. There is indication that his tendency to desire building physically is "primitive" behavior among less-advanced souls.

This, I believe, is a point that should be challenged. Are people necessarily more advanced on a mental level because they are in a less-solid condition? In a world where absolutely everything is created by thought, then it makes obsolete trades, skills, craftsmanship and the artistic ability that goes with those things. If one created a temple out of one's imagination on one of these mental realms; it would perhaps be created by someone without the appreciation and understanding of how such a structure is put together on a piece-by-piece basis. I cannot imagine a materialized structure having the same level of character as something with hours of work put into it, pieced together by hand or through teamwork among crafters.

Further, some people just innately have certain passions that are elemental to their soul's nature; for Harris it is building. Is it fair for such visitors to imply Harris is primitive for these actions? Is such behavior in itself perhaps *more* primitive due its judgmental nature?

So as we try to understand the afterlife, I don't think it's wise to look down upon astral residents who have less interest in those non-physical planes where everything is created as fast as one's thoughts can carry it. The more I study this topic, the more it seems clear to me that there's a place and purpose for everything; from our own Earth, the solid, nuts-and-bolts astral planes, to the entirely non-physical, mental planes of existence where form and function break away. Nor is any soul bound to any such plane for all of eternity. Personal preference ultimately determines one's desire; be it sculpting with physicality like clay, or creating everything through thought and indulging in the pleasures of that.

Finally, it's clear that in this plane of intermediate physicality that Flint's communicators reside, there is a mixture of both aspects. Among the citizens of these cities and neighborhoods, there is enough solidarity that houses and structures are permanent additions; as opposed to all matter fluctuating in and out in a state of impermanence, which is perhaps the nature of immaterial planes.

Communication Occurs Through Both Verbal Speech and Telepathy

Flint's communicators are using speech, which suggests people do not merely forget their language apparatuses. And, these vocal cords seem to still be active in the astral—or else there would be some very upset singers who cross-over. However, it seems much of communication is done through a mind-to-mind link.

In addition, there seems to be varying degrees of this skill. Starting out, it appears most newcomers prefer verbal speech. Later mental speech, and eventually more advanced styles of telepathy where information can be transmitted regardless of language.

During one séance, Rose describes this phenomenon:

"I understand there is a School of Learning there?" asked Woods.

"Oh, great schools, museums, places where you can go and turn up all history of nations and people. All sorts of marvelous places there are. Nothing is lost, you know," Rose answered.

"Do you talk?"

"Pardon?"

"Do you talk?"

"Well, it isn't necessary, but people do talk. But there again, it's like everything else in development. After you've been here a few years as Earth time, your time that is, invariably people advance and they realize there's no need to talk. They can send out their thoughts and be picked up. It's a kind of telepathy."

"Very advanced telepathy?"

"Oh, I'll say so dear. Yes, I'm not very good at it yet. I hope to be one day."

In our current world of mass-communication and Internet, where thoughts can be relayed anytime, to anyone, through our invisible wireless networks—is the concept of instant telepathy to anyone, anywhere that much of a stretch?

The telepathic powers also create a phenomenon where we become like "open books" to each other. Thoughts are no longer hidden. How you feel about someone is likely to come direct to the surface; which will make telling white lies particularly difficult. In a world of thoughts and feelings worn on our sleeves, it would be no surprise to believe that conflicts may arise in many human planes when suddenly old acquaintances finally know exactly how they feel about each other.

Physical Needs Are Neither Restricted Nor Required

So far in this chapter, there's been a frequent mention of tea. Which is good news for me considering how much I love tea. It should come as no surprise then that it seems people both eat and drink in the astral planes.

Firstly, some hypotheses about the astral body. Recall from chapter five that Alex Katsman postulated that the astral body has no need for digestive or circulatory systems, but likely contains a central nervous system (including a brain). This makes sense, when you think of the brain as a reducing valve for consciousness, something that is likely necessary to interact in any kind of physical realm.

But bodily systems for the purpose of keeping the body energized would no longer have purpose. At least, not an immediate purpose.

According to accounts from the afterlife, however, the astral body has all the same features. I would assume this also includes circulatory and respiratory systems, even though requirements for both breath and eating are eliminated.

During my few advanced OBEs, I've noticed unsurprisingly that there is no breathing required. I don't even realize this fact until I take note of it. Imagine you are on a full breath—it is like that state at all times.

Since form without function seems utterly pointless, what then would be the purpose of our mouths and noses?

Firstly, if we had no noses, I assume we'd resemble Voldemort from *Harry Potter*—no, not aesthetically pleasing, at all.

Next, the mouth enables the voice, which is still a necessary form of communication. Although it seems most people eventually move into telepathic communication, there are some people who may not be comfortable with that method.

Further, lower "near Earth" planes may require vocal communication. So unless you plan to be a hermit and never venture beyond your comfortable level in the astral, or you never plan to meet people of varying abilities, your vocal cords will be necessary. Finally, a face without a mouth would be as strange as one without a nose. In that case, one would be better with no face, at all.

Next is the ability to access our important two senses—taste and smell. We place great importance on these senses, as something that is required for our happiness and welfare. While food is cumbersome in our necessity to eat every-day to maintain the physical body; at the same time we have a love affair with the artistic properties of mixing flavors. Imagine a world where chocolate could never again be tasted? This is not a heaven I'd want any part of.

The same goes for breath and smell that comes with the nose, which is another essential sense. Just as everything has a taste, everything has a smell—so it's another fundamental way of observing the universe around us.

To make these apparatuses work, some form of circulatory, respiratory and digestive systems must be functional. While it's unlikely (and George Harris assures this) that we have to worry about defecating; there must still be proper teeth, tongue, throat, and finally stomach to process edibles. For breath, presumably we would need lungs and windpipe to process inhalation and exhalation.

Finally, who's to say that consumables have no effect on our astral bodies? If you choose to believe the Anthony Borgia testimonials in "Life in the World Unseen", he describes eating fruit with an important rejuvenating effect shortly after he arrived. Other edibles may have other effects, too. This is not a subject we can fully understand until we've actually arrived there, but I suspect food and liquids have numerous biological uses.

Here is a quote from Rose when asked about eating:

> "We have fruit and nuts. We have trees, I mean we have fruit trees, and nuts and all the things that you'd associate with your world regarding food, but you don't kill animals and eat [them] over here. You don't eat horse meat, or flesh or anything like that, you know." *(Editor's note: but if you really love bacon, who's to say you can't materialize some—without ever harming an animal in the process?)*

Another physical need that's eliminated seems to be sleep. However, as with food, drink and breathing—it remains as an optional thing to do, which your body is still apparently suited for. Rose elaborates:

> "Do you sleep?" Greene asks.
> "Oh yes, you can sleep if you feel so inclined. But it's not necessary," Rose answers.
> "You don't feel tired?"
> "Well, I haven't felt tired, no."
> "What happens when you feel mentally tired? Can you go away and ...? "
> "Well, if you're mentally tired, you just sort of mentally relax, close your eyes, and you rest and you open your eyes after a time. You don't feel tired anymore."

The function of the human body in these planes becomes a type of space-suit for our consciousness. Through taste, smell, sensations of touch, and everything we're already familiar with on Earth; an otherwise disembodied consciousness instead has the ability to interact dynamically in an environment. This is perhaps the true purpose of all physical form.

Nature Continues

A type of question repeatedly posed by Woods and Greene in the Flint séances concerned nature. Are there birds? Animals? Forests? Flowers? Rivers? Oceans? And so forth. The answer to all of these questions, based on numerous discussions from the Flint tapes, would appear to be "yes".

This is also a curious subject. The definition of nature, primarily, is the harmony of an ecosystem. This involves how creatures live on and feed from each other. Although nature in the astral, as with everything else, would appear to be a hyper-physical sort. According to the communicators, you can dive in a river, and leave that river perfectly dry; as like so many other things it's designed around human enjoyment. And, further, animals seem to quite readily get along with each other.

So this leads to the question of how nature functions. If there is no requirement for survival, what do wild animals do all day?

Or, for the purposes of maintaining a kind of harmony of nature, maybe animals are the exception and they do require organic nourishment to stay alive, creating similar ecosystems as here.

There is no way of saying with certainty. It's another mysterious topic that cannot currently be understood easily until new lines of communication and understanding are opened up.

Your Career May, or May Not, Be Relevant

It would seem jobs in social work and psychiatry / psychology will always have the highest demand in these astral planes. The world recounted in the Flint séances appears to be paradisiacal in nature. However, the communicators do not spend time elaborating on the often unspoken of "lower" planes. Not everybody, for whatever reason, ends up in, or chooses, to be in the paradise realms. By all accounts, there are planes that range from gritty and urban, to downright dark, dismal, or even "hellish".

And, according to the narrative presented, it's the residents of these mid-level paradise worlds who are typically assigned with rolling up their sleeves and going down into the lower pits to help out many of the worst examples of those who have crossed over. This is why careers in social work are clearly the most important. People must be adept at navigating the complex world of human psychology.

In addition, there are also many cases of people who die and have no understanding that they're dead. They become trapped in the in-between ether that separates our world and theirs (commonly encountered during OBEs). An example might be the Flint communicator Ted Butler, who wandered London's train system as a ghost before a woman, whose job it was to help the lost, located and rescued him.

And besides social work, other jobs appear to include architecture and construction; as with Mr. Harris. And, certainly there is no shortage of artists of all sorts, including concert musicians and playwrights. Both entities claiming to be Oscar Wilde and Lionel Barrymore recount that they are still dedicated writers and actors (respectively).

We can imagine certain careers would have no purpose in astral planes. A world without scarcity, and therefore without economics, would have no need for business, accounting, finances and all branches of those subjects. An exception, of course, would be some unknown Earth-like planes where these conditions continue to persist as a preference among its inhabitants.

Administrative positions may also be of great importance. Some souls doubtlessly must help to manage and organize the endless amounts of work required to collect the recently deceased, rescue the lost, and rehabilitate the broken.

You Have the Choice to Move

There are many more conditions to write or theorize about in this chapter. And, as I cannot cram in everything that I'd probably like to, I think it's important to wrap this exploration up with one last important point: nobody is trapped in some ecclesiastical prison.

The rainless, permanent sunshine of the English "Summerland" that Flint's communicators came from is just one plane. Based on some of the very limited perspectives of a few of the communicators (such as Rose, who rarely even left her cottage), I'd fancy a guess that even some of these astral residents are not entirely knowledgeable about broader horizons.

As I'll discuss a bit more in the next chapter, there are reasons why this world described may not be entirely my cup of tea (although at least there is tea in that realm). For starters, I'd probably prefer a majestic world of winter and frost, an exotic desert, or even a kinetic city as opposed to some endless plane of bright, sunny fields.

And, I have no doubt that I'll automatically line up with like-minded souls once I kick the bucket, and I'll end up in some corner of the universe that best suits me.

However, if friends and family members have instead chosen tea parties and country cottages with Flint's friends, I am certain visiting them will be as simple as focusing for a moment, and appearing there.

So-called higher-planes are more complex ventures, I assume. The non-physical worlds are in many ways alien to what we, as humans, are used to. These are planes that have likely existed far beyond the time frame of the humanoid form, and are in some ways incomprehensible to us. Yet, even these worlds can be visited and experienced with training.

So, What Happens When I Die?

Should we believe Flint's accounts?

Even if Flint is not credible, many other areas of evidence match up with everything Flint's communicators describe anyway. Near-death experiences, the most verifiable afterlife experience, regularly includes reports of entering paradisiacal worlds with deceased loved ones present—worlds that generally match the descriptions from the physical mediumship of Flint (as well as the accounts from contemporary physical mediums, like entities who appear in David Thompson's séances in Australia).

I think it's safe to say this is a type of realm you are likely to enter into. Even if all of Flint's communicators were coming out of his subconscious mind, it would still seem that his higher-powered mind was tapping into some type of knowledge about these realms to provide accurate information—even if the personalities were not real (however, I find this unlikely given the credibility of the Nanji tapes).

231

Therefore, upon dying and death, you could expect the following things to occur, based on accounts ranging from séances to near-death experiences:

- The first thing you will experience is the discovery that the pain you are in starts to cease. Your mind has started to disconnect from the physical. You may feel a sense of peace.

- If your sickness or injury is particularly severe, however; you may enter into unconsciousness. This unconsciousness will last until your astral body fully disconnects. Many of the below steps may be skipped and you'll simply wake up in another plane.

- If your consciousness remains present, as the pain begins to dissipate, you may find yourself drifting between use of your astral eyes and your physical ones. When your astral eyes turn on, you may begin to see shapes or figures in the room with you. These may be recognizable people you knew from life who had died.

- Initial experiences may be "dream like". When it is time to go, you will find yourself floating from your body as during any traditional OBE. The pain will be gone. You may experience a high-pitch sound, whirring or clicking as you disconnect.

- At this point, you will be greeted by people. Even if you had few if any loved ones from Earth, there will be "case workers" assigned to you. You will have companions.

- The tunnel and the light will occur. The tunnel is the wormhole to whatever plane you are being invited into. This place will feel very majestic by contrast to the dreary etheric in-between state. The light coming from the tunnel will make you feel rejuvenated and alive again. You will feel very drawn toward it.

- In most cases you will be surrounded by reunions. Friends and relatives will be showering you with attention. If you can keep your senses during this process, you'll find as you enter through the tunnel-wormhole, your dream-like etheric body will begin to regain substance which occurs as the vibratory speed of the dimension is now matching your physicality.

- As you land in this new plane, you'll find you're surprisingly weightless, but still grounded. You'll feel in very good health.

- You might not, however, be going straight to your new plane of residence. This experience of mortal death is being facilitated typically by beings on even higher planes, and it's time for you to receive your report card.

- This is where dying is not necessarily always going to be a pile of roses. Although not everyone experiences the "life review", it's a common enough occurrence that you should expect it—and be ready for it.

- You may find yourself being taken to a special facility or just a designated area of space in some astral realm, floating around in the presence of powerful minds. They are not judgmental souls, but teachers.

- What they will do is tap into the universal records of your life. Everything you've done has been recorded, and can be accessed. They will bring it to the surface, and telepathically send the entire "playback" into your mind. You will, almost immediately, relive most of your life's actions as if all your long lost memories have returned to the surface in a flash.

- In addition, however, you'll be experiencing the emotions you've created for others. Made some kid cry in fifth grade? Prepare to feel what he felt. Killed a bird for fun when you were 12? Prepare to feel those little baby chicks who died without their mother to feed them.

- What happens next is entirely up to however well you handle the life review. If it creates intense pain or sadness, there will be psychiatric help available for you. For many of us who lead reasonable lives, the life review may not evoke intense shame or remorse, and it can instead be a very positive experience.

- You may also at this point begin to feel pain or regret in relation to the family members who are likely grieving your passing. You may feel a desire to go back and see them as soon as possible. Your guides may advise against that idea.

- Given what could be the most emotionally intense period of your life, when it's all over, you may be advised to rest. You will be taken to your home that's been prepared for you, or to a hospital type environment for some new arrivals who need care.

- You will take a fairly long sleep. When you wake up, expect for a very surrealistic experience. You're suddenly alive and well in an entirely new, strange, but wonderful parallel universe that is oddly familiar yet also different.

- If you were not knowledgeable about the afterlife ahead of time, this could be a time of great confusion. You might not understand everything that's happened to you. You may have a hard time grasping that you were dying on some hospital bed, and those experiences would feel like a distant memory or a bad dream. Thoughts may race in your mind like "Where am I? Is this really happening? This is impossible."

- But fortunately, that's not you, as you're reading this book. Although you were skeptical when you read about the afterlife that time from some book you found on *Amazon.com*, it's in the back of your mind. Although you would have never imagined it possible, you do have some understanding of what's going on based on accounts you once read, and so slowly your mind begins to accept the bizarre things happening to you.

- And so, with that you can begin your new life. There will be great moments of jubilation in the near future; as everyone celebrates the welcoming of a new soul's graduation from the hardest school in the universe, Earth.

- Try your best at this point to not think too hard and enjoy yourself. Pain, guilt, remorse and other negative feelings bear consequences in the astral. If too many accumulate, it can make your vibration incompatible with the plane you're in. You don't want that to happen. If these feelings get out of control, it could boot you out of your new home. You may find yourself in a more dismal environment to match your state of mind. Try not to let this happen.

- We've been told many times that if, on Earth, you led a life that was unselfish and that you played by the "golden rule", this is not likely to happen to you. The joy you brought others will be compounded and you will not enter a dark state of mind. If, however, you spread a lot of darkness, those negative feelings may catch up with you— and have some dire consequences. This is the crux of the natural moral system that religions have tried (and failed) to teach.

XI – Conclusions about the Afterlife

Where does all of the information we've learned leave us? At the very least, even the most ardent skeptic could agree that there is "something" going on. It's only a small step beyond this point of view to see that the nature of our species, and universe, is not as we've been taught. Some of the grand mysteries of life are perhaps only inches from being peeled away and revealed. If we are to make any progress in regard to this area, we must look closely at the implications raised by the existence of a multi-planar universe.

One of the points of these next two final chapters is to shake up some of your preconceived ideas about the afterlife. I can't guarantee that you will make it through these without taking objection to one or two ideas presented. The point is to question some of our common assumptions.

There is No Afterlife

One of the most important lessons from 15 years of rigorously studying what happens to us when we die—is that there is no afterlife. This may come as a shock, but it's my determination.

Now, you may feel like there's been a sudden contradiction. This book is an argument in support of life beyond death, right? So, why would I say there is no afterlife?

236

What I mean is that the definition of life after death, as it's been culturally defined throughout the ages, is inaccurate in light of actual data and knowledge about the topic. The afterlife is currently understood as a religious, moral reward system taught through theological philosophy. Or, it is a purely conceptual thought-experiment, not designed to be understood literally.

The other hazy afterlife interpretations are conceived through near-death experience literature. "Into the light" books became popular in the early 1990s and aroused new public interest in literal interpretations of the afterlife. However, these books created their own type of ambiguity. Although the NDE is a legitimate excursion into the astral plane, the NDE is also a personal experience, and it's hard to draw accuracy from a single, individual interpretation. It is like trying to understand all of Europe based on the account of one person's 30-minute layover in Belgrade.

For these reasons, the afterlife is not considered a real place so much as some type of hazy blend of religious thought and abstract metaphysics. Maybe something happens when we die, maybe we see a light, or we blend with some type of universal Godhead, or maybe we don't. If we're Christians, maybe we see Jesus, or maybe we become a ghost who goes to live in some hapless person's attic, tossing dishware around at 1 AM.

By these definitions, the afterlife does not exist. There is no strange, vague and dream-like quantum soup that is our fate. Nor is there a quasi-religious eternity of any form. The atheists and skeptics are right in this sense. These are all mythological interpretations of something that most of us fail to understand, and so we look upon it with primitive interpretations.

So, in lieu of a traditional type of afterlife, as our cultures view the topic, what is really going on?

My outlook, based on available evidence, is that there is something more significant at work, which if revealed in its entirety, would call into question many of our most fundamental ideas about human existence. This is obviously a heavy pill to swallow, and it's no wonder that society at large is taking it's time to try to process such information.

Instead of an afterlife that places existence in a binary perspective of *life on earth* vs *reward / redemption after death,* the reality is that *human civilization is part of a much bigger universe composed of what are known as planes.* These are not abstract, thought-based dream worlds, but *literal other closely connected universes* complete with biological (albeit hyper-physical) life-forms, laws of physics, green grass, challenges, parties, schools, cities, lovers, jerks, and a host of other fundamental concepts that you and I are already familiar with.

The entire range of "paranormal" topics that most of us are familiar with are the result of the hints and shadows of these other realms that occasionally manifest. When a frying pan unexpectedly flies across the kitchen, this is a manifestation of a force in a neighboring plane that has decided to reach into this plane and scare the wits out of some poor guy trying to cook his omelet. The same can be said for many legends of ghosts, spirits, and goblins.

The idea of gods and divine beings is the result of life-forms in other universes with basic telepathic abilities who are poorly interpreted by humans as celestial masters. Mental communication has been identified here on Earth within the annals of parapsychology, but it's far more pronounced on other planes. When an individual influences another's thoughts, dreams, or hallucinatory states, we interpret these as "visions from Heaven"; whereas in reality it's a simple communication attempt by, most likely, another human in another universe who is no more Godly than you are.

In all likelihood, within the paradigm of inter-planar civilization, humankind on Earth are the equivalents of primitives who live on islands off the coast of Southeast Asia. Just as somebody who's never seen a telecommunication device before, we are no less significant and lovely than any other form of life, but we are sadly ill-informed to the point where we would be considered a developing form of civilization, still in its infancy and complete with the moral questions that would surround the idea of even interfering with us (would we drop a box of iPhones and satellite internet technology on an island of tribal natives? Equivalent debates would surround our planar counterparts revealing their power and knowledge).

Similar to the Star Trek universe's "prime directive", so I believe that more powerful forces from other planes could not ethically reveal themselves to us. It is instead up to us to reach out and discover them.

We Must Question the Entire New-Age Movement

In some ways, the New-Age is a redefinition of the Spiritualist movement. Both of these movements, in my opinion, suffer from flaws. They both lean startlingly close to the realm of orthodoxy and religion. They place ideas into our minds of exactly the way things are, and this gives us guidance so that we can follow something and place our faith somewhere.

An orthodox interpretation of perhaps the Leslie Flint tapes that we discussed at length in the prior two chapters would present the idea that the Summerland described by his communicators is an absolutism. The rules and conditions described is the truth for everyone who crosses over, and that it's the one type of afterlife we can all expect. This, of course, is ridiculous.

Similar assumptions have been made about books like "Life in the World Unseen" or, with the South American Spiritualist churches, Chico Xavier's "Nosso Lar" ("Our Home", an excellent book, by the way). Some may read these accounts and believe that it's an orthodox truth about where we go when we die.

The same thing has occurred among individual near-death experiences. One person's journey into the astral becomes the only way it is for everyone. People may even read a particular favorite NDE story and say "This is what happens" and then reject another popular story because the experiences seemed less favorable to personal preference.

Worse yet, people prescribe judgments of different afterlives. "Earth-like realms are undeveloped and primitive," I hear them say. "We must aspire to shed the individual self, merge with the Light and join as one with the cosmos." Well, I'm glad you're so well-informed. The idea that one condition is necessarily better than the other is absurd because it discounts unique conditions, motivations and desires.

Some refuse to acknowledge the negative exists. "Negative emotions don't exist in the afterlife," they say. "You can't get sad, or angry, or anything like that. Those are all low-level feelings. We merge with the Light and we become harmonious." If this were true, I'd lose part of my soul. I'd rather just disappear after death. Fortunately, this assumption is not true whatsoever.

I've heard people place unusual conditions on planes based upon unfounded hypotheses rather than fact. "In the astral world, you are just waiting around to reincarnate. You must keep reincarnating until you shed your ego, only then can you move on." What? Seriously? Who's making these rules?

I've seen writers or adherents of the New Age movement, in some form or another, say all of these things. And, a further problem is the tendency to merge unverifiable phenomena with the evidential. Not every medium is a bringer of truth. There are charlatans.

The only truth is that there are no absolutes. Just like our lives right now. Mormonism is not the absolute truth. Nor is Hinduism, Islam, socialism, libertarianism, veganism, paleo-enthusiasts, humanists, or anything else you can think of.

The same goes with life in the other planes. When we project our biases onto them, we greatly restrict the potential of the things that are out there waiting for us. It seems more likely that almost anything we can imagine is probably possible. And, this is rather scary. It means not everything is always pleasant and cheerful. There are beautiful planes, for sure. There may also be dark and menacing ones. And countless in-between. There are human planes, and planes inhabited by alien life-forms that we could not even comprehend. And much more.

The Next Planes Have Enormous Potential for Artists and Storytellers

Looking at the planes beyond in a multi-faceted way, many potentials become apparent. Least of all the ability to actually *create your own planes*. The artist's passion to create worlds could be manifest—and even more exciting, it means we could populate and explore those worlds as a way of limitless adventure and fun.

Think for a moment about the whole process in its grandeur: A filmmaker, author or video game developer is born on our world, has limited resources, but learns all the intense dramas, struggles and adventures that come with life in the rigid, physical Earthly condition. Then, using the tools of illusion at his disposal, he creates artistic works to peer into worlds of his own imagining, shares them with others, and if fortunate—makes heaps of money in the process.

Now, he or she transitions into the planes. It's unlikely they will be content to settle into a cottage and sip materialized tea all day (as with Flint's communicator Rose). Fans of this person's work will be eager to see their worlds realized. And so, the artist becomes the *planeshaper*, creating a realm that may involve a fair amount of role-playing among its inhabitants to make it possible.

Although in a sense illusionary, this is not necessarily a bad thing. Doubtlessly there are swathes of *Lord of the Rings* fans currently cleaving Orcs with broadswords somewhere. Since this world is more an elaborate theatre, you won't have to deal with the karmic repercussions if you were really slaughtering life-forms (Orcs or anything else). In fact, the Orc was either a kind of sophisticated artificial intelligence created for that plane, or another "actor" with whom you can enjoy cocktails with back at your astral home when the season's adventures are over.

If you're not a fan of science fiction and fantasy, I imagine every literary world you can think of can also be explored. This could be your chance to finally go hunting Moby Dick with Captain Ahab.

It seems unlikely that anyone with an imagination could be bored for very long. The afterlife planes, I strongly suspect, are above all else going to be *fun*. Every fantastic idea you can think of can be brought to life and explored to some extent.

The Paranormal Paradigm Hinders Human Progress

Somehow, humans in our infinite wisdom, decided arbitrarily to divide subjects between "normal" and "less important" without putting much thought into the categorization process. So long as anything stays in this fringe, then it's acceptable to not take it seriously, or even denigrate it.

This is understandable for some subjects. For instance, Bigfoot. Totally up-in-the-air, and for me personally—not altogether an interesting subject. Many UFO sightings may fall into this range, as well.

Life after death is not a paranormal topic. It's an apparent phenomenon that has the same amount of evidence (or more) as regular scientific principles and facts. The only reason it's put into this area is because it's beyond the comprehension of critics and mainstream institutions. It's better to just ignore it or pretend it's not there.

As soon as this book is released, I predict strangers and acquaintances alike are going to scoff. "Why did you write a book about THAT? I thought you were smarter than to peddle the paranormal."

This is, plain and simple, socially conditioned brainwashing. Life after death is pushing itself, slowly, out of this box. I think this is because many people exist "in the closet" who believe in it because of personal experiences, but they don't share their belief openly. The majority of people I talk to, after I pry beneath the surface, have had some out-of-body experience, apparition of a loved one, ghostly encounter, etc that made them think twice about the topic.

But even people with personal, unexplainable experiences don't have a way to understand or reconcile what happened. It becomes an anomaly. Many are not even aware that there is literature available to study that can provide answers that are removed from the wishy-washy paranormal world. So many people experience afterlife related phenomena but are forced to keep it hidden. If life after death were not considered fringe and taboo, people would be more willing to look at the data without feeling they are reducing their intellect for crossing into forbidden territories.

For now, however, everything written in this book is still "forbidden"; at least according to the ruling class of ecclesiastical scientism. There's a long way to go.

Physical Mediumship Could Be the Key

Flint and the Scole experiments were the physical mediumship circles that I discussed at length in this book. However, the truth is there are many more unpublicized ones where two-way communication between our side and theirs is normal and verifiable. Some believe physical mediumship is now the greatest form of evidence for survival of consciousness, and perhaps one of the greatest discoveries in human history.

The problem is that it's far beyond the "boggle threshold" of many people, even those who already have an interest in the subject.

I was like this for years, until I scratched beneath the surface and gave my own skepticism a chance to peel away.

Apparent distortions of facts from physical séances back in the 1900s could be attributed to hysteria that was caused by what I believe was an initial wave of legitimate phenomena. After that, everybody wanted to create their own physical séances. Many wanted to form their own religions around it. And certainly more than a few people, faced with WWI and depression-era economic turmoil, wanted to make money off it anyway they could.

Today, conditions are different. Although physical circles are uncommon, the ones I know of are motivated by a genuine desire to connect with the deceased. Or, in some cases, explore scientific possibilities, as in Scole.

Unlike the heyday of Spiritualism, today in an age of Photoshop and Adobe After Effects, people know that even if they caught an apparition on camera, it's not going to make anyone money, nor will it even help their credibility (in fact, it may hurt them). There is no rush to be the first discoverer of the astral planes with some type of photographic proof to create a claim to fame for oneself. And so, naturally, 1900s hysteria is not poised to return.

What's needed, then, are more physical circles, like Robin Foy's Scole group, or Flint's. These don't necessarily have to be publicized affairs. Anyone with an interest could give it a shot. From what we understand, physical circles take some years to develop. And, it requires two-way cooperation between both sides, as well as the medium him or herself possessing some type of natural ability.

However, this ability may be more common than we think. What's needed is for people who know they are mediumistic mentally to go ahead and brave the physical séance. While mental mediumship, as demonstrated in earlier examples in this book, can be extremely evidential—it's physical mediumship that allows actual, verbal communication to occur, which is obviously extremely important.

Personal Experiences Are Needed For Anyone on This Journey

Some skeptics say that a problem with the afterlife is that we "want" to believe in it, and so we will clutch at straws and put pieces together that don't fit to make it real.

My sense is that the opposite is true. Most people don't want to be deceived. Even if we read about the best possible evidence to support this topic, we'll still have lingering doubts because it's something so disconnected from our day-to-day reality. More people lean toward realism in our day and age. We don't want the wool pulled over our eyes.

This is why it's hard to fully process this information without finding your own experience. For me, some of the OBEs I talked about a couple of chapters ago were the key to put all the proper pieces together and finally obtain a fairly clear understanding of how it all works. Before those experiences, I still found myself pandering to a type of personal faith, which I did not feel entirely comfortable doing. A healthy mind wants evidence.

Seek out a mediumship circle, start to practice OBEs, or even try something a bit kookier like ghost-hunting or EVP communication. Many minds have been changed over the years after seeing an object hurl across the room by the hands of some invisible poltergeist in an old house.

Afterlife Knowledge Could Create Needed Changes in How We See Death and Dying

The idea of non-existence after we die, or its near equivalent of religious heaven or hell, is so deeply rooted into our culture that everything from funeral practices to how we treat the dying is a consequence of these beliefs.

We can try to pretend our fear does not affect how healthcare workers see patients or family members treat their ailing loved ones, but let's face it: the culturally accepted notion that death is unknown and ultimately "bad" affects our decisions. It's why it might be acceptable that somebody exists in a vegetative state versus allowing that person to die naturally. It's also why it's more acceptable to desperately prolong someone's life even if it means they are suffering. For instance, a cancer patient, already terminally diagnosed, undergoing brutal and ultimately futile dosages of chemotherapy. This is because of the belief that even life that includes intense suffering is better than the alternative which is non-existence.

Another issue is euthanasia. Somebody under intense pain, faced with inevitable death, could die in a very difficult way as a result of the illness, or through a painless injection (or as is done in Oregon and Washington, take a couple of pharmacy prescribed pills that results in sleep in 5 minutes, death after 30 minutes). Again, the first option is preferable by society, because of the belief that another few weeks of life, even if the life is spent in horrible conditions, is preferable to death—which is the ultimate bogeyman.

From the afterlife point of view, this is dangerous. What we know about the transition process is that nothing is fundamentally different. We keep our memories of everything that's happened to us. In fact, those memories may even be enhanced. A traumatic experience, like extreme pain, could leave a person traumatized even after death. In Flint's afterlife reports, there is common mention of hospitals and recovery wards. Many arrive on the other side in poor mental condition as a result of trauma they incurred in the physical body.

The next way that ignorance of this topic is hurtful is that it's accepted for hospital staff to be skeptical or dismissive of: near-death experiences, shared death experiences, and deathbed visions. The reaction by nursing staff is to increase dosages of morphine or whatever other chemical is needed to drown out the "hallucinations". This is an injustice to both the patient as well as the patient's family.

People who have near-death experiences must also undergo the humiliating process of withholding their experience from not only family members, but hospital staff as well. At a time when some needed psychological support would be great, instead the ND experiencer is faced with bias and dismissive attitudes. Or worst of all, to be told they're crazy.

This ignorance is unacceptable considering the amount of mainstream attention the NDE has received in past decades. But, even with that, there's a long way to go.

The Afterlife's Existence Could Greatly Assist With Grief Support and Mental Health

Everybody will always grieve, and some consider it a good thing. Elizabeth Kubler-Ross, afterlife proponent and pioneer of the well-known five stages of grief, considered it the healthy psychological process. Psychologists agree that suppressing grief is what's dangerous.

But grief itself can turn dangerous, too. A couple of weeks of a grieving process is to be expected. However, for some people this is extended into months or years of agony. For grief that's precipitated by death, it's the existential fear of death that reinforces it. People report being in a type of daze, unable to cope with reality, unable to believe what's happened could even be real. It's a face-to-face with oblivion that sends people into such deep despair; attempting to conceptualize that a person you once loved no longer exists.

By contrast, some psychologists argue that grief does not have to even occur. George Bonanno, clinical psychology professor at Columbia University and proponent of the controversial "resilience" model, argues against the Kubler-Ross design and proposes that the healthy outcome of a situation is actually no grief, at all. A very positive environment may induce a lack of grief altogether, which is a better option than the suffering that is commonly expected with the Kubler-Ross model[45].

One way that grief could either be lessened or completely removed, is with concrete understanding of the afterlife. For instance a family medium, with a long history of veridical information, could be a tool to ensure communication with the deceased remains active, as well as other areas of assisted after death communication (in Martha Copeland's case, it was through EVP. See her book *I'm Still Here* available on Amazon). Overall, it's been established that after death contact greatly assists in eliminating grief[46].

So how do we use the afterlife knowledge to begin healing our emotional wounds? As I discussed earlier in this book, short of a personal experience—merely studying a subject like the NDE is one of the best ways to begin a process of deprogramming the belief that death is terrible, and it can have a long-term positive impact on how a person handles death, dying, and grief.

I recall a particularly good MSNBC investigation of near-death experiences from some years back (please navigate to the following YouTube URL: **http://tinyurl.com/pbvquhl**) which highlighted the case of Pam Reynolds. The actual surgeon involved with the famous NDE case is interviewed. He was the one who performed an intensive operation that completely ruled out any form of conscious activity; and yet the veridical accounts by Pam occurred, anyway.

At the end of the segment, Pam demolishes current fears about death. "If at the end of our lives, this is what's going to happen to us— I don't see the problem," Pam says. "I really don't get it. I mean, I fear pain, but I don't fear death."

Experiencers like (the late) Mrs. Reynolds lost all fear of death from their experience. It's safe to assume someone who has completely lost all fear of death and the negative associations of death, will be significantly less prone to grief as a result of death. We cannot all have out-of-body ventures from near-fatal circumstances, but we can at least take the matter seriously enough that we can draw conclusions from accounts like Pam's, and accept the benefit of those conclusions which is the emotional relief of no longer being terrified of the existential crises of the myth of "oblivion".

There Are No Spirits and "Non-Physical" is a Misnomer

Humans have been using some variant of the term "spirit" since Babylon and long before. This is an inaccurate term. Terms like "spirit communication" are used by many of us (including myself) for simplicity's sake, but at some point we have to move past this habit. Likewise, "non-physical" as an accurate description is commonly used, but it's not accurate, either.

A spirit is a shadowy incarnation of a dream-like "spirit world" that is unattached to our world, disconnected from physics, and more imaginary than anything else. From everything we've learned about the multi-planar universe, we've come to find there is no room for superstition like this.

By contrast, the astral body is organic, made of bones, muscles, a nervous system, and functional organ systems. What happens, though, is that this matter can get stuck in the etheric in-between state. Vibrations do not match, the astral person becomes shadowy and ghostly. They can't touch objects, they drift around, and may exist in a dream-like stupor. This tragic circumstance is the exception and not the rule, and they are assuredly rescued at some point.

This age-old phenomena has created thousands of years of superstition about life in the planes. But it's born from a fundamental misunderstanding of how these high-level physics operate.

Further, it's confusing to refer to other planes as non-physical. This term implies that you can't shake someone's hand, eat fruit, or pick up a musical instrument. **Physical merely means the ability for matter to solidify and interact with other matter**. And, in general, to be able to interact physically, some type of body is required. Now, I am positive entirely non-physical planes exist. These are the "mental realms" described frequently among some NDEs. It makes sense that after a person experiences everything they can imagine they could experience in a physical body, they will desire to move beyond to a more ancient and primal existence, closer to the source of all consciousness.

But there is no rush or need to get to that point right away. Nor is there any reason to assume those in that realm may not eventually return to expression in some type of physical form—or perhaps even reincarnation back to an Earthly world to begin a long journey all over again.

Finally, there is no reason to assume the "Earthly" style of existence pre-dated the astral counterpart, and so humans are somehow inferior to non-physical wisps of light (which is another argument I have heard). Although I cannot vouch for the book's authenticity, in "Life in the World Unseen", the writer describes encountering a very ancient being—billions of years old—from an ancient and sophisticated plane, who came one day to visit his realm. That celestial being, however, had seemingly always maintained a human form, suggesting that the mold of the human organism and perhaps even human civilization, could have existed in other parts of the cosmos for eons before the apes on Earth grew opposable thumbs and began developing such characteristics, as well.

The Afterlife is More Logical Than the Alternative

In our lives on Earth, we are plagued by "the great mystery". How come a bunch of meat evolved out of nothing and became conscious and self-aware? Further, why are we here on Earth? Why is there even life in the universe? What is the relationship between soul and biology? How does life first appear? Is there life elsewhere in the cosmos? And so forth and so on.

We are born without any understanding of these things. We are living in a complete mystery that most hard-working people try to ignore or supplant with religion or narrow philosophies so one does not have to think too hard about it.

Now, by contrast, let's look at existence on an astral plane. Unlike our lives here, it's no longer so unfathomable and bizarre. The astral plane is designed around life. Life is fundamental to the universe. People exist there because they were born on Earth and brought into a new part of the universe.

In other words, an existence in the so-called afterlife makes more sense than life here. It's a more logical existence without so many problems of comprehension. It's our lives here on Earth that are bizarre to understand.

I bring up this argument to people who say that the afterlife itself is somehow "illogical". By contrast, the proven post-Earth planes are a much more practical, understandable form of life no longer interwoven with questions about biology, purpose and the nature of what life even is, as the source of life as energy is immediately apparent and self-apparent.

Afterlife Awareness Does Not Inhibit Life Quality

"You are selfish to believe in an afterlife," I've heard critics argue. "Why would we want more than what we have?"

The argument is that we will become less centered on our current life, and instead chasing after some idyllic life beyond the veil. We should be thankful for our lives here on Earth. Afterlife belief is therefore dangerous.

This is rubbish. Afterlife awareness, at least in my personal experience, amplifies my life. What I discovered was that the ordinary lingering fear of death was at least partially lifted from my shoulders. And you don't even realize how pressing that weight is until some of it is finally lifted.

That extra bit of negativity and uncertainty that follows us around does absolutely no service for us. If awareness of the afterlife in any way works to lessen the common death-related anxiety in our lives, then the afterlife can only be beneficial to us.

Even with belief in the afterlife we still keep the understanding that death means a huge transition. It's a total shift in lifestyle, environment and consciousness. Therefore, what we have now on Earth should still be enjoyed to the fullest before the game is up. No matter what, death will probably always have powerful social implications and be considered a finality. For anybody of a healthy state of mind, afterlife knowledge in no way will precipitate a desire for suicide or an obsession with seeking death.

In short, it's a lot easier living life to the max when you're happier and less fearful.

Interest in the Afterlife Grows With Age

I've met people who used to be card-carrying skeptics who would quickly denigrate any of the topics brought up so far as delusions by crazy people. Those same people, today, are firm believers in the multi-planar universe.

The thing that changes and sways people toward taking this topic more seriously is life experience. A parent dies, your child dies, your spouse dies, your brother or sister dies. Suddenly, your former position of scoffing and feeling intellectually superior is dimmed by a shocking sense that you might need to go back into that material and find some answers to reconcile your grief.

By contrast, I notice how many younger people I meet are less open-minded about this sort of thing. It's interesting what a difference a few tragedies can make to change people's perspectives around.

Our Higher-Self is the Subconscious Mind

It's impossible to go too far into the world of NDE accounts in particular without reading about epic encounters with one's "higher-self". This is when your own persona is separate from your singular conscious identity. It then begins communicating with you. Sometimes it's the higher self that orchestrates the life review.

The best I can grasp is that the higher-self includes our subconscious—all the aspects of our consciousness that operates "behind the scenes". And in some way we don't quite understand, it can also exist in multiple form and incarnations at once. A typical soul may have divided itself into numerous versions of itself, all linked together by what is really a single unit of consciousness, divided by an illusion of separateness.

Your higher-self is you, but it's also countless other identities and aspects of itself that it's learned through countless incarnations. The higher-self operates in the background on purpose. The goal of any incarnation, on Earth or in the astral, is to meet people, have interesting experiences, and learn as a separate, unique identity. So our higher-level consciousness understands this enough to be continually dividing itself across different realms, to experience new things and occasionally reunite and share the collected knowledge.

This is all speculative. Some of the Flint tapes hint at this process, suggesting even that souls can be in multiple places at once in this way; or reincarnated on Earth while still existing in the astral at the same time. We are told that with time and space as illusionary in nature, one's different existences (reincarnations) exist simultaneously, operating out of the higher-self, versus existing chronologically.

It's believed the higher-self exists in the so-called "mental plane" above and beyond all physical planes. The mental plane may not be as inaccessible as we think. Eastern spiritual practices involve ascending to that state simply through meditation. Within that state of consciousness there is a deep sense of interconnectedness, not only where you are once again aware of yourself as your higher-self, but also you are aware of the consciousness of others, as well. This is when separations between consciousness begin to break down, the programming code starts to peel away, and we see that all awareness stems from a single source.

There's a Reason Love is a Universal Message

Do you ever wonder why "universal love" is such a common theme in more advanced NDEs? (Dr. Eben Alexander's comes to mind). They are repeatedly reporting that the very fabric of consciousness and the cosmos, are these positive feelings that we identify as kindness, love, compassion, and so forth. These lessons are usually taught by the most advanced entities.

To the more scientifically minded, these reports sometimes seem unappealing. It just feels like philosophy, and it's hard to understand what the big point of these claims are.

However, I eventually realized the importance of this message. Studying the afterlife does not come without its own form of existential crisis that is equal to (or worse) than even adherents of eliminative materialism and other soulless (literally speaking) philosophies.

The crisis is the issue of permanent existence. With our current death paradigm, as grim as it is, it at least puts a starting point and finishing point on our existences, just like any good story in a book or on TV. We are very used to this way of looking at our lives.

Replace this with the concept of eternity. That's *eternity* as in *infinity*. Afterlife intelligences downplay the importance of time, but it's hard to ignore the possibility of not a million years, not a trillion years, but a trillion *trillion trillion* years—and still we are not even close to the length that infinity represents. Whatever consciousness that animates us right now in our present identity will still be active even after all of that time. Doubtlessly some other unrecognizable, perhaps incomprehensible form—but it will still be there. You will still be there. Forever an aspect of a multiverse that never began, and will never end, but has always existed. For that matter, you have always existed.

This can be a burden. In fact, there's a chance the above paragraph may have just made your head explode. I don't think it's something many of us even want to directly confront or think about.

However, there is one way—one and only way—to reconcile this existentialist crisis; and it relates to that message of universal love.

Can you recall a time you were truly happy? Maybe when you were in love with someone, and everything around you just felt amazing and there was a bounce in your step. Forget the subsequent breakup and throwing out all your former partner's photographs, just think about that period of love and happiness, even if it was fleeting.

During these moments, the idea of eternity is not only bearable but it's desirable. Time famously does seem to either speed up or become not entirely noticeable during moments of joy. You feel a bit like your soul or spirit is too large to fit inside of your body. You want to express your love with that person on every scale imaginable.

And so eternity becomes something we can welcome when within a state like this. A universal message we receive from the other side is that feelings like this are the substance of progression to new, more powerful planes. And, anybody can access this type of happiness.

Yet, at the same time, we also sometimes need the flipside— we need the despair and sadness, to contrast and allow us to recognize the love, happiness, tenderness, and so forth. The negative creates a polarity that actually reinforces the positive. This was a message often taught by famous afterlife intelligence "Silver Birch".

Maybe our existences will always consist of a dance of emotions like this. However, it's those moments of being in love that we are connected to the greater planes and to the concept of eternity itself, which exists in resonance with these emotions, allowing existence to span effortlessly for infinity. It's the only way the idea of eternity doesn't seem so terrifying.

XII – Debunking Afterlife Myths

"There are many spheres, this business of spheres and conditions of life and planes ...and 'Summerlands' and all these other phrases that people have created ... sometimes people on this side have used those terms, because they couldn't think of anything else to use ... there is no way of depicting or describing, because all these different planes, in a kind of way, intermingle, I mean there are millions of them, not just one or two or three, or the seventh plane ... all this is just talk, it doesn't really matter... it's only to give you some sort of vague idea ... but every plane is a series of many planes, interwoven ... and according to a man's evolution development and his consciousness widening and expanding, he will be receptive and aware of and conscious of different vistas, different aspects and so become a little wiser and a little more understanding, a little more evolved or developed." - Mickey (Leslie Flint's Spirit Guide), Leslie Flint Direct Voice Recording

In general, any attempt to limit the afterlife makes me cry foul. Beliefs and biases shape worldviews, and those are projected on to the planar-verse. Mythology of heavens have perpetuated this for a long time.

For some, I assume because of limited human reasoning, one thing has to exist to the exclusion of others. The planes have both purely physical and purely energetic qualities. So anything within those spectrums can exist (which ultimately consists of everything imaginable).

Let's go over what I perceive as myths. Some of these are taught by authors in the New Age field, some by theologians, but all of it is quite bunk. Further, I would not be surprised if you disagree with me or otherwise feel uncomfortable by what you are about to read, especially if you are used to reading contradictory information from the New Age shelf at the bookstore.

Myth 1 – The Higher Quality, More Evolved a Person You Are, the Higher, Less Physical and Happier the Plane You Call Home

This kind of spiritualist orthodoxy teaches us that life is about progression up plane after plane, until we finally reach the "top" where we rejoin the universal Godhead, become light-beings, and fade forever into that existence. They may even give a specific number, like there are seven planes of ascending magnitude, and it's our goal to reach the seventh heaven.

This orthodox teaching also attributes physicality of matter to happiness and quality of the individual soul. The more connected to the "Earth" a spirit is, then the less spiritually "evolved" that person is, however the less "physical" a plane is—the more we need to strive to enter that condition. I notice this teaching is spread very commonly among authors of New Age books, but less so by actual sources from the other worlds.

This is a myth because, firstly, it discounts individual motivation. One of the most dense, lowest physical planes we can imagine is here on Earth. Yet, spiritual "masters" of all sorts exist here. In fact, it seems to be a primary location that we desire to reincarnate into. The reason is to learn lessons and have important experiences to help us mature.

This teaching also supposes that materiality is to be distrusted. A belief that I think may stem from eastern spirituality, including Buddhism, which teaches people to limit Earthly influence.

The philosophy, however, fails to see matter (materiality) as something that is fundamental to the universe just like non-materiality (energy and thought). A more developed perspective, I think, is to see both camps as integral to our existences.

Physical astral bodies exist because to live in worlds of matter, we need "space suits" for our consciousness to interact with that world. This gives us benefits that we may not necessarily have if we become pure energy. Energetic forms may have advantages, too. But no one form is superior to the other. Further, the human form itself appears to be a constant in the universe, beautifully designed (ask any portrait artist) and so it is no wonder that we desire such bodies.

This also stems from the belief that any kind of restriction is a bad thing. Although a pure energetic form may technically have no restrictions, this does not mean it's always a soul's preference. There are various reasons we may choose a more restrictive environment, which leads perfectly into the next myth:

Myth 2 – Higher Planes Are Superior to Lower Planes

Not only is this myth prevalent here, but I sense it is prevalent in many of the planes that we initially cross into, as well. Conventional wisdom suggests that we want to avoid "lower" conditions and aspire for purity of "higher" conditions that are less physical, more beautiful, and with even fewer things that could interrupt our happiness.

However, to be perfectly frank, the view that we must limit ourselves to nothing but what makes us feel happy all the time, or that feels initially "pleasant", is an immature perspective. And it's not a perspective shared by more advanced spiritual teachers, like Silver Birch, who responds to complaints of basic day-to-day difficulties of jerks, less advanced souls, and so forth:

> "There will be always some less evolved than others. How else would you have it? Would you have all humanity reaching the same stage of evolution at the same time? Would you have every human being moulded to the same pattern at the same point of progress at the same time? Would you reduce all life to a state of monotonous equality in regard to its

development? Would you have only light and no shade? Would you have only sunshine and no storm? Would you have only virtue and no wickedness? Would you have laughter and no tears? How would you regulate your world unless it be through an infinite variety of expression?"

I personally may prefer to find myself in "lower" planes; jerks and all. More Earth-like, more limitations, and less paradisiacal. There are two reasons: one is to keep myself challenged and developing as a person, and the second is to live in a world a bit more random and less ruled by group consensus in regard to what is "pleasant" and what is not. This is so you can experience diversity and new things; as opposed to existing within an echo chamber.

I made this determination reading many of the Flint transcripts. It was a conversation with Rose the flower-seller that really caught me:

"When you walk out in the country, do you see animals?" Betty Greene asks.

"Oh, I've seen animals in the fields, of course I have. And I'm not scared of them. Over here they're as gentle ... And it's almost as if they can talk to you. Of course I could never stand crawly, creepy things like frogs. I haven't seen any of those, and I'm told they're on a very low vibration or whatever it is. I don't know what they mean, but they don't exist here. And I haven't seen anything like gnats and flies I've seen butterflies though, that's strange."

"I bet they're lovely ones too."

"Oh, lovely, beautiful. I'm told they don't - there again they don't ever die. Funny business, you don't die you know. Nothing dies. When I first came here, once I settled in that was, I thought, well, how long is this going to last, you know? I wondered if it was another sort of life where you go on for so many years, you get antique again, and then you kick the bucket. I wondered if there was anything beyond that. But there is no dying here. It's most peculiar.

It seems as if you can go on and on and on, and then you get browned off, or fed up, or think you know all there is to know or all you want to know of where you are, then you can sort of just go off into a kind of sleep or something, and then you go on to a different [plane] ... of course I'm scared stiff of that in a way. I don't want to go, you know. A lot of my friends say I should, but I can't see any sense in it."

There are a few important points from this conversation. The first is that Rose's so-called "higher" plane feels *sanitized*. I take mild offense to the notion that a frog is necessarily from a lower plane. For those strange people like myself, a frog is perhaps one's favorite animal. Just because it's not as perfectly reproduced from a Maxfield Parrish painting does not mean it's somehow an imperfect specimen, or that its less pleasant qualities make it something to be avoided. This is the mentality of a squeamish soul, scared to venture beyond one's comfort zone. Is that really the hallmark of an advanced character?

And this also perfectly describes the Rose character. Throughout the Flint transcripts, Rose describes dwelling in her cottage, scared to leave her Summerland plane despite frequent encouragement by her peers who suggest for her to not spend eternity in that particular abode.

It's understandable why many would want to leave. Although this realm may seem very beautiful by description, the fact that it's a subjective interpretation of "perfection" raises my alarm bells. It's almost like it's where people conceptualize paradise using a limited frame of mind, and have then made that into a reality.

As any author of fiction will tell you, sometimes what we need is *conflict* and *imperfection*. A realm of perpetual sunshine and the censorship of life-forms that might cause mild offense to those scared of negative emotions is not necessarily a paradise for someone who values and respects diversity of experience. Fortunately, as we learn from Rose herself, it's very possible for people to move beyond those initial planes and find one that is perhaps more suitable for a mature character.

Myth 3 – When We Die We Become Formless Light Beings

This myth is hard determine the origin of. However, it's repeated among groups of New Age types often enough that I see people claiming some version of this on almost any afterlife-related internet community I go to.

One example I've seen recently: "A loved one may appear to us as a human to provide comfort. Their real form is formless, pure energy."

We've shown throughout this book how the astral body maintains both form and function. Also, I know this is a myth because it's another absolutism (or orthodoxy), and it's alarmingly limiting to the afterlife experience. It negates concepts of physical universes, civilizations, and identity based appearances.

I think what happens is that this is another misinterpretation of people's experiences. An NDE may involve a story of becoming a "pinpoint of light" and shooting through the universe. Or, we hear stories about orbs of light, for instance. Neither report is a conclusive be-all, end-all to describe what happens after death. Some OBE accounts, for instance, suggest that we can go in-between energetic and physical forms. The idea of one being better than the other cannot be defined in this way. Most likely, more advanced souls happily switch between both materiality and immateriality.

Myth 4 – Those in the Afterlife are Immediately Made All-Knowing, All-Powerful

This myth is ridiculous because it suggests human progression ends in the afterlife. It also suggests all souls are removed of flaws and are instantly converted into perfect beings regardless of their own path and progress in life. In other words, Jeffrey Dahmer, far from being accountable for his behavior, is instead immediately turned into some perfect all-powerful light-entity.

This idea is also perpetuated among people afraid of things like negative emotions or imperfection, and it goes hand-in-hand with mythologies of ascension to "perfect" spheres removed of physicality, uniqueness, imperfection, and so forth.

The reality is that conversion into higher vibratory matter gives a "spirit" abilities that could be considered God-like to us densely physical humans. For instance, expanded consciousness, immortality, the ability to transcend spatial distance, and so forth. However, these abilities are simply designed to fit these other worlds. It doesn't speak anything of how psychologically fit a particular soul is.

Traditionally, "spirits" have been worshipped as God-like. Therefore, this myth could even be the origin of many religions.

Mickey, communicator of the Flint séances, shuts the lid on this myth, and also attempts to idealize the afterlife or create perfection;

"No one's perfect, and we're all striving for something, and we don't quite know what it is we're striving for. In any case, everyone would be uncomfortable and bored in a perfect world, I'm not in a perfect world, and I've never met anyone over here who would say that they are in a perfect world. We are in different states of being according to our evolution and our development, and we're happy in that environment, because that the environment to which we have achieved over a period of what you call time. People have got funny ideas, they think that because you kick the bucket, you suddenly become very angelic, well how boring we'd all be if we were all that angelic. We wouldn't want to be here, we'd want to be somewhere else. The point is there are different levels according to one's evolution and consciousness and, people have got funny ideas, they really have about us, we're real people, we're not conjured up and made from imaginary things."

Myth 5 – There Are No Negative Planes or Problems

This is yet another variation of other myths outlined so far. There are some who adamantly believe a "negative" environment cannot exist in the planes beyond. Everything is light and love, for all eternity. It's also a step away from claiming other planes are not physical (it's all pure energy) and that "lower' level entities cannot exist (frogs, snakes, other life-forms that gave you the willies once).

By contrast, great OBE explorers like Jurgen Ziewe have chronicled the endless variation between planes basked in positivity and loving entities, and planes born of selfish desires and ambitions. This fact, logically, *has* to be true or else we'd be defaulting to myth 4—suggesting that even the worst of society will migrate to love-and-light planes upon death; environments that are certainly not adaptable to the hateful and selfish of the world.

In addition, negative can be very subjective. A Norse afterlife where those deceased are engaged in ever-lasting warfare may seem "negative" to the mind of a play-it-nice housewife who passes away. However, for a Viking warrior such a plane is heaven whereas lilies, tea parties and perpetual summertime is closer to a nightmare. It would be highly closed-minded to then cast judgment on the aforementioned Viking warrior for desiring something that is different, and then labeling his plane as "negative" or "unevolved".

But even worse is the idea that alternative views and desires are not permitted altogether. "Such negative notions of war or conflict cannot exist in the heavenly realms!" I've heard more than one Spiritualist say.

They certainly cannot exist in the realm you choose to dwell in. But we are dealing with an infinite potential for different realms of existence. And therefore, endless opportunities—including things you don't feel comfortable with. If the idea of something you don't like bothers you so much that you have to argue that it doesn't exist—then it might be a good idea to evaluate your own level of tolerance for foreign ideas.

As for problems and challenges, I will leave you with this quote by famed afterlife intelligence Silver Birch, when asked if there are problems faced by astral residents:

> "Oh far more than you face on Earth. We have problems such as you cannot possibly realise. We have to deal with millions of souls in many parts of the spiritual

universe- sick souls, young souls, forgotten souls, lonely souls, malformed souls, ignorant souls. Have we got problems! We have them because you send them to our world... It is very hard for me to convey to you what life in our world is really like. I speak truthfully when I tell you that there is so much to explore on this side. You have no knowledge of the infinite richness of the life in the world of spirit. There is no beauty anywhere, no majestic scenery, nothing you have visualised that can compare in its grandeur and in its infinite variety to that which can be seen in our world

Myth 6 – We Immediately Reincarnate

Among the most persuasive afterlife evidence that is even taken seriously by more ardent skeptics, is Ian Stevenson's reincarnation research. An assumption that I sometimes hear (a combination of Ian's factual examination and Buddhist theology) is that reincarnation is inevitable and will happen to all of us.

The truth is we don't really know much about reincarnation, except that it occurs. The majority of spirit sources do not talk a great deal about the subject. Although some astral residents (like Rose) have explained how many friends and fellows "move on" to other planes eventually. This may include going back into an Earth body.

Further, other sources have indicated that reincarnation may involve the splitting of a collective soul into another fragment. In other words, you're conscious of yourself right now, but another part of your consciousness diverges into a reincarnation, and then re-merges with your collective after it dies. So you may be reincarnated but not even consciously aware of it.

A lot of this is conjecture, though. The big point is there's no evidence to suggest we are forced to reincarnate X number of times until we finally "get it right". This is a Buddhist teaching that I have heard taught before like a gospel. There are certainly grains of truth in this philosophy, and notions of karma certainly play into the concept of the life review. Reincarnation may in-fact be a way to rectify past ills and learn important lessons, but that it's inevitable and forced upon you is a myth.

Myth 7 – Our Higher Selves Absolve Individual Identities

An abundance of afterlife accounts and evidence points to our higher-selves that operate on a higher level of consciousness. The higher-self works a bit like imagining consciousness as a pitcher of water. You can pour it in multiple glasses, dividing it up, but it all came from the same source. One pitcher of water is the higher-self, and perhaps the ocean is all consciousness (or God), while every glass is an identity.

The higher-self may pour itself into a few different glasses to explore different realms simultaneously. Some people during NDEs have reemergence experiences where they find themselves rejoining with what they view as past or even concurrent lives (the glass of water is returned to the pitcher). Based on this definition, it's even possible to "meet yourself" on Earth!

Your higher-self, however, is your identity and all other identities. And, from what we understand from the simple act of socializing with people, everybody is extremely unique and elemental in nature. Every personality widely differs in nature. Your own personality is as fundamental to the universe as the color blue.

Therefore it does not make much sense to assume who "you" are is eaten up by some greater power at death. This kind of "spiritualist existentialism" is something I've heard on a number of occasions. I may hear arguments like "Yes, there is an afterlife, but upon death we just merge with a higher consciousness, who we once were no longer matters and it's hardly any different from the materialist notions of oblivion."

Sometimes this assumption comes from certain NDE accounts; the very transcendental variety where people report merging with a God-like divinity. Similar stories also arise out of trips on Ayahuasca and other psychedelics.

However, this assumption ignores all other afterlife evidence that proves, by contrast, who you are is almost unchanged at the moment of crossing over. You're simply in the new astral body, that's it. There's no great change or assimilation that will happen. So, this idea is clearly just paranoia.

Myth 8 – There is No Physical Action (Food, Drink, Etc)

We've already covered the topic of food and drink extensively, and there's no point in rehashing previous material too far, but just to be clear: We have our full sensory apparatuses, which are only heightened by comparison to what we have on Earth, given our filtering mechanism (the brain) is no longer restricting us so severely. You can taste things, smell things, and so forth and so on. The main difference, however, is that we (probably) do not depend on substances consumed for energy to power us. It's theorized that instead we absorb energy from the environment around us to keep our astral bodies going. (However, maybe in "lower" planes we do have to eat regularly. Who can say?)

Myth 9 – Everything in the Afterlife is Impermanent or Spectral

This is the notion that if you build something, it will be gone as soon as you no longer care about it. Understandably, the Flint séances offer a lot of contradictory evidence about this, and so it is a confusing topic. On one hand, Rose describes her tea cup disappearing once she doesn't care about it anymore. On the other hand, many of the other intelligences say it is a physical, tangible world where people create things and those creations are permanent additions to the environment.

It's possible that some things are impermanent and other things are not. Materialized objects (a cup of tea) may be prone to disappearing back into some kind of mental matrix from whence it came from. By contrast, a temple constructed through a team effort becomes a permanent addition to the countryside. Possibly a regular object, if constructed through the environment, will also remain a permanent addition. However, if the same object were instead created through a mental power, it may be more vaporous in nature.

This is just speculation. It will be hard to understand this concept until we kick the bucket and find out.

Another facet of this myth is the idea that we are all of us spectral or "ghostly" in nature. For instance, we are in translucent bodies that are not really developed in a human sense. In other words, we are as vaporous as Rose's cups of tea. Perhaps constantly shifting to different forms without any type of permanent solidarity.

Some afterlife accounts reflect this description. It's likely certain "higher" planes are this way. Some entities in certain planes may be very alien in nature to what we're used to, and may not have any regular physical apparatuses.

However, these planes are perhaps more prone to very old souls who no longer identify with notions like a human form (or any form). It's not everyone's preference, and it's unfair to base one's entire view of the afterlife (which consists of endless styles of realms) on a very specific place recounted from a particular NDE or mediumship transcription.

Myth 10 – There is No Sex in the Afterlife

I decided to save my very favorite myth for last. I've been waiting to address this topic for a while as I've written this book.

Sex itself is a topic viewed negatively by large swathes of society. In fact, even the implication of sex is condemned; to where violence hardly affects the MPAA ratings, but just a brief sight of a woman's breasts will push a film up to PG-13 or R.

Given that sex, and the power that sexual attraction has over us (sexual desire) are both considered forbidden topics, it's no surprise that people carry this feeling over into their ideas of "paradise". You may hear arguments like: "Sex is of the flesh. A physical impulse with no bearing on higher, spiritual realities where we can finally transcend these lower-level thoughts and exist in purity."

Obviously, this raises some questions, such as "on who's authority is it that sex is lower-level at all?" These assertions are very limiting and damaging to people's conceptions of other planes. However, it's my determination that "sex negative spirituality" is just a belief system.

Sex is really a complex subject, and it has many links to topics that are explored in the context of an afterlife. Namely, how sexual desire and exchange seems to have both a physical and energetic element (including but not limited to the orgasm); which is something that has been explored at length through ancient tantric practices. By all accounts, sex is an awesome gift. So, why the bad press?

Religion is the main culprit behind anti-sexual feelings. However, there are a few more I can list, as well:

- **Anger or jealousy:** Sex on Earth is not very fair. As we age, our sexual attractiveness fades. Many of us are also born without body types that most would find attractive. This can breed deep resentment as we find everyone else enjoying such a fundamental human need that some of us seemingly cannot access. Anybody who's ever had years-long "dry spells" can testify how maddening this is.

- **Frustrating relationships:** The sexual desire in a relationship may also fade, leaving one or both partners feeling resentful against sex itself after the spark finishes.

- **Negative experiences:** Rape, molestation, and abusive relationships can all attach deep negative feelings against sex.

- **Toxic sexual culture:** Some grow to hate sex as a result of depictions of violent pornography. Or, "hook up" culture amongst youth becomes extremely frustrating as it seems exclusive based on never-ending standards of attractiveness or relates to game-playing, ego gratification and other immature behaviors.

- **Lack of control:** Some grow to dislike sexual desire because it can hijack our behavior, seemingly as a result of biological impulse. For this reason, monks of various sort practice celibacy.

- **Religious shaming:** Religion then stokes the flames of above listed reasons to dislike sex. It gives people a rallying call against a subject they are already biased against. A child growing up in a household influenced by this may be indoctrinated against sex without even understanding why.

266

The interesting thing about sex and the afterlife is that all of the above reasons could be mitigated in an afterlife context.

Understand that sex is really an entire experience that encompasses not just coitus, but the initial desire, interest, feelings of heightened desire even leading to attachment and romantic thoughts, increasing physical intimacy, foreplay, the sexual act itself, shared orgasm, post-coitus intimacy, and even the subsequent sexual and romantic relationship.

On Earth, this process has an important secondary function: replication. We don't know if the same process can be used to create offspring in other planes (many reports say "no", but we cannot know with certainty). However, if nothing else, sex would then be important for the same reasons we value it in our society outside of just having kids: it's fun, adventurous, and brings us toward passionate, heated experiences, romantic, loving relationships, or combinations of the two. Anybody who's experienced sex in its greatest forms would feel that it's one of the best experiences of being human. The entire process, beginning with initial attraction, is phenomenal. Further, as one discovers their own sexually attractive qualities, it has powerful self-developmental benefits, as well.

Simply imagining the afterlife as we understand it, leads us to conceptualizing how many of the hang-ups and difficulties we experience with sex can be eliminated on crossing over and entering into the appropriate plane.

- **Heartbreak:** In a universe where time is pure abundance, we would not have the scarcity complexes that we have here. Therefore, there would be less judgment between lovers and less risk of getting "dumped" as people race to find the best long-term, exclusive partner.

- **Attraction:** In a plane where everyone regresses to the most beautiful versions of themselves, it would be an even playing field where nobody is bound to a physical disadvantage that prompts a lack of attraction. Anybody who wants to be sexually attractive and have such experiences can then have that door open for them. And if everyone is beautiful, the standards of attraction will likely shift more toward personality and energetic factors.

- **Culture:** As like-minds join in particular planes, there would be no culture of abuse, game-playing or ego-fulfillment. Lovers would meet in greater abundance in an easier, more natural way.

- **Jealousy:** I am sure there's still jealousy to contend with. However, in a world not burdened by extreme scarcity, most healthy-minded people could "move on" from rejections, past lovers, and so forth.

- **Religion:** Unless you choose to enter a Christian or Islamic plane, this won't be an issue. And people who shame others for expressing their sexual side for any reason would exist in their own subculture far away from yours, so long as you choose it.

- **Past negative experiences:** Through the life-review system and high-level psychiatric care, it's more likely to be able to move onward from past sexual traumas.

- **Sexual pleasure:** On Earth, some sex is pretty bad. And, some who suffer from impotence or inability to orgasm can't even enjoy it that much. As outlined in books like *Astral Intimacy* and among those who have experienced sexual encounters in astral states can testify; the pleasure experienced is phenomenally more powerful. As the afterlife is a more energetic realm than ours, it would seem sex can very much be a combination of physical and energetic action (like so many other subjects over there). The energetic, mental element means lovers may find new heights of ecstasy together that could not even be comprehended while on Earth. Imagine that.

The Bottom Line: Far from being a world devoid of sex, it's very possible human astral planes are *designed* for great sex. However, those people with preconceived biases against sexual energy won't find any of it because they'll be magnetized into a corresponding plane of existence with like-minded individuals who also distrust sexual energy. This, tragically, means that such people may be caught in an "echo chamber" for a very long time; being unable to experience one of the greatest divine gifts. A similar threat exists to any soul with a strong bias.

I'll leave the rest of this subject to Oscar Wilde (or a discarnate voice that claimed this identity), who communicated through Leslie Flint in the 1960s and was rather opinionated and humorous about a number of subjects. It's the closest we get to a more sexual person arriving in Flint's séance and he implies a naturalness free of the dogma of sin.

"I am sure you are much more pleased to have me through than I am to come" the mysterious voice said. "At least, it would perhaps be more correct to say that I am quite happy to come, but I certainly wish that it were much more congenial trying to converse, to pass through to you my thoughts through this particular method of communication. It's like using an actor on your side."

"Ah," said Betty Greene. "You wrote plays."

"Oh, you might as well know. My name is Wilde"

"Oh," said Woods. "I've read your books."

"How fortunate you are! I suppose I should be highly flattered. Not that I'm getting any royalties. No doubt you belong to a very good library."

"Mr Wilde," said Greene, "can you tell us something of your life on the other side? What are you doing?"

"I must admit," he replied. "it's a relief to be asked to discuss one's life over here in preference to one's own life on Earth. Because in any case my life when on Earth is pretty well known among the gossipmongers. If I were to say to you that my life here is not unlike my life on Earth, you'd probably be horrified. But it happens to be perfectly true. And I've no regrets about it whatsoever! I'm perfectly happy and perfectly contented, and I live a life of delicious sin. But only as the world sees sin. It is no longer sin here to be human and to be natural. But on Earth to be natural is to be sinful. Over here one can be sinful because it is natural. The world has strange ideas of sin. I live a natural existence here, and I'm perfectly happy."

Final Thoughts on Myths

There is a simple litmus test that we can perform to separate fact from BS as we try to understand this most complex of matters. Simply ask: is a source of information attempting to limit the scope of the afterlife in any way? If the answer is "yes", it's likely subjective information with little or no bearing on reality.

This can be identified most easily by statements that begin like "In the afterlife, X, Y, Z can occur but A, B, C cannot". When you hear something like this, it's important to critically evaluate "why", because most likely what you're hearing is nonsense. Remember that one person's paradise is another person's hell. So just because their personal preference is that everybody plays harps and there's no rock 'n roll, doesn't mean that their preference is some type of divine astral law that applies to all planes, everywhere.

Recall from the previous chapter the important conclusion that we're not necessarily dealing with "the afterlife". That is just human civilization's primitive terminology for the way life in the universe really works; which is that life is separated into near infinite realms. There is such a great variety in the multi-planar verse, and with thousands from Earth joining the realms every-day, we can be certain there's as many things to do over there as exists diversity of personalities on our side. In other words, very little if anything at all is restricted in the astral settings.

It was our tendency to place limitations, rules and regulations on the planar-verse which is what created religious dogma and eventually religious persecution; thus bathing the vast amount of mankind's history in blood. Therefore, this habit is more than just annoying, it's quite dangerous.

XIII – The Path Forward

Not all readers will have arrived at this point necessarily convinced of the afterlife. And, it would be worrisome if everyone did, because a subject this weighty does not deserve to be accepted into one's worldview at first glance. I certainly did not arrive at the point I'm at simply from reading a couple of New Age books and watching an episode of some flighty performance medium cold-read an audience. It took many years of studying and, eventually, personal experiences to solidify what I sort-of already knew.

However, this topic also exists in shades of grey. Not necessarily subscribing to the full-on belief in the afterlife is an acceptable and sometimes necessary position to take, especially for the sake of the scientific study of related phenomena. A good example of this is Dr. Sam Parnia, leading NDE researcher and director of the AWARE studies. In interviews, Parnia always stops short of subscribing to the idea that the NDE is really an afterlife experience. This is in contrast to many other medical colleagues (Long, Morse, Sartori, to name just a few) who are quite public about the afterlife's existence. The point of this strategy is to court the mainstream scientific establishment, who are much less excited to work with someone who openly admits a taboo subject.

Although an argument can be made that all paths lead to Rome; and even a topic like psi is directly indicative of consciousness beyond the brain (AKA, the afterlife), there is a more accessible and apparent conclusion that science is moving toward which exists somewhere short of full awareness of the multi-planar universe. This is the notion that the universe, at its most fundamental level, is not a purely mechanistic phenomenon. Before we can possibly think about connecting the dots all the way to assuming post-mortem survival, we have to first try to establish the prerequisite that the materialists are wrong in their assumptions. The current paradigm is not going to go down without a fight. In fact, not just a fight but the academic equivalent of WWIII.

We are watching as this fight is beginning to occur. The proverbial shots have already been fired and the war is already being waged. The end result when materialism finally folds could include everything from a completely different view of humanity, consciousness, why we are here, to further developments in both science and medicine that we could not dream of right now.

Materialism's Origin

Materialism, as a philosophy, has nearly always been present. Aristotle argued in favor of a mechanistic universe, while Plato argued against that idea. Through the ages, dualism, vitalism, bio-centrism and other non-materialistic views of the universe have also historically had a slight allegiance with the church. The reason is that it's very hard to justify a theocratic universe ruled by a supernatural God, a host of angels, and afterlives while subscribing to the idea that everything is made of its constituent parts, randomly sewn together and born out of further randomness, chaos and nothingness.

The enlightenment represented a widespread rebellion against theocratic ideas. Humanity, until the enlightenment, had suffered from centuries of pathological belief in supernatural forces and an unwillingness to yield to scientific facts. As those tables finally turned, mechanistic materialism resurrected itself as the new dominant worldview. And with the scientific revolution of the enlightenment, we rapidly advanced toward the industrial age, leading up to modern society with its vaccines, high life expectancies, abundance of food, and the ability to not die from things like childbirth or tooth infections.

Materialism's power would have never taken root had it not existed as a type of response to religion. It is the reason that non-materialist philosophies are oddly married to religion or "supernaturalism" despite all efforts to separate the two. It's the reason proponents of materialism indiscriminately lump these points of view together, considering them all to have come from the same basket of bad apples that led to the Dark Ages.

Of course, logically this is a very bad thing. The way the universe works has nothing to do with mankind's religions or anti-religions. Science, as a methodology, is not the same as materialism as a philosophy. Science is just how we learn and understand things. It's science that is pointing us towards non-materialism. It's the philosophy of the enlightenment, however, that is keeping things rigidly in place. It's the church all over again—and the hero living long enough to see itself become the villain.

The Taboo

The effects of systematic materialism comes in the form of cultural taboos. Materialism as a philosophy is not concerned about whether something is right or wrong, it cares about preserving its own type of theology. Most people today cannot conceptualize that alternatives exist between religious thought and materialism to explain topics like consciousness. And so, in an effort to make sense of a confusing universe, materialism is upheld by very passionate supporters of it.

Absolute, unequivocal evidence (or proof) of other worlds (planes) or non-biological powers of consciousness could be discovered tomorrow. And, it would not make a single ripple in any scientific institution.

The reason is that despite all of the emerging ideas in quantum mechanics, with experiments that prove far-flung theories such as how consciousness directly affects matter, scientific materialism is still the status quo. Proof or evidence be damned, this conviction is the ruling body in academic / scientific institutions.

This hidden taboo is strong. Have you ever had a conversation with someone, only to find they start adding legal addendums before attempting to bring up topics related to non-materialism?

"You know, I'm not one of those woo-woo types, and I might be completely wrong about everything I'm going to say, and I'm probably uninformed about the topic, but I read this interesting study about near-death experiences, how…" You get the idea.

People talk like this to avoid getting socially ostracized. Going against "common knowledge" is a dangerous thing to do for one's reputation, career and social life. And this is the problem. Although many people have an interest in these topics, we can't just openly admit to it. The materialist bias may have its origin in academia, but it leaks into how we approach these topics on a daily basis. The "supernatural" becomes a secret, guilty pleasure.

This is also why media pseudo-skeptics can get so much attention (and make so much money), because they are defending a status quo that *wants* to be defended. They don't even have to do a particularly good job. They just have to show up with whatever half-baked theories they conjured up while they were in the shower that morning, and suddenly they're the experts.

This taboo personally affects me. Finishing this book has been a major accomplishment. However, I won't be sharing that joy with just anyone. Certain friends and people in my family may look at me differently for a long time if I reveal that I wrote a book chock-full of descriptions of the afterlife. If I had written a book about motivational theories, business, travel or nearly any other topic, I'd be saluted by just about everyone. If I were to announce that I authored this book on my Facebook, by contrast I'd watch my Facebook friends-count slowly dwindle downward as various people start labeling me a nutcase.

Already I'm taking a major gamble by publishing this with my real name. If I should ever desire a mainstream job again, I'll be getting Googled and bearing the consequences of representing such a forbidden topic.

As with all taboos and moving against common knowledge; there are consequences. It's one of the reasons many are hesitant to carry the torch of a blacklisted subject.

Prying Out of Materialism

So how do we pave a path forward and crush these taboos? Certainly, worse taboos have been vanquished in ages past. For instance, it was once an executable offense to suggest that the world was not flat or differed from any other Biblical description. Or, more recently in 1950s America black people couldn't share breathing space with white people.

The best way to crush a taboo is always with logic and facts. These two things tend to influence people's sensibilities far more than any other argument or philosophy.

The next important point is to pick your battles wisely. People have the right to be skeptical, to make skeptical blogs, or even to be aggressive and unreasonable. However, when a cultural taboo directly affects you in a negative way, that's when you have to fight back. An example could be a family member labelling you as a crazy person for coming into the open about an NDE, or when one of those negative people on the internet singles you out and attempts to smear your reputation.

The purpose of debates in these cases is not so much to convince another person (who cannot be convinced) but to influence the opinions of third-parties; who are able to evaluate both sides of the argument and become educated as a result. This is how we can move forward—by education through discussion and dialogue. Hard-liners will never change their minds, but for every one hard-liner there are ten fence-sitters.

So far in this book, I have presented a great deal of evidence to support life beyond the brain (a fundamentally anti-materialist proposition). But I worry that the subject itself is so far past the boggle-threshold of many people that it's not effective as a way of dismantling the materialist agenda.

For this reason, we need to get back to basics and focus on step 1, which is eliminating the credibility of materialism as a philosophy. Not necessarily by upholding the afterlife, but by highlighting the very best examples of evidence that calls materialism into question. Any incident where the mind demonstrably operates outside of the confines of the brain is a death-punch to the materialist world-view.

Further, developments in quantum physics are merging materialist and non-materialist scientific institutions at a rapid pace.

Turning Paranormal to Normal

College classes that discuss the psychology of religion link paranormal phenomena with a belief in a spiritual premise. If that premise is removed, then the subject is no longer paranormal. Further, if the subject is explained successfully, it reverts to a non-spiritual, materialistic / physical explanation.

The paradigm that has not been explored is that both materialism and non-materialism can exist together. Materialism is persistent because it is perceived accurately. Or that natural phenomena have no philosophically "spiritual" assignment unless we do it ourselves. On a macro level, it feels like matter is a reducible and fragile structure. On a quantum level, we are now learning how this is not true. Certainly matter, however, has a strong effect on reality, and even "mind stuff" (get a person drunk and observe the differences resultant from brain chemistry changes).

However, as argued at the very beginning of this book, one set of rules in nature does not mean a contradictory phenomenon is automatically not true. Just because materialism can be observed as real, does not mean that immaterialism is false. And, vice versa.

Non-materialism and its philosophies (such as dualism, that the mind and brain are not the same, ultimately relating to the afterlife) become suggestive after (literally) going beneath the surface and entering quantum, energetic levels. Here, concepts like telepathy are not far-flung but normal. It then makes the macro level phenomena (like telepathy, or for that matter anything outlined in this book) seem far less alien in nature.

One of the most famous experiments is double-slit experiment. This experiment is now commonly repeated by quantum physicists. These have also been carried out by Dean Radin (consciousness and psi pioneer) and his colleagues, and published in the journal *Physics Essays*[47]. The experiment, as described by Radin, is simple in concept. Electrons are shot through a filter (shaped like a vertical slit). Predictably, electrons should come out on the other side in the shape of the filter. Instead, the electron interferes with itself, presenting a wave-like pattern (a bullet is shot out, and seems to "scatter" in various places). The variable of observation, however, changes how it spreads. When it's observed, the act of observation causes the electron to shoot through the slit in a predictable way as it appears on the other side of it. What this means is looking at the electron changes its behavior from wave-like encompassing multiple possibilities, to a "collapsed" form with its outcome determined.

Another unusual phenomenon is the ability for a particle to understand the relationship of its corresponding particle despite any amount of distance separating the two. So a particle fragment spinning in a certain direction will match the corresponding rotation of its linked sister-fragment even if they're in different parts of the galaxy. This unusual phenomenon was predicted very early in the founding of quantum physics, and the action was dubbed by Einstein (who was skeptical that such phenomena was really possible) as "spooky action at a distance". Spooky because, well—such notions really shouldn't exist in a materialist world.

In summary, the behavior of matter is determined and influenced by both conscious awareness, and also instantaneous information transfer. Understand that an action like telepathy is considered impossible because without wires or at least some type of delay per the speed of light, transference of anything is impossible. These quantum rules show that it's not the case. If a remote viewer can accurately detect information from far away, instantaneously, this is not something so far-fetched according to the laws of advanced physics. We just don't understand the relationship yet.

And the double-slit experiment has shown the role of consciousness on a quantum level. Remember that what occurs on the micro-scale is just a reflection of what occurs on a macro-scale. Tiny fractions of matter—like electrons—are literally everywhere. It's what everything is made out of. We have now learned that everything is therefore subservient to consciousness. From this point, it's not a stretch to say telepathy, intuition, and psychic phenomena of all sorts are just the natural processes of how consciousness interacts with the material world.

And if the psychic is natural, then a whole host of "paranormal" phenomena are perfectly natural, as well. The problem is that materialist philosophy is trying to impose an "unnatural" label to something that does not deserve it.

"But there is no application to these quantum phenomena," some skeptics decry. Which is absurd. The future of quantum-level computer-processing may revolve exactly around instantaneous information transfer, independent of the laws of space. Further, day-to-day phenomena we take for granted may relate to "psychic" quantum processes, such as our very health.

Every Day Non-Material Laws in Effect

How material is our universe really, when consciousness at the very least can alter the physiology of our bodies? One example of this is the placebo effect. It's one of the most recognized aspects in medicine that the majority of drug trials must account for, by including placebos as a variable. In short, when we believe something has an effect on our bodies, our chemistry changes to match the belief.

A skeptic would say that the placebo effect's power is thin. A strong belief could send a mental signal that creates some chemical reactions or hormonal changes that could mimic an effect. However, what researchers have come to find is that placebos are really much more powerful than we think. Our mind can change the body's physical makeup.

One case that sheds light on the awesome power of the placebo was a 2002 Baylor School of Medicine study (published in *The New England Journal of Medicine*) that explored the usage of placebo *surgery* to fix chronic knee pain due to arthritis[48]. Unlike placebos that involve consumables and pills, this experiment involved doctors carrying out an entire fictitious operation among patients, using the real operation as a control effect.

- The first group received a treatment where the damaged cartilage was shaved from the knee.

- The second group removed material from the knee joint responsible for inflammation. These are both the standard procedures for treating the condition.

- And the third group received an entirely fake operation. The team brought the patient under general anesthesia, passed operating tools back and forth, and watched as a real version of the procedure took place on a monitor. Incisions were added to the knee, and then sewn up to make it impossible for the patient to know whether they received the placebo or the real surgery.

Normal materialist science would predict that without an actual operation, the placebo surgery would have no effect. However, that was not the case. The placebo group generally improved from their knee condition. One of the patients had a follow-up interview many years later by a reporter, who claimed that his arthritis was still cured and that he owed a great deal of gratitude to the doctor for performing such a remarkable operation that restored his quality of life again.

Non-material science, however, shows that this effect is very possible with the dominant relationship of consciousness over regular matter.

To watch an awesome documentary segment that includes the follow-up with the patient, please navigate to the following address (YouTube): http://tinyurl.com/nkvqbmc.

Similar to the placebo effect is the "nocebo" effect documented in medical literature as "medical hexing"—when a misdiagnosis actually creates the physical condition on the patient as a result of that patient's subsequent belief. One famous case in the 1970s involved a man misdiagnosed with metastatic cancer, although in reality his tumor was benign. Just as the doctor said, the patient died a few months after diagnosis. Upon autopsy, they discovered the tumor never did spread; despite that he came down with all the symptoms of the illness. He died as a result of his belief.

This phenomenon should cause some serious thoughtful consideration about the effects—and potential damage—caused by a doctor's prognosis being believed without question.

Thoughts Affecting Matter

The placebo effect demonstrates the power of thought over our bodies, but telekinetic powers simply take the concept a step further to demonstrate how thoughts can change matter outside of our bodies.

Mystical and impossible under our current paradigm, but normal and common-sense in the new paradigm.

One of the most interesting were the experiments carried out by Dean Radin at the Institute of Noetic Sciences at Sonoma State University[49]. The experiment, which used a double-blind protocol and was a replication of similar studies conducted by other researchers, consisted of attempting to alter the formation of water crystals using thoughts; including the focused attention of thousands of people in a "prayer group" far away in Tokyo, Japan who were assigned with the task of directing their "energies" toward the water. According to Radin and his team, far beyond chance—the positive thoughts created symmetrical and more "beautiful" crystals compared to disheveled crystals that formed as a result of negative thoughts.

This experiment, of course, makes us pause for consideration on how thoughts can affect external objects—like the bodies of others. By ignoring non-materialist science, it's evident that we are also ignoring important advances in medicine, and potential causes for sickness. Non-material science shows that concepts like prayer should not be discounted; nor should energetic healing principles (such as Reiki). In addition, negativity and depression may profoundly affect molecules of any substance, causing patterns of disarray.

Non-Material Effects are Subtle but Noticeable

The important takeaway point from all of these topics is that, under controlled conditions, we can observe how non-material effects occur (ie: how our thoughts affect the world around us), and through quantum mechanics we have a sort-of clear understanding of "how" these effects are possible. However, our minds are noticeably "filtered" by the density of this material plane. What we think (fortunately) does not simply pop into existence. Instead, it's a process that occurs very much beneath the surface.

Materialism is still there. If we get exposed to battery acid, it's still going to harm us, no matter how much we try to think it away. This is because physical universes are bound by natural laws. However, the non-material effects are still there, even if it takes a long time to manifest, or the changes are only occurring on a quantum / molecular level.

In addition, some people are clearly more advanced than others at manipulating this ratio. While if we are diagnosed with a terminal illness, it may not be possible for we ourselves to will it away, it might be possible for an advanced energetic healer to perform such a feat because they are much more trained compared with what a normal person is capable of.

One way to conceptualize the afterlife is to consider to what degree materiality vs. non-materiality is present. For instance, as a rough speculation we can imagine that our world is 95% physical and 5% non-physical. This means our thoughts are still affecting things, but it's not readily apparent, or it requires a great amount of practice and focus. Materiality is the dominant force.

On the other hand, common astral plane environments could be more like 50% materiality and 50% non-materiality. This means your thoughts can actually change the world around you in real-time. This isn't to say that it's immediate, but while it may take hundreds of people in a type of prayer-state or focus to change the consistency of matter here, in an astral world it would only take a single person a short amount of time. Or, as another example, an astral body may (as is commonly reported) slowly regress to a different age (an elderly man will eventually reach his 20s). This would occur as a result of a subconscious desire to appear this way, which slowly changes your physical structure.

And based on reports, it would seem every plane has a physicality to non-physicality ratio to consider. The so-called "mental planes" we sometimes hear about could be more like 90% non-physicality. In these realms, recounted by certain experienced astral travelers and some near-death experiences, you create things (matter) as fast as you think of it. So your own thoughts, and those of others, are endlessly materializing concepts, ideas, and experiences all around you in a space of hyper, nearly omniscient consciousness.

You may have guessed by now that my opinion of this subject is that whether materiality or non-materiality is better, is about personal preference. It would certainly seem, however, that our Earthly lives are extremely rigid and material perhaps to a point of extremity. However, as we read about in much spiritual literature, perhaps these tough conditions works as a type of "bootcamp for the soul", and after we transition to the next world where these strenuous physical conditions lessen; we can greatly appreciate it.

Accepting the Non-Material

Whether or not people believe in life after death is not relevant to the argument about non-material function in the universe. And acceptance of an afterlife is by no means necessary to study, research or explore non-material phenomena. Throughout this book, all of the evidence put together, at the absolute minimum, proves a non-material aspect of the universe exists. The sooner this is accepted, the sooner we can begin to reap the benefits of these "new" laws of physics. As we speak, possibilities of advanced medical care and possibly even mind-blowing technological equipment are all eluding us because of our rigid inflexibility in exploring these topics and accepting them into our field of knowledge. Today's studies that range from changing water crystals with thought, to remote-viewing and mediumship, are all relegated to fringe experimenters. Mainstream funders refuse to acknowledge such things are even possible. And "skeptic" groups continue to lobby against this information being taken seriously in any public sphere.

However, the "divide" is growing, and the inevitable civil war in academia is beginning to come to light. One of the more interesting developments in recent months has been the Manifesto for a Post Materialist Science[50].

The manifesto was written by eight PhD scientists and medical doctors, including Mario Beauregard, Larry Dossey, Rupert Sheldrake, Lisa Jane Miller, Marilyn Schlitz, Gary Schwartz, Alexander Moreira-Almeida, and Charles Tart, plus 130 scientists, doctors and philosophers who agreed with the manifesto's assertions.

The manifesto states the case for the "post-materialist paradigm" and cites some of the topics discussed so far in this book, including the NDE. The manifesto proposes that:

- There is a deep connection between the physical world and the mind.

- The mind can influence the state of the physical world.

- The mind can work through the brain, which operates as a transceiver, but is not necessarily a result of the brain.

- Non-materialism does not exclude matter but both elements are part of nature.

- Spiritual experiences are a central part of the human condition, and therefore deserve to be taken seriously by scientists.

- Because of the non-local effects of consciousness, the intentions, emotions and desires of an experimenter are not isolated from the results of experiments. In other words, a strong negativity toward the chance of a particular outcome could increase chances of negative results—our minds may be constantly meddling with the universe around us.

- The mind is fundamental to the universe and is not a reducible phenomenon.

- The shift to a post-materialist science could be extremely important for the evolution of mankind.

Although not every researcher chooses to look at the evidence at face-value and accept the possibilities of the afterlife (or the greater planar universe) as outlined in this book, the investigation of the afterlife undoubtedly is something that opens up so many possibilities of non-materialist science.

The quest for the acceptance of any non-materialist idea (let alone life beyond death) is ongoing. However, it would seem that the link that will finally connect these two worlds is quantum physics. Public interest in QM has caught fire in recent years. It has created a newfound interest in non-material concepts that could defy the mightiest attempts by the detractors to suppress. QM is the first scientific branch that places emphasis on the importance of consciousness and how it directly relates to all forms of matter. This is the primary function of non-materialism and brain-independent life-forms.

XIV – Final Thoughts

We are left now asking: what is it that we can do with this information? How can we apply it to our lives?

My sense is that we do not have to stress about conforming our Earthly lives to any kind of servitude of worship of these other planes, because the fact of continuity has little to do with the religious notion that we must live our entire lives devoted to ascension to some superior, heavenly abode. That's all nonsense.

The reality of the situation is that the afterlife appears to be such a normal, natural and even mundane thing that today you might be lounging around reading a book; and by this time next year, or next month, you may be lounging around in another plane, also reading a book, amazed how easy and nonchalant the whole *dying* thing turned out to be, and being just as curious and perplexed by the nature of reality as you were on Earth.

Since the fundamentals of who we are does not change, a major premise of our existence would not change, either—which is making our shared reality better for everyone around us.

Living on Earth presents unique challenges and opportunities to perform this type of charitable work. Although other planes are superior for pleasures, enjoyment and exploration—our Earthly world is superior for discipline, self-development, and the chance to do good things for people. It tests our wits, strengths, and abilities and

285

continually presents options for right and wrong, selfishness versus inclusiveness, or avarice versus charity.

And these natural dramas exist in other planes, too. However, perhaps never quite as dramatically as in our universe where we are dense and bound to not only physical laws and restraints, but also widespread confusion about who we really are and the nature of the universe.

So, in regard to how we can live our lives with knowledge of the afterlife; the answer is that how the information affects you is entirely up to you. However, the general need in society to uphold the golden rule remains all the same, whether one chooses to accept the information about life after death or not. There is no requirement to accept this information as a prerequisite to leading a good, honest life.

To Be Grounded in Objectivity, and the Danger of Dogma

The New Age movement has certainly been a double-edged sword on society. On one hand, it has allowed information about other realms to become widely accessible. For instance, one of the most successful New Age books of all time, *The Secret*, introduced to the entire world the concept of thought manifestation—a basic non-material concept (albeit presented in a way that was arguably very flawed).

The problem with *New Age* anything, however, is that we can too easily lose our balance and start accepting any idea or notion without examination of objective elements.

Something that is subjective is a belief system. A real event that occurs is objective and independent of belief. An example is a near-death experience which is an objective event, where perhaps the experiencer even leaves his or her body and observes the surroundings in a veridical way. On the other hand, interpretations about the entirety of the afterlife based on that experience turn into belief systems— which are subjective and cannot be proven wrong or right.

The quickest way to understand the nature of reality is to examine the objective elements first. Figure out what is really going on. And then, after all of the information is accessed, begin to create philosophies to help make sense of it, and to help the facts apply directly to your life in a meaningful way.

It's not wise, however, to begin first at a philosophy without objectivity to back it up, and then perform reverse-assessments of the objective information to back up your belief.

This is the nature of how dogma manifests. And, it's dogma which has held back our ability to digest this information for thousands of years.

No source has all of the answers, and that includes this book. That's because reality, by its very nature, is open to interpretation. You could read a hundred books about life in Tokyo, but without ever actually going there, your experience will never be entirely accurate. I think we must learn to be comfortable with this lack of knowledge and not always yearn for absolute understanding.

However, there is one element of the afterlife that I'm quite certain of, and it's that there are far fewer limitations in the planes than many of our interpretations suggest.

In recent years, I've found a book called *The Afterlife of Billy Fingers* to be very popular. The book (which I think is a very good one) recounts an interpretation of the afterlife through a particular mental medium who brought forward a deceased individual who seemed to go through great effort to make contact with his friends and family again.

It's an entertaining and delightful read. The book is well-written; and written concisely with a clear beginning and end to the story. In the book, Billy Fingers describes that he has no astral body as the one I discuss that we possess. The medium also describes Billy ascending into some much higher sphere toward the end; where he re-merges with God, the "Light" (or what have you) and is absorbed of his prior identities to rejoin the cosmic consciousness. It makes a poignant finale for a narrative.

Since this book released, I've had many arguments with people on Facebook and in afterlife related reading groups and communities who take exception to my interpretations. "The idea that we have astral bodies with mass is absurd," some say. "We become formless beings of light, just like Billy Fingers. And, we are only in these heavenly realms for a certain amount of time before we rejoin God on the seventh plane. All this talk of denser vibrations or Earth-like realms is absurd, and even if they exist; who would want to go there?" (This quote is a recollection based on memory, but a near match to something somebody wrote to me not long ago.)

On the flipside, I had a woman write to me with this message: "Dear Cyrus, my teenage son passed away. I recently read *The Afterlife of Billy Fingers* and I feel a little upset that my son would not be able to enjoy teenage activities in the afterlife. I understand we are all supposed to shed our material selves and merge toward a universal consciousness, but it would be nice if my son could still be enjoying his hobbies, continue his education, and maybe even have a girlfriend. I know it's unevolved to be thinking this way, but the idea that he has no form now makes me sad."

The particular mother who expressed these concerns to me is completely justified. When these singular interpretations of the afterlife rise to prominence, almost without fail it's like the adherents of that faith are quick to shout down people who think otherwise. And if I lost a teenage child, I too would be terrified that they'd be subject to the *Billy Fingers* afterlife against their will. This is when afterlife research can go from healing and therapeutic to anxiety inducing.

And the reason these dogmatic interpretations arise is because of the way some of these New Age books are written. They are not written as potentialities or interpretations, but as *facts*. A mental medium, which is by nature one of the least reliable channels of communication to the other side, does not necessarily have all of the answers. Even in the case of *Billy Fingers*, I doubt what the real discarnate individual was trying to convey was a hundred percent relayed with accuracy. And even if it were entirely accurate, there are millions of varieties of astral planes. His experiences matched only his own preferences and needs.

The afterlife is such a personal experience that it's folly for not only people to cling to singular interpretations, but it's also a mistake for astral people to try and teach their experiences to us in a one-size-fits-all fashion. A mature teacher is going to explain that there's diversity and that their descriptions are limited only to their own personal experiences, and not necessarily of other people with different needs, desires, personalities, and so forth.

And there is also the issue of credibility. How do we even know when X medium is receiving accurate information or not? This is why I found myself more drawn toward the Leslie Flint tapes. The reason is that Flint could demonstrate what many contemporary mental mediums and channelers are hesitant about; which is scrutiny under scientific pressure. Flint was tested and found to be credible even by stiff skeptics. And the nature of his mediumship allowed communicators to manifest in their own voices and provide long, detailed and *objective* accounts about what life is like on the other side.

These accounts can then be scrutinized. As I described earlier in this book, some of the communicators, like Rose, seemed highly limited in their understanding of their new world, and even quite naïve or frightened. On the other hand, other communicators, like Flint's guide Mickey, seemed to provide the most balanced, rational assessments of the nature of their world.

It's not until we learn to push aside dogma will we ever make much progress in this area. And, that work begins right within the New Age communities. There is no "path" to follow to obtain divine knowledge about the afterlife. Following a specific medium at the expense of other mediums is, for instance, a mistake. Selecting a single NDE account as "the truth" and discarding all others is also silly.

Another way that dogma rears its ugly head is with interpreting communicators or powers from the astral and beyond with godly reverence. No astral entity, no matter how old or wise, should be bowed to. If any channeled entity presents itself and claims to some select group of followers that they are the "masters" with the answers for humanity—I suggest to RUN. No wise astral resident would ever impose this kind of egoism or desire for reverence.

We may also elevate the messengers of the beyond (for instance, the mediums or channelers) onto pedestals of reverence, perhaps even against their wishes. Another great mistake. History is marked by many saints and prophets, some perhaps quite legitimate, but who were regarded as divine figures requiring worship. We sometimes continue this practice even today. Much earlier in this book, I talked briefly about my favorite artist, Akiane Kramarik, who many believe draws her abilities from some type of astral, channeled source, and is a perfect example of a modern day "saint" (and given her popularity in religious communities, may certainly finish her life on Earth with a saint's title). It's hard to deny this when looking at the profound paintings and poetry created by what was then an eight year-old child. It's heavy, mind-blowing stuff.

Akiane, as a result, has drawn many followers who believe she is a connection to some heavenly realm, a reincarnated angel, a divine being, a supernatural phenomenon, and so forth (a perception that may be exacerbated by the fact that she's also very physically beautiful). Some of these claims may be "true" from what we understand about these astral dimensions. She could be an ancient soul with great power and understanding. However, even if that is the case, there's no reason to put even her on a pedestal. Among the first and most valuable spiritual principles is that everybody is equal. And even ancient, divine beings have wishes, desires, hopes, flaws, problems, and other "human" qualities. And, virtually none of them would appreciate being worshipped, unless they are egotistical or desire some type of reverence (in which case, it would be best to be very wary of them).

I do not know if Jesus Christ truly existed or not (I would lean toward "yes"), but if he did—it seems the last two millennia of worship of him have been quite ridiculous. If the real Jesus appeared to me, I'd be curious, but I'd have no reason to treat him any differently from the cashier at Whole Foods. Both Jesus and the cashier are immortal fragments of consciousness with unique personalities and essences. One is not more important or powerful than the other.

I feel the same about modern day spiritual leaders or eventual saints. I'd treat them as regular people first and foremost, and then be curious about what I could learn from exploring that relationship. No reverence, no worship.

This attitude, I think, is the key to keeping dogma at bay. It's an attitude I'd suggest for readers to think about adopting, as well. It's a mature way of treating people around you.

At the same time, in the spirit of reducing dogma, even this advice is not a hundred percent. Maybe some people need gurus, masters and / or followers. That could be part of their individual situations in life. We can never judge. However, dogma and worship does, objectively, cause a lot of problems that we must be mindful about.

The Benefit of Reduced Fear

The fear of death is crippling for so many of us. Grief is enhanced to levels of debilitation in our culture. Sometimes it feels as if everything is built around a foundation of fear caused by the shadow of death.

What we have learned about the afterlife teaches us that while some fear is inevitable; debilitating fear is not necessary. Irrational paranoia of "oblivion" is no longer something we need to concern ourselves with.

To ensure the fear is reduced, we must develop personal relationships with the afterlife, with our deceased loved ones, and to seek to expand our understanding of this topic. As the fear is reduced, I've personally found life to be far less troublesome. We all have this existential crisis of mortality on the back of our minds that some of us never even look at for our entire lifetimes, until the day death comes knocking.

This should not be you. Any psychiatrist in the world will tell you how toxic it is to push away and suppress these types of things. The afterlife paradigm creates a much healthier attitude of continuity instead of panic-inducing finalization, and it allows us to then confront the subject of death head-on without intimidation.

Your thoughts and actions no longer have to be born from nihilism, with the belief that the void from whence we came we shalt return. Instead, every goal, ambition, and creation we can see as something that will be forever an addition to the infinite multiverse. And most importantly, as we develop ourselves, and grow our personalities and creative potential, we get to keep those fruits with us after our physical body dies, and we transition to the next plane— wherever that may be.

We can start to lessen the fear today. It starts with you.

The Burden of Proof

Finally, with this much evidence accumulated in support of the afterlife, to make the claim that the afterlife does not exist is a burden that requires addressing all of the areas of evidence listed so far. This ranges from veridical perception during the NDE to Stevenson's reincarnation research, and many more subjects outlined in this book. If a single study, like the Medium 7 work or the Archie Roy / Tricia Robertson mediumship research is left unaccounted for, then the position the afterlife does not or cannot exist will have a glaring hole in it.

I don't envy the skeptics who pin their careers on trying to disprove this topic. Much like the world's hardest game of "whack-a-mole", every time one subject is smugly dismissed, three or four more pop up in its place. Indeed, one can fit an entire career into trying to keep track of every development and constantly doing battle with them.

If the proper areas of afterlife evidence cannot be addressed and factually rebutted, then it remains that all of the evidence—taken together as a whole—provides justification for the afterlife hypothesis. A phenomenon that is of vital importance to mankind and is easily the most important discovery in history.

To say the afterlife does not, or cannot exist, must therefore be understood as a belief system that runs contrary to objective evidence. And if this is a belief that a person chooses to adopt based on a moral or philosophical imperative, then it's not something that can be swayed. Much like I won't go to a Mormon temple and start telling everybody that Joseph Smith was not a real prophet, I would not attend a James Randi "Amazing Meetup" in Vegas and start trying to tell everyone that their narrative that all non-material phenomena are created by charlatans and con-artists is not an objective or rational assessment. There's no swaying true-believers.

And, to be fair, if someone felt absolutely certain that the afterlife cannot exist, it would be rather futile for them to try to tell me that this is so, because I've already studied the same evidence and made up my mind in a different direction.

This is the nature of how we process information. Beliefs are an inevitability, and even those people who profess a rejection of all beliefs, by contradiction, are just aligning themselves with a new belief (the belief of non-belief). The only way out of this rat maze is to attempt to, at the very least, align one's beliefs with where data and evidence points. The afterlife hypothesis is such a subject, reinforced by a seemingly endless amount of evidence that reinforces it as being much more valid than any belief born merely from dogma or faith.

This discussion leads us to perhaps one final question, and it's if everything presented in this book could somehow, in fact, be untrue. After everything we've explored—from the Anni Nanji tapes, to mediumship research, to testing spirits in laboratories, to personal experiences and much more—could somehow the afterlife and the existence of the greater planar universe be invalid?

My personal assessment is that there is a 99% chance the afterlife is true, but it's wrong to ever deal in absolutes. The only alternative explanation that I can possibly rationalize at this point is that if, somehow taken everything we've learned the afterlife is still not real, then at the very least there is some powerful force at work that *wants* the afterlife to be real. The only other explanation is that the universe, working as some type of conscious entity, is fabricating all of these experiences in the minds of its human subjects in an attempt to manifest something into existence. It's the only explanation for how so many people can hallucinate the same thing or experience so many life-like contacts with entities from beyond, or to be able to leave one's body in such a convincing way. It would mean some form of super-psi theory is true, and that all of our minds are linked, creating a narrative built on some type of collective subconscious desire.

But I don't have any interest in being caught up in miniscule chances and abstractions. While some prescribe to this idea, I feel it's even more far-fetched than the afterlife itself. It's a lot more practical to call a spade a spade.

I believe now that with so much growing evidence for this field, the far future is going to be very different from what we experience now. Someday, maybe not in this lifetime, there is going to be a shift where topics denigrated now as "fringe" or "New Age" will have finally crawled out into the realm of what is considered self-evident and a part of nature. This will vastly change how we perceive our own lives, and will certainly have profound effects upon the sacred narrative of life and death that has remained unchanged for all these thousands of years.

It would be exciting to see what this world would be like. Fortunately, based upon the afterlife research outlined, it seems likely that I may in-fact still get to see such a world unfold, whether it's within this lifetime or in several hundred years from now. In fact, all of us may be around to see what direction the world goes, whether positive or negative, from the safe vistas of other planes and the astral civilizations within the realms that we are all fated to eventually experience.

It would seem this journey of life is much bigger than we ever gave it credit for.

Coming Soon: "Understanding Spirit Communication"

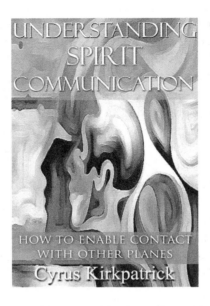

It's possible to build a bridge with the other-side that allows us to develop personal relationships with residents of other planes. This is done through understanding basic concepts of how the multidimensional human mind really works. Like an advanced form of wireless internet, consciousness itself can immediately tune-in and detect the frequencies of other people. In our material universe, this is much more difficult, but it becomes practicable when making connections with other, unseen universes. In addition, residents of other planes are slowly developing and learning new methods of making contact with us. As these connections open up more and more, the possibility of staying in permanent contact with deceased loved ones, or learning from those who have passed on decades or even centuries before us, become possible. Long considered the realm of the occult, gradually our civilization is evolving to embrace "spirit" communication for what it is – a part of the natural universe.

"Understanding Spirit Communication" by Cyrus Kirkpatrick and AfterlifeTopics.com is due out in early 2016. Add yourself to

the mailing list so that you can pre-order a copy (for cheap) when it becomes available. You can do so at www.afterlifetopics.com/newsletter.

Additional Links and Videos to Continue Your Education

Websites and YouTube links tend to change or go obsolete over time. Depending on how long ago you ordered this book, there's a chance some of these links no longer work.

Links Related to the Author and This Book:

Afterlife Topics: www.afterlifetopics.com: A new informational resource to explore the afterlife from a non-religious, non-New Agey perspective.

Afterlife Topics Facebook Group: https://www.facebook.com/groups/afterlifetopics/, This is a safe space. Please discuss your encounters with the beyond, the supernatural, or with deceased persons, and what you learned from those experiences, as well as your opinions about life in planes beyond this one.

Cyrus Kirkpatrick: www.cyruskirkpatrick.com, my personal website. Stay up-to-date with my writing, or my travels as I wander the world. I also write non-fiction books about business, career, and personal development. Coming soon, I'll be releasing my fiction series, as well. (Fantasy-adventure, for those interested.)

My author page on Facebook. If you liked this book, please come by and give me a "like" which is always appreciated. https://www.facebook.com/cyruskirkpatrickauthor

Cyrus@cyruskirkpatric.com : My e-mail address.

https://www.facebook.com/cyrus.kirkpatrick My personal Facebook page.

@AuthorCyrusK (https://twitter.com/AuthorCyrusK) – My Twitter. I rarely use Twitter. People are trying to drag me into it kicking and screaming, and I finally submit. Give this page some love with a "follow" and I'll try to return the favor.

More Resources:

A Lawyer Presents the Case for the Afterlife (www.victorzammit.com): One of the most recognized afterlife resource sites today.

Institute of Noetic Sciences (www.ions.org): Dean Radin's institute that has become the materialist-skeptic's worst nightmare as they make continued progress in areas of consciousness research including telepathy.

Michael Prescott's Blog: michaelprescott.typepad.com. Michael, a reputed novelist's long-running blog that often includes critical examinations of otherworldly topics.

Multidimensional Man: (www.multidimensionalman.com): The website of out-of-body explorer Jurgen Ziewe. Fantastic information, including visual depictions of other planes. Also see: www.vistasofininity.com for further depictions.

Near Death Experience Research Foundation: (www.nderf.org). This is by far the best resource available for browsing user-submitted NDEs and having your mind repeatedly blown away.

Paranormalia: The blog of Robert McLuhan (monkeywah.typepad.com). "Randi's Prize" author McLuhan explores one of the greatest mysteries of the universe—what makes materialists and organized skeptics tick.

Skeptical About Skeptics (www.skeptikalaboutskeptics.com): An important resource for examining the media skeptics who attempt to position themselves as the final word about the afterlife.

Skeptiko (www.skeptiko): Alex Tsakiris' long-running paranormal and consciousness themed podcast that includes interviews with researchers, skeptics and other thinkers. The afterlife is an ongoing theme in his show.

Spiritual, Skeptic? Evidence For the Existence of the Afterlife Facebook: (https://www.facebook.com/groups/evidenceforafterlife): Moderated by Caroline Sloneem, Victor Zammit and others, this group is approaching 10,000 members and remains one of the most active afterlife discussion communities on the web.

About the Author

Cyrus Kirkpatrick was born on a ranch in the Sonoran desert outside of Tucson, Arizona. He graduated from the University of Arizona in 2010, studying journalism, film and business. Since then, he's made it a point to become a globetrotter—living in Thailand, Central Europe, and producing a documentary in troubled North Korea. He enjoys parapsychology, photography and eating his way through various countries. His personal website is www.cyruskirkpatrick.com.

298

BIBLIOGRAPHY

[1] Devinsky, J.; Schachter, S. (2009). "Norman Geschwind's contribution to the understanding of behavioral changes in temporal lobe epilepsy: The February 1974 lecture". *Epilepsy & Behavior* **15** (4): 417–24.

[2] Thacher, George A. and Hyslop, James. The case of Lieut. James B. Sutton. Journal of the American Society for Psychical Research, 1911, 5, 597-664.

[3] Wagner, Stephen. "Edison and the Ghost Machine - The Great Inventor's Quest to Communicate with the Dead." About.com. Web.

[4] "Marconi and EVP" – New World Science, 2013

[5] Tart, Charles T. "A Psychophysiological Study of Out-of-the-Body Experiences in a Selected Subject." *Journal of the American Society for Psychical Research* 62.1 (1968): 3-27. PsyWWW. Web.

[6] Sicher, F et al. "A Randomized Double-Blind Study of the Effect of Distant Healing in a Population with Advanced AIDS. Report of a Small Scale Study."*Western Journal of Medicine* 169.6 (1998): 356–363. Print.

[7] Lobaido, Anthony C. "Inside the CIA's Psychic Program." World Net Daily, 3 July 2000. Web.

[8] Bowman, Carol, and Steve Bowman. "Scientific Proof of Reincarnation: Dr. Ian Stevenson's Life Work." *The Reluctant*

Messenger. 1997. Web.
<http://reluctantmessenger.com/reincarnation-proof.htm >

[9] Hennacy Powell, Diane. "Evidence of Telepathy in a Nonverbal Autistic Child." *DianeHennacyPowell.com*. 27 Aug. 2014. Web. <http://dianehennacypowell.com/evidence-telepathy-nonverbal-autistic-child/>.

[10] Betty, Stafford. "When Alzheimer's Victims Suddenly 'Perk Up' Just Before Death -- What's Going On?" The Huffington Post, 29 Sept. 2014. Web. <http://www.huffingtonpost.com/stafford-betty/the-miracle-of-terminal-l_b_5863492.html>.

[11] Greyson, Dr. Bruce. "Consciousness Independent of the Brain." *YouTube.com*. Plato's Cave, 9 Nov. 2014. Web.

[12] Moncrieffe, Donna. "Life After Death From a Non Believer's Perspective." *YouTube.com*. Medium 7 Project, 21 May 2012. Web.

[13] Roy, Archie E., and Tricia J. Robertson. "A Double-Blind Procedure For Assessing the Relevance of a Medium's Statements to a Recepient." *Journal of the Society for Psychical Research* 3.65 (2001): 74-161. Print.

[14] Beischel, Julie. "The Reincarnation of Mediumship Research." *Edge Science* 1 Apr. 2010: 10-12. Web. <http://www.windbridge.org/papers/BeischelEdgeScience3_p10-12.pdf>

[15] Beischel, J., Boccuzzi, M., Biuso, M., & Rock, A. J. (2015). Anomalous information reception by research mediums under blinded conditions II: Replication and extension. *EXPLORE: The Journal of Science & Healing, 11(2)*, 136-142. doi: 10.1016/j.explore.2015.01.001

[16] Neko, Eteponge. "Exploring The Veridical Cases of Psychic Detective Dorothy Allison." *Eteponge's Blog*. 29 Aug. 2007. Web. <http://eteponge.blogspot.com/2007/08/veridical-cases-of-psychic-detective.html>.

[17] Oliver, Myrna. "Dorothy Allison; Volunteered to Aid Police as 'Psychic'" *Los Angeles Times* 7 Dec. 1999, Obituaries sec. Print.

[18] "Detective Psychic Dorothy Allison Dies before 75 - as Predicted." *Amarillo Globe News* 9 Dec. 1999, Stories sec. Print.

[19] Schurman-Kauflin, Deborah. "Psychic Mediumship in Law Enforcement." *Psychology Today* 9 Nov. 2012. Web.

<https://www.psychologytoday.com/blog/disturbed/201211/psychic-mediumship-in-law-enforcement>

[20] Zammit, Victor. "UK MEDIUM EDDIE GRENYER RECOUNTS HIS EXPERIENCES OF MATERIALISATION WITH MEDIUM RITA GOOLD." *A Lawyer Presents the Case for the Afterlife*. 2011. Web. <http://www.victorzammit.com/articles/eddiegrenyer.htm>.

[21] Roll, Michael. "A First Hand Account of Materialisation Mediumship". *The Campaign for Philosophical Freedom*. Web. <cfpf.org.uk>

[22] Mackenzie, Grahame. "Exclusive Interview with Michael Roll – What Is Life after Death All About?" *Spiritoday.com*. 28 Dec. 2012. Web. <http://www.spiritoday.com/exclusive-interview-with-michael-roll-what-is-life-after-death-all-about-3/>.

[23] Keen, Montague. "The Scole Investigation: A Study in Critical Analysis of Paranormal Physical Phenomena." *Society for Scientific Exploration (SSE)* (2001). SurvivalAfterDeath.info. Web. <http://www.survivalafterdeath.info/articles/keen/scole.htm>.

[24] "International Association for Near Death Studies." *About IANDS*. Web. <http://iands.org/about-iands.html>.

[25] Cunningham, Janet. "Ancient Egyptian Mythology: A Model for Consciousness." *The Journal of Regression Therapy* Vol. XIII.No. 1 (1998): 86-96. *JanetCunningham.com*. Web. <http://www.janetcunningham.com/Ancient-Egyptian-Subtle-Bodies.html>.

[26] "Chapter 6: The Tibetan After-Life The "Bardo" or Intermediate State." *The Bardo Thodel - The Egyptian Book of the Dead*. Kheper.net, 24 Apr. 2001. Web. <http://www.kheper.net/topics/bardo/tibetan.html>.

[27] Van Lommel, Pim, Ruud Van Wees, Vincent Meyers, and Ingrid Elfferich. "Near-death Experience in Survivors of Cardiac Arrest: A Prospective Study in the Netherlands." *The Lancet* Vol. 358.No. 9298 (2001): P2039–2045. *PimVanLommel.nl*. Web. <http://pimvanlommel.nl/files/publicaties/Lancet artikel Pim van Lommel.pdf>.

[28] Long, Jeffrey, and Paul Bernstein. "Dutch NDE Study Attracts Worldwide Attention." International Association for Near Death Studies. Web. <http://iands.org/research/important-research-

articles/464-dutch-nde-study-attracts-worldwide-attention.html?task=view>.

[29] "Results of World's Largest Near-death experiences Study Published." University of Southampton, 7 Oct. 2014. Web. <http://www.southampton.ac.uk/news/2014/10/07-worlds-largest-near-death experiences-study.page#.VERpycnRjkg>.

[30] Knapton, Sarah. "First Hint of 'life after Death' in Biggest Ever Scientific Study." *The Telegraph* 7 Oct. 2014, Science News sec. Web. <http://www.telegraph.co.uk/news/science/science-news/11144442/First-hint-of-life-after-death-in-biggest-ever-scientific-study.html>.

[31] Clark Sharp, Kimberly. *AFTER THE LIGHT: What I Discovered on the Other Side of Life That Can Change Your World.* 2nd ed. Lincoln: iUniverse, 2003. Print.

[32] Sartori, Penny, Paul Badham, and Peter Fenwick. "A Prospectively Studied Near-Death Experience with Corroborated Out-of-Body Perceptions and Unexplained Healing." *Journal of Near-Death Studies* 25.2 (2007). International Association for Near Death Studies. Web. <http://iands.es/bibliografia/Sartori_Fenwick.pdf>.

[33] Kevin, Williams. "Some People Were Dead For Several Days." *Near-death experiences and the Afterlife*. Near-death.com. Web. <http://www.near-death.com/science/evidence/some-people-were-dead-for-several-days.html>.

[34] Greyson, Bruce. "Nature of Mind and Consciousness: Is Consciousness Produced by the Brain?" *Cosmology and Consciousness*. ScienceForMonks.org, 7 Dec. 2014. Web. <http://www.scienceformonks.org/SciencePrograms/MonasticGraduates/Conference/CosmologyAndConsciousnessI/Resources/Text_Is_Consciousness_Produced.pdf>.

[35] Sunfellow, David. "Dr. Penny Sartori's New Book: 'The Wisdom of Near-Death Experiences'" *NHNE Near-Death Experience Network*. 28 Jan. 2014. Web. <http://nhneneardeath.ning.com/forum/topics/dr-penny-sartori-s-new-book-the-wisdom-of-near-death experiences>.

[36] "Where Is Consciousness? I've Lost It!" *Is the Brain Really Necessary?* Flatrock.org.nz, 2009. Web.

<http://flatrock.org.nz/topics/science/is_the_brain_really_necessary. htm>.

[37] Lewin, Roger "Is Your Brain Really Necessary?" *Science* 210 December 1980, page 1232

[38] Gutschner, Mareike. "Discovery of Quantum Vibrations in "Microtubules" Inside Brain Neurons Corroborates Controversial 20-Year-Old Theory of Consciousness." *Elsevier* 16 Jan. 2014, Research and Journals sec. Web. <http://www.elsevier.com/about/press-releases/research-and-journals/discovery-of-quantum-vibrations-in-microtubules-inside-brain-neurons-corroborates-controversial-20-year-old-theory-of-consciousness>.

[39] "Planck 2015 Results. I. Overview of Products and Scientific Results." *Inspire* 36 Pp (2015). Web. <http://www.cosmos.esa.int/web/planck/publications>

[40] "Dark Matter." *CERN: Accelerating Science*. Cern: About, 2012. Web. <http://home.web.cern.ch/>.

[41] Motta, Leonardo. "Ether -- from Eric Weisstein's World of Physics." *Science World*. Wolfram Research, 2007. Web.

[42] Lodge, Sir Oliver. "The Mode of Future Existence." *Linking Life After Death To Subatomic Physics*. Rense,com (Michael Roll), 11 Nov. 2000. Web. <http://www.rense.com/general32/sub.htm>.

[43] Katsman, Alex. "Physical Model of the Parallel Ethereal World." *The Campaign for Philosophical Freedom*. Michael Roll, 1 May 2004. Web. <http://cfpf.org.uk/articles/rdp/physicalmodel.html>.

[44] "The Mediumship of Leslie Flint." *Leslie Flint - The Voice Box*. The Voice Box (orig. published by the Ark Review, 1998), 2007. Web. <http://www.the-voicebox.com/flintleslie.htm>.

[45] Stix, Gary. "Http://www.scientificamerican.com/article/the-neuroscience-of-true-grit/." *Scientific American* 1 Mar. 2011. Web.

[46] Beischel, Mosher, and Boccuzzi. "The Possible Effects on Bereavement of Assisted After-death Communication during Readings with Psychic Mediums: A Continuing Bonds Perspective." *Omega (Westport)* Vol 70.2 (2014): 169-94. Web. <http://www.ncbi.nlm.nih.gov/pubmed/25628023>

[47] Radin, Dean. "Double Slit Experiment Results" *Institute of Noetic Sciences* (2010)

<http://media.noetic.org/uploads/files/PhysicsEssays-Radin-DoubleSlit-2012.pdf>

[48] "A Controlled Trial of Arthroscopic Surgery for Osteoarthritis of the Knee." *The New England Journal of Medicine* 347 (2002): P 81-88. Web. <http://www.nejm.org/doi/full/10.1056/NEJMoa013259#t=abstract>

[49] Radin, Dean. "Double-Blind Test of the Effects of Distant Intention on Water Crystal Formation" *Institute of Noetic Sciences* (2010) <http://media.noetic.org/uploads/files/Double-blind_water.pdf>

[50] "Manifesto for a Post-Materialist Science." Open Sciences, 1 Feb. 2014. Web. <http://www.opensciences.org/about/manifesto-for-a-post-materialist-science>.